PAINT AND
PREJUDICE

PAINT AND PREJUDICE

by

C. R. W. Nevinson

R.B.A., R.O.I., N.E.A.C.

WITH 32 GRAVURE PLATES
FROM THE AUTHOR'S PICTURES
at the end of the book

METHUEN PUBLISHERS LONDON
36 Essex Street Strand W.C.2

First published in 1937

PRINTED IN GREAT BRITAIN

ILLUSTRATIONS

v

AMONGST THE NERVES OF THE WORLD
London Museum

THE SOUL OF A SOULLESS CITY
In the possession of Williamson Noble, Esq., London

THE TEMPLES OF NEW YORK
Purchased by J. Rosenberg, New York

WALL STREET, NEW YORK
Birmingham Art Gallery

THROUGH BROOKLYN BRIDGE, NEW YORK
Purchased by Sinclair Lewis, New York

NIGHT DRIVE
Purchased by Mrs. Fox Pitt, London

HENRY IV, L'ILE DE PARIS
Dublin Art Gallery

CHRISTINE
Purchased by G. Besky, Esq., London

FILLES EN FLEURS
Purchased by Alec Waugh, Esq., London

NOTRE DAME DE PARIS
*Purchased by the Northern Arts Collection Fund for the Laing Gallery,
Newcastle-on-Tyne*

A STUDIO IN MONTPARNASSE
Tate Gallery (reproduced by permission). Presented by H. G. Wells, Esq.

ENGLISH LANDSCAPE IN WINTER
Walker Art Gallery, Liverpool

SATURDAY AFTERNOON IN ENGLAND
Manchester Art Gallery

THE CHARLADY'S DAUGHTER
Purchased by Miss Evelyn Sharp

CLOUD SHADOWS OF SPRING
Purchased by Hamilton Fyfe, Esq., London

STARLIGHTER
In the possession of the Artist

BATTERSEA TWILIGHT
Purchased by R. Temple, Esq., London

THE TWENTIETH CENTURY
In the possession of the Artist

PAINT AND
PREJUDICE

NOTE.   The illustrations appear together at
the end of the book.

1

On sort, on crie, c'est la vie

I came out on a sultry night of 13 August, 1889, and wailed piteously and lustily. Two battling cats squalled in through the open window of the room, fell into and polluted a bathful of water which was meant for other purposes, and fled noisily out again into the night. The witches had come early to see the brood, and I greeted them stormily.

The nurse had come on from another case and ignored the quarantine into which she had been put. She gave my Mother a fever, and this later caused weaning to be difficult. Psychologists of to-day say that these shocks may be responsible for much of my character. I accept their views: it is always comforting to have somebody to blame.

My childhood is half-forgotten. When eventually I learned to talk it was in three languages: German, French, and English. For some reason I invented two imaginary dogs who were my constant companions. One, called Hampstead, was my guide, philosopher and friend. The other, known as Herod, was evil company, but extremely useful, as I held him responsible for all my crimes. Even to-day their names stamp them. For those few who read their Bibles the name of Herod must still stand for wickedness; while Hampstead is known throughout the world as representing just what is right and proper. In addition to this early appreciation of values I was truly Trinitarian in my beliefs and endowed my imaginary beings with only three legs. But those creatures were my very own, and when Canon Barnett heard of them from my Mother and inquired after their health I suddenly destroyed them, disconcerting the

I

poor gentleman by informing him that they were all horrid lies and rebuking him for encouraging me to speak of them.

Our house was in John Street, since re-christened Keats's Grove, and was an old, white, Hampsteadean monument of stucco, dampness, bad plumbing, and immense kitchens, and set in a garden of lilac and may. Opposite was Keats's cottage, a place of pilgrimage; behind was the Freemason's Arms, where the shrieks of ejected drunks at midnight made 'Appy 'Ampstead what it was. Beside us were the Asquiths, the father then a rising barrister, and on one occasion I nearly lost an eye through an arrow which had been shot into the air by one of our junior neighbours. Perhaps the archer was Elizabeth, now Princess Bibesco.

Shortly after this escape the Thames froze over and I was taken to see the ox roasted near Waterloo Bridge. I remember being struck by the great number of sea-gulls near the Adelphi and being told that this was the first time they had come so far inland. I then became the pride of the pond, on skates. In those days the Hampstead Ponds stretched right down to the bottom of Keats's Grove.

Although both my Father and my Mother came from old English families, I was brought up in a spirit of inter-nationalism. My Father had only lately given up a post he had held as a professor at Jena; his friend and neighbour Professor Goodwin, the classical scholar, was more than pro-German, like many people in those days; while my Mother's French was as correct as her English. Both my parents were as much at home in Europe as they were in London. Our servants were usually German or French.

Unlike most artists, I was born into the most exquisite and intellectual ambience, and in my early years at home I was surrounded by scholarship and all the brilliance and wit of the 'nineties. ' Fin de siècle ' was a phrase getting almost as tiresome as ' mot juste '. The Fulleyloves would come down to repeat the latest bon mot of Whistler or of Oscar Wilde, and Mrs. Fulleylove would linger to tell us of the bold bad doings of The Langham, the famous art club, and how some artist was carrying on with a model or two. Nobody worried about my long ears.

2

Gordon Craig lived somewhere near with Martin Shaw, and I heard a good deal about them.

I was sent to a kindergarten school, but I have little recollection of it beyond the fact that I met the daughters of some R.A. architects and that my Mother was in a white fury because their parents had not returned a call. It seemed that they lived in 'Upper' Hampstead and that my Father was only a literary man with no academic honour. The eighteen-nineties had as much snobbery as the nineteen-thirties; I well remember that; and some of the precious aesthetes of Kensington, the Adelphi, and Well Walk, would often roll their eyes in horror because my Mother went to work among the lower orders at Toynbee Hall and taught them French. I must have been completely beyond the pale, for in addition to this my Father was secretary to the London Playing Fields Association and an officer of a cadet corps in the East-end; and the docks, the lower river, and Whitechapel High Street were as familiar to me as my native heath; an early experience for which I have always been grateful, as in consequence I have no English fear of the poor or 'the uneducated'.

In due time I went to a large school, a ghastly place from which I was rapidly removed as I had some sort of breakdown owing to being publicly flogged, at the age of seven, for giving away some stamps which I believed to be my own. I was not only described as a thief but as a fence. From this moment I developed a shyness which later on became almost a disease. During my sufferings under injustice a conflict was born in me, and my secret life began.

Shortly afterwards I was sent to University College, where I rapidly recovered from the immediate effects of this experience and became a normal, healthy child, quick at learning, with a passion for engineering, and a capacity for painting imaginary and historical subjects which were so far from bad that I was eventually given a prize by Professor Michael Sadler, representing the Board of Education.

Meanwhile we had moved to a modern house in Parliament Hill. My Father had now become a journalist, and when the Greco-Turkish war broke out he 'covered' it for H. W.

Massingham, who was then editor of the *Daily Chronicle*. For a time my life was quiet and nearly orthodox. I worked steadily and nothing much happened until the outbreak of war with the Boers, when my Father was seen at pro-Boer meetings on Parliament Hill, at which all manner of cranks were present. Morris, the slum reformer, was one of them, and I think another was G. B. Shaw. Whether my Father was present in his capacity as a journalist or as a pro-Boer made no difference to the young men of Hampstead. I became a pariah and several times was thrown into handy ponds by patriots. On one such occasion I returned home soaked and sick at heart to find my Mother in a state of ecstatic delight because Lloyd George had been rough-housed when he attempted to address a pro-Boer meeting at Birmingham. Her jingoism did little to revive my dampened spirits.

Fortunately my Father soon left for South Africa as a war-correspondent and was besieged in Ladysmith. I got accustomed to seeing Nevinson in the newspapers and on the placards, and was grateful indeed that I could now walk alone without fear of further persecution of Kipling-minded Beggars.

But I was soon to learn that patriots are not the only misguided people in the world. Full of anticipation I went with my Mother to France, where I saw the Dieppe of Aubrey Beardsley, Sickert, and Conder. To my great surprise I also had soda water squirted over me and fish thrown at me for being an English pig. However, in spite of black looks, and threats, we went on to Paris, where in our hotel at the Odéon I first saw electric light. At that time three-horse buses used to run from this point to Montmartre, and the band played nightly in the Luxembourg Gardens in a pavilion illuminated by fairy lights, while *les étudiants* would leap about in wild serpentines. Because of my Mother most of my time was spent in Notre-Dame.

If I had little childhood I had far more liberty as a child than most of my contemporaries. The literary lights of the 'nineties did not mask their thoughts before me, and my Father was behind the scenes. While quite young I knew

4

the truth about many matters which were incomprehensible to the public, and I was trained in war long before my doomed generation. I went to a great many places, and from the press box saw a great many sights. The memory of Queen Victoria's Diamond Jubilee, which I viewed from Whitehall, is still vividly with me, and from that time until I left home for a public school I witnessed nearly every important event because of my Father's profession. In those days the Press was not, as it is now, an advertising medium rivalled only by Radio Luxembourg, with a dash of jazz news thrown in for relish. It was a respected institution which attracted brilliant men. But that was when truth meant more than circulation and before it was decreed that as women take more quack medicines and buy more clothes they must dominate the news. Women must be in everything these days, and if fifteen men were to fall to death from the dome of St. Paul's we should certainly see the heading, ' Woman Spectator Faints.'

In the days when journalists were literary men the papers were put to bed with hotter news and more truth at a far later hour than they are to-day, and my Father seldom arrived home before three or four in the morning, usually having shared a hansom with Vaughan Nash, who was later to become Campbell-Bannerman's secretary. I nearly always woke up when he came in, and this nocturnalism has left me with a complete indifference to night or day, whether for work or play. When I was at school I was out of the way, but when I was at home I was driven out early in order that my Father could sleep. It was then I roved London in a ' motor-car' which consisted of a plank, four pram-wheels, and a ' stay rib' or two that clicked against the spokes of the wheels and made a noise which I was satisfied resembled that of an internal-combustion engine. I am proud to say it was my own design. On this contraption I careered about the streets, travelling miles a day. As any mechanically propelled vehicle was an object of interest in those days, I was given a certain amount of attention, not always polite. I had a peculiar horror of pedestrianism, a horror which persists to this day.

Then one magic morning I became the possessor of a bicycle. They were the fastest things on the roads and a boy could be allowed to roam without the present fear that he may never return. At a music hall I had seen some trick cyclists and I practised hard in an attempt to copy them. In time I could ride on one wheel, stand on the saddle and on the handlebars, ride backwards and in reverse: feats I would never attempt now. But games always bored me. Instead of playing cricket or football I spent my time in exploring London, and my knowledge for a boy of my age became encyclopaedic.

Since an early age I had been receiving the best possible training in drawing from Fulleylove, R.I., the distinguished architectural water-colourist rival of David Murray, a pillar of The Langham club. He was an old and valued friend of the family and a fine tutor for any boy to have.

Gradually I had become familiar with most of the current art exhibitions in London and Paris, and my instincts leaned more and more towards painters and painting. During this period I was happy and industrious. Sometimes I stayed with the Massinghams in Grosvenor Road, near the Houses of Parliament, and once I painted from their window a landscape of the Thames with the Doulton factory on the other side of the water. It must have had something in it, for it was described in a whisper as a Maeterlinck landscape. How I wish that now, when I have a greater technical accomplishment, I could do industrial scenes with the same lyrical quality.

At about this time I was beginning to discover that conformity to other people's opinions was necessary for happiness. My Mother, always a pioneer, was shingled, and she used distemper instead of wall-papers. She could not abide Nottingham lace curtains and Victorian knick-knacks, and our home was full of Italian Primitives in reproduction, pre-Raphaelites, and English water-colours. Therefore I was booed in the streets because our house looked different from the others.

Then came the *débâcle*. I was sent to Uppingham.

My Mother, like other people, was influenced by the

6

appalling jingoism of the South African War, and by the fanatic and almost music-hall patriotism that found its expression in the celebrations over the relief of Mafeking, when, draped in red, white and blue, we wandered from Ludgate Circus to Piccadilly ringing a dinner bell.

Before that, when Ladysmith was relieved, my Father had returned on short leave before going to Pretoria, and there is no doubt he was impressed by the charm and brilliance of the Army staff, and the nobility and altruism that seemed to be founded on the public-school spirit. It was much later on in life that he became Socialist. In those days he was a polished Englishman of culture, and said he wanted me to go to Shrewsbury, his old school, and on to Balliol, if not into the Army itself.

Perceiving that I had little interest in the classics, but was enthralled by modern mechanics, and above all by the internal-combustion engine, my Mother compromised and in my Father's absence chose Uppingham. It was a great public school with the traditions of Tring, and it was more modern than other public schools of that time. Science was not merely regarded as 'stinks', and music and painting were not looked upon as crimes. In fact, David, a German pupil of Richter, was almost head master owing to the importance in which music was held.

I had no wish to go to any such school at all, but nevertheless Uppingham did seem to be the best. Since then I have often wondered what the worst was like. No qualms of mine gave me an inkling of the horrors I was to undergo.

Bad feeding, adolescence—always a dangerous period for the male—and the brutality and bestiality in the dormitories, made life a hell on earth. An apathy settled on me. I withered. I learned nothing : I did nothing. I was kicked, hounded, caned, flogged, hairbrushed, morning, noon, and night. The more I suffered, the less I cared. The longer I stayed, the harder I grew.

I attended endless divine services ; listened to strange sermons delivered by doctors of divinity in which Englishmen were confused with God, Nelson with Jesus Christ, Lady Hamilton with the Virgin Mary. The German Fascists of to-day are fed on no greater confusion of patriotism and religion. English Nationalism was a creed which defined Americans as cads, Frenchmen as libertines, and the rest of the European races as a great deal worse—with the possible exception of Germans, who were regarded merely as dangerous rivals in trade.

As a result of my sojourn in this establishment for the training of sportsmen I possessed at the age of fifteen a more extensive knowledge of ' sexual manifestations ' than many a ' gentleman of the centre '. It is possible that the masters did not know what was going on. Such a state of affairs could not and does not exist to-day. It is now the fashion to exclude ' the hearties ' from accusations of sexual interest or sadism, or masochism; but in my day it was they, the athletes, and above all the cricketers, who were allowed these traditional privileges. Boys were bullied, coerced and tortured for their diversion, and many a lad was started on strange things through no fault nor inclination of his own.

Games and the practice of games were the order of the day, but I was able to escape grim afternoons of chasing a ball by going to a studio to paint and draw, and by accompanying my art master in a gig to draw the lovely architecture of Rutland. I also joined the Cadet Corps, a move that made it possible for me to escape the main object of the school, which undoubtedly was cricket and perhaps rugby football. Fortunately, too, I was a good runner, and I seldom was whipped by the hunting crops of the ' hearties ', who would ride beside us lashing out at any fellow with stitch or cramp. I was also able to follow the hounds on foot in that great hunting county and thereby escape many a flogging.

It is only just over thirty years ago, yet the latrines were outside and of the bucket-and-earth variety. That was bad enough; but in the cold weather the younger boys were employed to sit for ages to keep warm the seats for the seniors. The appalling food and the general atmosphere of misery gradually numbed me.

I think it was the kicking which finally settled matters. In this popular pastime known as the ' flying kick ' the cricket eleven wore their white shoes and any junior was captured

8

and bent over for their sport. They took running kicks at our posteriors, their white shoes marking the score and a certain place counting as a bull. A period of this marksmanship left me inflamed and constipated, and eventually I developed acute appendicitis, an illness much dreaded in those days, as the operation was thought to be extremely dangerous.

Thank God, I became so ill that I was moved to London, where I suffered attack after attack. I was in a wretched state, septic in mind and body. Largely encouraged by my Mother, who was always against surgeons and believed we should appear before our Maker in entirety, the doctors refused to operate. I became even worse, my life was despaired of, then the problem was solved by an abscess and perforation. A difficult operation, but I survived.

I had made many cycling tours with my Mother about England, throughout Brittany and France, and we had left hardly one church unvisited. In the art colonies at Pont Aven, Concarneau, Quimper, St. Pol, Caudebec, and St. Michel we always associated with the painters. The name of Monet had been familiar to me for some time. As my Mother had been in Paris from about 1870 she was particularly versed in the Impressionist school; and I had already devoured, by the age of fifteen, the books of Camille Mauclair on Renoir, Manet, Degas, Sisley, and Pissarro, and had heard of Gauguin and Cézanne. I had even heard of the ' mad ' paintings of Van Gogh some five years before their ' discovery ' by Roger Fry and the dealers.

When we stayed at Pont Aven, Mortimer Mempes, whom Whistler dismissed with, ' Who is Memps ? ', was perfecting the three-colour process; and one of the jokes of the family was that Cézanne, Gauguin, and Van Gogh had in the past presented him with some of their canvases, which he considered the work of ardent bunglers, so put aside and lost. I wonder how many thousands they would now be worth.

After my illness we went a ' *Grand Tour* ' to Spain, Northern Africa, Genoa, the Lakes, and Venice. I sketched day and night; but what was best of all, a German, an artist who was of some standing in Munich but whose name escapes me, was much struck with some seascapes, and gave me sound advice and encouragement.

During this period my Father was abroad, chiefly in India, in Central Africa, or in Spain, reporting the Spanish-American war. My Mother was then a very religious woman, and she was in perpetual indecision as to whether or not she should become a convert to Rome, a grave step at all times, but particularly for her, as she was the daughter of the Rector of St. Margaret's at Leicester. She was not the kind to hold her peace during spiritual conflict, and this no doubt accounts for my wide knowledge of the Bible and of the various dogmas. But religion has always left me untouched, my public-school training having killed the mystic that lurks within me, though my intimate friends always say I will yet become an intensely religious man !

I had long been accustomed to an ecclesiastical atmosphere and was familiar with Cathedral Close life through frequent visits to my uncle, Canon Lloyd Jones, at Peterborough, and to my paternal grandfather at Leicester. I have the recollections of an old gentleman sitting in a brougham wrapped in shawls ; an antiquarian whose house was packed with Chinese furniture, dragons, and other treasures, and whose walls were graced by Italian paintings and Constable landscapes. He used to take me on visits to county families near Leicester, where the tradition of the squire lingered on, where every form of class snobbery was worshipped, and where reverence to birth was paid in a way which is now only to be found among the paying guests of Kensington boarding-houses, and writers for *The Times* or *Daily Express*.

What would they think, those Nevinsons who lie in peace in our old cathedrals, or those others on the soldier side of the family, what would they think if they knew we were now called Jews ?

Possibly through my life in the streets I have never been class conscious. At Uppingham I was often in trouble because I had been seen talking to ' cads '—boys or men of the county town who were not considered so well-off as the sons of the newly rich of Yorkshire or Lancashire : a type peculiarly numerous in the school at that time. Some of he little brutes had as much as a pound a day for pocket money. The profiteers in the Boer War did almost as well as in the last one.

The gross Edwardian days were in full swing, and every one was conscious that money was rapidly taking the place of breeding, birth, and culture, and that achievement in the arts or science was about to count for nothing. Even Americanism, as we know it, is not new.

By this time I had become the most hideous, bespotted, cracked-voiced goup it is possible to imagine; broken in spirit, overwhelmed by a thousand conflicts, bursting with energy, yet indescribably bored. I devoured every kind of literature, with a partiality towards the morbid. I was suicidal, a tendency which shocked my Mother, but I can understand now that my spirit had been knocked out of me.

I had an adoration for the theatre, and especially for musical comedy, and I used to stand in the queue ridiculously dressed in a white starched collar and shirt, with a school tie and a huge straw hat of black and white, for such shows as *The Belle of New York, Floradora* and *The Catch of the Season.* My shyness and self-consciousness were terrifying; and once, whilst waiting for my Mother at the Restaurant des Gourmets, I was petrified when a beautiful and befurred Frenchwoman spoke to me.

I went scarlet, but I bowed and replied with seeming aplomb in my best French:

'Madame, je regrette, mais j'ai déjà un rendezvous.' !

For a week afterwards I sweated at the thought of it.

The monastic life I led would be quite incomprehensible to modern youth, which regards the opposite sex with a beautiful ease. I was a self-made prisoner. Not that now a great deal of my time wasn't occupied in the pursuit of girls: the pursuit, not the capture. I have walked countless miles on the promenades of France and Belgium, Italy, Holland, in Brighton, the Spaniards' Road, Earl's Court Exhibition, St. John's Wood, Oxford Street, and Brixton. In spite of my appearance I was given every encouragement; but I was always too shy to speak, and after a vain attempt to screw my courage to the talking point I would salve my conscience with the plea that the girl was not sufficiently good-looking, and would go home, footsore and weary, cursing my cowardice.

I seem to have had a confused training. I lived in a household where literature, politics, art, and music were everyday topics. Eminent people would drop in and lightly discuss the weighty problems of the day. War correspondents would tell what really happened during some advance or retreat, politicians would discuss secret intrigues and unsatisfied ambitions. Artists would take me aside and talk painting for hours. I had suffered three terrible years at a public school, where I was supposed to learn everything about a gentleman, shut my eyes to corruption, kick the weak, and glorify the rich. Behind this there was a background, a noisy accompaniment, of music.

Chopin, Schubert, and Beethoven were played at all hours by my Mother and sister, and at Uppingham the more severe Germanic music of Bach and Handel would be drilled into me by the school orchestra and choir, which were directed by German masters. Towards the end of my summer holidays Monday nights would be devoted to Wagner at the Queen's Hall, and to this day I am thrilled by the realistic dynamics of this 'not quite pure' giant, so unlike the Pure Bloomsbury Pigmies.

Considering that my sister was training at the Royal Academy of Music and that students were all over the drawing-room practising, it is an extraordinary fact—for which I now thank God—that I failed to learn anything about musical technique or construction. This is the one art of which I have no 'backstage' knowledge, and it has, therefore, a real emotional appeal for me. One curious effect of this familiarity with the great masters of music is that I often know what is going to happen ten bars ahead, even when the piece is new to me, and because of this I have a leaning, nowadays, towards the more modern compositions. Every note gives me something of a shock of surprise; and after years of anticipation it is a pleasure to find oneself wrong: an Athenian emotion, perhaps, but an enjoyable one. And, of course, after years of the deadly unescapable jazz bands

12

on and off the wireless, and the reiterated clichés and monotonous rhythm of Jewish and Negroid music, the surprise
comes as a greater relief with modern music.

As an idle speculation I sometimes wonder what effect
wireless will have on the classic music. It has made dictators
possible: what will it do to music? No works of art can
stand up to endless repetition. The youth of this country is
hearing more and more music. I am aware that this art is
now discussed by mathematicians and neo-philosophers as
a science, but I am still convinced that it is an emotional
expression common to any race, creed, or class, and emotional
expression cannot go on day and night.

My escape from school gradually drew to an end and I
felt that my life was going to be wasted once again. By
this time I had definitely decided to be a painter and not an
engineer. In fact, I had reached the stage when it had
become impossible for me to be anything else. Abroad I
had been fired with an enthusiasm which precluded any
other consideration. I was a modernist. The plethora of
artistic training and my revolt against public-school traditions
made me bored with old masters; in Venice an international exhibition of contemporary art had interested me
more than anything I had ever seen. I really was excited
about it, although it is significant that now I can recall no
single picture I saw there except those which introduced me
to the technique of a Neo-Impressionist, Signac.

I returned to Uppingham for a term; then my Father,
who was at the moment in England, came down to consult
Selwyn, the head master. My illness seemed to have interrupted my Father's dream of Balliol, and my future had to
be decided all over again. Most fortunately for me, Selwyn
recommended fruit-farming in California, a suggestion which
caused such indignation on my Father's part that he realized
the school was no good for me, and I left immediately.

2

From Uppingham I went straight to heaven: to St. John's Wood School of Art, where I was to train for the Royal Academy Schools.

I suppose it would take a psychologist to explain it, but whenever I am sent to hell—which, unfortunately for me, is an English institution, into which fits exactly the national code of snobbery and sport—a lethargy settles upon me, I lose all interest, and a morose dumbness paralyses me, making it impossible for me to have any human contact, and shyness and loneliness begin to form a circle. This has happened to me throughout my life. But at St. John's Wood School of Art I became, within half an hour, almost unrecognizable as the same character that had been at Uppingham. The whole of that ghastly school life, with its monastic habits, its sports, its religion, its façade of tradition which hid the most cunning commercialism and clerical opportunism, might never have existed for me.

The Principal, a Mr. Ward, who I suppose had brought the Royal Academic honour within the grasp of more artists than any other tutor of his generation, had already seen my work; and one or two artists had recommended me as a more than likely candidate to be successful in entering the Royal Academy Schools, a position very much valued by 'the Wood' at the time. However, I spent my days not in the life class, but stippling away in 'the Antique' with chalk stump and pointed indiarubber, only drawing from the model at night: a tremendous grind, demanding a completion of tonal effects and tightness of technique unknown among students to-day, involving also a study of facial anatomy and of construction through anatomy. Classic

14

casts were mostly the source of inspiration, and I remained in this stage for a long time. My work up till then had been almost entirely architectural or landscape, and undoubtedly I was sloppy in my technique, as I had studied far too much of the work of De Wint, Claude Monet, and the later Turner water-colours. It was lucky for me that I had not gone straight to Paris as had been suggested, because already I was running before I could walk.

Eventually, however, I became a worker in the life class. The method of teaching there was very similar to that of Julian's. The draughtsmanship was essentially a painter's method of drawing, and often colour and tone were used rather than the pure lineal draughtsmanship associated with the old masters such as Leonardo and Raphael.

We used to meet at Orchardson's studio—son of the Sir William Orchardson, R.A.—at least once a week, and there we held a sketch club and did compositions of a set subject, without, of course, any models, but making the pictures 'out of our heads'. Archibald Barnes, who was later to become a very fine portrait painter, and Longstaff, were the hopefuls of the School. I was an appallingly bad student; but during the vacations I painted and painted, occasionally doing as many as four sketches from nature a day, in all kinds of weather, and at night I often employed some model I had met at the School and worked in a ghastly little studio I rented for seven shillings a week, just off the Marlborough Road.

What energy I had in those days! I cannot think how I packed so much work and pleasure into eighteen or twenty hours a day. Often I cycled violently about loaded with easel and paint-box. My shyness went, and I spent a good deal of my time with Philippa Preston, a lovely creature who was later to marry Maurice Elvey, the film producer. There were others, blondes and brunettes. There were wild dances, student rags as they were called; strange trips with Johnson, an immensely fat man, to the opera; and various excursions with exquisite students, young girls and earnest boys; shouting too much, laughing too often. We usually travelled by four-wheeler, but seldom inside, and wherever we went we made our presence felt.

Grand days ! Those lovely meals at French restaurants, how good they were ! The Café Royal, Gambrinus, would always have to be visited, and although the Café Royal had been familiar to me since the age of eight, I felt most beautifully self-conscious as we strutted in. We were more familiar with the life of the great cities than any *vieux marcheur* or ' gay girl ' from the promenades. With Hill, who eventually departed for America, I formed the music-hall habit. The Metropolitan in Edgware Road, the Bedford at Camden Town, the Tivoli, the Oxford, and the Pavilion were visited regularly, while on some nights we strolled in the most *blasé* manner about the promenades of the Alhambra and the Empire, occasionally condescending to glance at the dancing of Genee, or the hundreds of great, big girls, who pranced their way through such productions as *Les Cloches de Corneville*.

I always seemed to be meeting friends of the family, as the promenades were used by the Intellectuals as well as the *demi-mondaines*. Not that I ever spoke to them; they all seemed far too old and far too correct, with the exception of Arthur Symonds, whose book on Beardsley I had read with such enthusiasm while I was at school. He would generally nod to me in a vague way, stand me a ' trinity ', a three-colour layered drink of *crème de menthe*, brandy, and gin, and sometimes even talk to me in an excited manner about the beauty of some woman or other. Unfortunately I was never able to follow his sentences, he was so strangely inarticulate, even more so than when he became an old man.

The Rothensteins were, I fancy, of the same epoch. I must have seemed an impossible creature, yet Albert Rothenstein, a great promenader with Innes Lees and John, was kind to me then as he has been since. I was only seventeen, but I had my own banking account and often earned five or ten pounds from the sale of my landscapes, most of which were sketches of the Thames and wharves, Paris, Rouen, and Le Havre.

My first commission came from Ramsay MacDonald. He

was visiting my Mother in connexion with the Poor Law, a subject to which she devoted a great part of her life, and he noticed a drawing entitled 'Revolt', inspired by my Father's visit to Moscow on 'Bloody Friday'. He was impressed by it and asked me to the House of Commons, where he gave me lunch and described to me the type of thing he wanted as a poster for a party called the Independent Labour. It was to show a working man looking at a new dawn, and hint at the great future of peace and prosperity which lay before him.

He then introduced me to Keir Hardie, the pioneer of Labour in this country and a man with a head like a lion. I warmed to him. He took me out on the terrace and pointed out to me what he thought was a glimpse of the picturesque—a view of the dreadful slums and Salvation Army hostels which in those days jostled the House of Lords. Of course, I spurned the picturesque: it was already too Proutish for a young man such as myself.

The influence of a certain student was then strong within me. Whistler, one of my gods, had been dismissed by him as a man who could not draw, an amateur painter of old houses and old women. I devoted myself entirely to figure work and the accurate painting of heads. Messina, Holbein, and Dürer became my craze; a reaction for the boy who only a year before had taken little interest in the old masters he saw in Venice. Naturally in this phase of artistic prejudice my poster for the Labour Party was a dismal affair: too black, too overworked, and the hands of the labourer were more Dürer than Dürer. It was rejected.

St. John's Wood School of Art was essentially a school for academic training, and I had begun to do well. Sir David Murray awarded me a prize; Charles Sims was kind about a pastel; and other Academicians, Hacker and Sir James Lynton, had given me encouragement. For a time I had a swollen head because Sir John Clausen had praised a landscape. But in spite of all this a feeling of despair began to well up in me. I had difficulty in creating realistic pictures of the model or still life, and my work suffered from over-painting. My first shot was always the

17

best one, after it would become glutinous and oily, timid and dead in the handling, and my drawing would go from bad to worse.

Most of the people around me were older than I, and through them I became aware of a reaction against what they called the 'pussy' paintings of the Royal Academy. A change was due. We were all obsessed by Fabianism. One man greatly my senior was incessantly preaching Bernard Shaw, and he it was who first showed me drawings by Augustus John. They were reproduced in a publication called the *Slade*, and there were some sketches by Orpen as well. These drawings completely upset my apple-cart. I studied them for a time and then showed them to Orchardson, who, something to my horror, dismissed them as no good. John was simply a posing charlatan who wore gold earrings, 'long hair like Christ' and a Salvation Army jersey, for advertisement; while Orpen, what was he after all, but a flashy trickster?

A period of doubt descended on me. By upbringing I could never accept the 'established'. At that time my family seemed to be always in trouble. My Father had been chucked out of more meetings than any other man in London and had achieved the distinction of being publicly rebuked by Lloyd George at the Albert Hall. My Mother devoted the whole of her life at this period to the under-dog, the scallywag, and the fallen woman, and she fought tooth and nail against the smug powers that were. At home I heard little but a lucidly expressed contempt for the grossness of Edwardian days and its worship of all things which were established, be it prostitution or painting. Our house seemed to be a meeting-place for French, Germans, Finns, Russians, Indians, 'Colonials', Professional Irishmen, and Suffragettes, and none of them had any respect for the things that were. It was, indeed, clear to them that England had nothing to be proud of; a belief which was in sharp contrast to the apparent self-righteousness of all other classes. Puritanism, with all its lusts and cruelties, had created a suspicion of beauty and a reverence for commercial success. It did not matter what a man did for the world. What would he leave ? A poem ? A picture ? Nonsense. Look at his will. What had he made ?

The knowing ones said that if an artist wanted to make his way in the world he must cater for the merchants of the North by illustrating in pictorial form copybook ethics that would now make Ethel M. Dell blush. No details were spared to me. I must paint Darbies and Joans, deeds of daring-do or of sacrifice, or perhaps young girls praying while dogs looked on with human eyes expressing reverence mixed with envy. True-blue religion, sudden death, and beef-on-the-hoof or hunting, were also good themes. Occasionally, I was advised, sex might be allowed, provided it showed coy and pretty maidens fleeing from wicked conquerors, while loot and rape had been known to succeed if and when they were daintily wrapped up in the theme that ' men would be men in the Good Old Days '.

All this talk had its effect; England was obsessed by a material vulgarity and, in addition, my travels abroad, which were now made on every possible occasion, had led me to view my own country with a clearer eye. I saw what was happening throughout Europe, and I could find nothing to compare with what was then the fashion in England. I read literature far beyond my years and was familiar with Tolstoy, Dostoievsky, Zola, Maupassant, G. B. Shaw, Hardy, and a host of others whose work shouted for a better appreciation of art.

The trips abroad were nearly always made with my Mother, and I was beginning to know Paris besides its churches and galleries. I was familiar with all French art and I had already met Toulouse Lautrec, a dwarf in a frock-coat. It was at a private view at a Gallery in Lower Regent Street and we were the only visitors. Lautrec was somewhat tipsy, although it was in the morning, and like the old aristocrat that he was he refused to sit in the presence of a lady although he was quite unable to stand. I suppose I looked at him far more than at the pictures, for I only remember one or two of Yvette Guilbert, of whom Arthur Symonds had told me so much about. They roused my curiosity about Montmartre, where ' Life ' was. We always stayed in the Latin

Quarter in Paris, but Montmartre was my romantic magnet. At that time Montparnasse did not exist except for the studios in the rue de la Grande Chaumière. Raspail was still incomplete, but every afternoon when my Mother lay down, off I went on foot to Montmartre; down rue de Seine from the Odéon, over the Pont des Arts, up the Place de l'Opéra to the Grands Boulevards, through rue Lafitte to glance at the latest Monets and Pissarros at Durand-Rouel, and see the glistening Sacré Coeur—still with the scaffolding on it—against the dark silhouette of Trinité. Here I always made a mistake through studying the map of the Metro too keenly, and instead of going straight on I would turn to the right to reach rue Faubourg Montmartre, thereby adding at least a mile to my walk. I would arrive at Place du Tertre, via the steps, more dead than alive, and eventually find myself at Place de Clichy. Having gazed at the shut doors of the Moulin de la Galette, sipped a *syrop* at the Pierrot, and looked at the dead windows of the Royal, the Monico, and the Rat Mort, I would lapse into the Metro and so home. As far as I recollect the Nord-Sud was not then working. Perhaps it was as well that I was always too tired to get to Place Blanche and the apéritifs at the Moulin Rouge. That was a joy to come.

Doubts about conventions in art grew into certainties; and when Sargent, the god of St. John's Wood, stated that John was the greatest draughtsman since the Renaissance, I think my mind was made up. It became obvious to me that the Slade method of draughtsmanship had a liveliness and intention unknown in the misapplied energy of the old-fashioned dogmas that came to England through the salons of 1870. Nevertheless, I owe much to the idealism of those old Academicians, especially when they took us to Kew to paint the river, or the trees and flowers of the gardens, with an almost unholy accuracy. In summer we also went to Frensham, girls and boys, painting in a barn in bad weather, but otherwise we were left to ourselves to sketch on the moor or in the lanes. It was a strangely beautiful time for me, especially as I was also busy falling in love, usually with two or three girls at the same time.

20

This was probably the wildest and most joyous time of my student days, but I will say no more about them than this: the mothers, and even the grandmothers, of the so-called modern girl managed to live a life strangely like that of the much-abused contemporary. Perhaps they were a little more secretive; perhaps a little less innocent; certainly a little more cautious, but so promiscuous.

I left for the Slade and abandoned any attempt to get into the Royal Academy Schools, a grave step which I took lightly, a step which undoubtedly altered my career, whether for better or worse I still do not know, because of the undying persecution of Tonks. In these later years I have often regretted that I did not stick to the conventional course. Who knows, I might have been a smug portrait-painter now, respected, rich, and respectable, with little more than a sixpenny packet of artistic wild oats withered and forgotten.

My departure from the Wood was marked by the first and, I think, the last occasion on which I was drunk. We had a party of some sort, the usual joyful affair artists seem to have made their own, and I had to drink rather more than was customary for me because I was the excuse for the festivities. Afterwards I went to say good-bye to Johnson in Maida Vale. He was leaving for Scotland by the night train, and he pointed out how necessary it was that we should finish the drinks instead of leaving them to the landlady. We finished them to the last drop, then made for King's Cross with his luggage inside a four-wheeler and ourselves, as usual, on the roof, urging all and sundry to their congenial tasks with loud cries of ' Och aye ! ' We were duly decanted on the platform for the express, which he just managed to catch; and, in a burst of affection unusual in me, I raced alongside the departing train, urging him in what I imagined to be broad Scotch to come back again. Then I fell down, and was picked up and scolded by a sympathetic porter, who led me away to be sick.

Acting under orders from the porter I walked to Hampstead, where I was accosted by a young girl in purple plush and a hat full of feathers. By now I was fairly sober. She said she wanted a drink, so we went into Jack Straw's Castle, where we had two drinks each. The girl was calling me 'sir'; but, for all that, she led me out, I fear with immoral intentions. She must have been disappointed when I was violently sick again, but she took my arm and propped me up a good part of the way home. When I felt able to walk alone, with splendid largess I gave her half-a-crown, which at first she refused to take; then she spat on it and slipped it into her stocking, blessing me as a kind gentleman and advising me to keep off the booze. It was very like Satan rebuking sin.

With great determination and fixity of purpose I got home and to bed, but as soon as I put the light out and lay down the bed became like a raft in an angry sea. I was tossed, spun, heaved, and lurched, and in desperation I put on the light again. My Father, seeing the light under my door, came in resplendent from some regimental dinner. He told me *all* about it, then started to talk about art. Then my Mother came in from a political meeting, and a long argument took place as to the exact words of some quotation from Juvenal. By now I was queasy again and keeping up appearances by an effort. Eventually I was left alone, but only just in time to make a dash for the lavatory, where I was terribly ill.

It was years before I tasted whisky again.

3

University College in Gower Street was familiar to me, as I had been there to school for a time, and Goodwin—Professor Goodwin's son and now a famous gynæcologist—and others I knew, had become medicals or scientists there.

On my first morning at the Slade I showed my life drawings to dear old Professor Brown, who looked at them and at one or two of my portrait heads and remarked that as art was long I could skip the antique and go straight to the life class.

I went. It was a large, gloomy vault of a place, and on my entrance I was greeted with embarrassing enthusiasm by a girl model who frequently sat at the Wood. Immediately I was aware again of that terrible disapproving atmosphere of the public school. Once more shyness and uncertainty came back upon me. The room seemed to smell like a chapel and I did an awful drawing. However, I had sufficient presence of mind to turn over my piece of paper and start again just before rest, and so cheat the students who crowded round to see the work of this old hand with the large bow tie, bewaisted coat, socks and handkerchiefs of a delicate peacock blue, and a slight growth of whiskers à la Rapin about his ears.

At this time the Slade was full with a crowd of men such as I have never seen before or since. There were two outsize Germans, who were dwarfed by a giant of a Pole with scowling brows, tight check trousers and whiskers eight inches long. Mr. Fothergill was an exquisite in dark blue velvet suiting, pale-yellow silk shirt and stock, with a silver pin as large as an egg, and patent court shoes with silver buckles. It was possible in those days, of course, to

23

be a dandy without being thought a pansy as well. The two things are more than distinct, yet completely confused by the present younger generation. There were Claus and Ihlee, a retired major or two in white shirt-sleeves and cuffs, and Stanley Spencer with uncombed hair and a cockatoo, looking like a boy of thirteen. Mark Gertler was there, looking, with his curly hair, like a Jewish Botticelli. There were several very old gentlemen; a completely civilized-looking Gilbert Solomon—now secretary of the R.B.A.; a long, thin fellow named Helps; Benson, already yellow with cigarette smoking; and I think Paul Nash and Ben Nicholson, very correct and formal. The atmosphere was as solemn as it was uncouth: self-consciousness ruled. In order to attract attention Fothergill developed a fit of temperament and tore up his drawing, then struck several matches which he threw in the air, and departed, I learned later, for his studio in Fitzroy Street. Presently he returned in changed clothes—a black coat, chef trousers and sandals, with a whippet at his heels—and prepared to make a fresh start upon the long road that leads to artistic achievement.

Then Tonks came in to criticize and stopped to have a long social talk with the retired majors first, discussing the vintages at some dinner-party they had attended the night before. He then came on to me and was not unpleasant. He asked me to define drawing, a thing I was fortunately able to do to his satisfaction, as I neither mentioned tone nor colour in my stammering definition but kept on using the word outline. But he nevertheless managed to shatter my self-confidence, and I was wringing wet by the time he left me to go on to Stanley Spencer.

For a whole term I felt thoroughly out of it. I was wretched, subdued, and only escaped at week-ends to enjoy painting. At this period I used often to meet Duncan Grant staggering along with canvases to some other art school, and this gave me the idea that while the Slade was undoubtedly more professional than St. John's Wood, I was not learning to paint; so I used to drop into Heatherly's, and paint *croquis* in the French manner, receiving no tuition but learning from the people around me. I had already done this at Colarossi in Paris and did not mind the atmosphere. During the lunch hours I associated, not with the Slade students, but almost entirely with the medicals, often going with them into the dissecting-rooms. I must confess that for a time I yearned to become a medical. Perhaps they were more lax in those days, but I seem to have spent many happy hours in the hospital with the students.

In spite of the fact that I still had many girl friends, I became morbid, introspective and shy again. The society of the opposite sex usually has a good effect on the young, but my trouble went deep. Most of my friends had gone on to the Royal Academy Schools and we saw little of each other. I spent a whole year of dullness, although I still went to all the French restaurants and sat about in the French cafés. It is queer to think nowadays that sometimes I never spoke a word of English during my evening's amusement.

I still kept in touch with Philippa Preston, who, owing to the sudden death of her father, had become a journalist. In those days Maurice Elvey—her future husband—was an actor, under, I think, Fred Terry. He was a highbrow, very interested in a new theatre, and was obsessed by Ibsen and G. B. Shaw. He ran a Sunday Society for impossible plays, and it is interesting to note that he was the first man to put on *Peer Gynt* in this country. This connexion put me in touch with a theatrical set, and I joined a strange club called the Arts and Dramatic, with its headquarters at Allan's bead-shop and tea-rooms at Oxford Circus. For some reason I have always got on with theatrical people. I like their quick conversation and endless talk of shop. Nothing interests me more than other people's shop; and owing to my almost incessant attendance at theatres and music halls, both at the front and at the back, my life became more like that of a student of the Royal Academy of dramatic art than that of one at the Slade.

Gradually I came to feel more at home at the new school, largely because of Wadsworth and Allinson. I formed a real friendship, too, with Gertler, who was the genius of the place and besides that the most serious, single-minded artist I have ever come across. His combination of high spirits, shrewd Jewish sense and brilliant conversation are unmatched anywhere. He is now famous enough to need little description, but in those days he had come on from the Polytechnic through the Jewish Education Society, and even as a young man he was an outstanding figure. His father had been an innkeeper in Austria and was then a furrier in Spitalfields. Through my early association with Toynbee Hall and the current Oxford movement, Whitechapel had no terrors for me; and being what Augustus John called a man cursed with an educational tendency, I was delighted to be able to help Gertler, I hope without patronage, to the wider culture that had been possible for me through my birth and environment. At any rate, I loved it, and his sense of humour prevented me from becoming a prig. Often, indeed, the pupil was able to teach the master a great deal, and it is impossible to convey the pleasures and enthusiasms we shared in the print room of the British Museum, in South Kensington, and in the National Gallery. We also shared the joys of eating, and I am proud and glad to say that both my parents were extremely fond of him. Never shall I forget his description of his visit to the Darwins at Cambridge, where he was painting a portrait. At dinner he was offered asparagus for the first time. Being accustomed to spring onions, he started at the white end first, and the beautifully mannered don followed suit in order not to embarrass him. He was a boxer, besides, *au fait* with every turn at the Shoreditch Empire, fond of the girls and adored by them.

By now Wadsworth, Allinson, Claus, Ihlee, Lightfoot, Curry, Spencer, and myself had become a gang, sometimes known in correct Kensington circles as the Slade coster gang because we mostly wore black jerseys, scarlet mufflers, and black caps or hats. Sometimes we were joined by the one-armed Badger Moody, who was the toughest of the lot. We were the terror of Soho and violent participants, for the mere love of a row, at such places as the anti-vivisectionist demonstrations at the " Little Brown Dog " at Battersea. We also fought with the medical students of other hospitals for the possession of Phineas, the bekilted dummy which stood outside a tobacconist's shop in Tottenham Court Road and was rightly or wrongly considered the mascot of the University College of London. I believe they still fight for it. This often entailed visits to Tottenham Court Road police station, Bow Street, and Vine Street. There is no doubt we behaved abominably and were no examples for placid modern youth. Fortunately we were well known to the police, who in those days treated ' college lads ' with an amazing tolerance. I could not mention the number of occasions on which the crowd turned on our gang and pursued us up Greek Street and round the Palace Theatre. They were usually actuated by a frenzy of patriotism, as the eccentricity of our clothes proved we were dirty foreigners. Why they should have felt like that in Soho, of all places, heaven only knows.

It was rare for us to see the end of a music-hall performance, and we would have considered it beneath our dignity to leave in a voluntary manner. This method of exit led to my first introduction to Charlie Chaplin. We never missed a show of Fred Karno's ' Mumming Birds ', and after being duly ejected we would go round to the pub at the back to meet the performers, for there was no malice aforethought in our demonstrations. In those days Sid Chaplin was more important than his brother and I met them both. Charlie was a quiet, little, dark man, who played a small part. He had nothing much to say for himself and gave no hint that he would one day prove to be the world's greatest clown. I can recall nothing funny that he did or said. He was just the ' pro ' off-stage, one of a crowd doing the work he knew, and probably thankful he was able to get it. I say this in no spirit of underestimation.

The Bedford Music Hall was our Mecca, not only because it was painted so much by Sickert, but because the twice-nightly performances possessed a vitality, a full-blooded, god-blessed vulgarity, that would horrify the B.B.C.-fed audiences of to-day. War has been blamed for many things, but who ever thought it could make a nation prim ?

Once a month the management would announce that in its Search for Talent it would hold an Amateur Competition Open to All. This was always a heart-rending, side-splitting affair. A coy person who had never sung anywhere

27

but at the piano in the parlour would pipe ' The Maiden's Prayer ', with as much chance of getting it across as a dumb girl. At the third note ' the bird ' would be heard and in half a minute the uproar from the audience would drown the orchestra. If the performer continued to sing bravely, an enormous hand with a policeman's brassard on the sleeve would be thrust from the wings and the offender dragged from view. Sopranos usually ran. A few minutes' pause and on would come, say, a local butcher's boy, full of cheek and a determination to give an impersonation of Albert Chevalier, with ' Knocked 'Em in the Old Kent Road '.

Sometimes an aspirant would lose his temper; sometimes, I am afraid, she would burst into tears. There were even times when a good turn came on and got applause, for the whole affair was *meant* to be good-natured. If the performer thought the audience harsh, he was learning something that every one in the theatrical profession knows from birth: the audience has always the right to be rude.

At the time of the Slade gang I was also working at sculpture under Harvard Thomas. He was a bad teacher but a great man. Rightly or wrongly he always claimed to have helped Epstein, who according to him was ignorant of the technique of architectural sculpture. From what I know of Epstein as a craftsman I should say this is completely wrong, but when Epstein's work in the Strand was attacked by all the press of London, Thomas defended it as if it had been his own. After a good deal of experience I imagine Epstein has become accustomed to defending himself.

All this time I was evolving from the chrysalis stage and beginning to look like a normal young man. The years fled and I discovered myself to be on the eve of twenty-one. A birthday is always an excuse for a party, and so I ' flung ' one. Everybody came; all the Slade gang, the Academy students, men such as John and Strang, and a crowd of professionals, singers mostly, men, women, and girls. We had a whole dancing troupe to keep the party going, and one of the girls danced naked. No doubt we all felt very Harry Thaw-ish and tried to look like decadent geniuses with a strong tinge of the anti-*bourgeois*. At that time such

28

a thing was as unusual as it is now commonplace, the only difference being that when I say naked I mean naked.

It is amazing that we managed to be so serious in the midst of these high-spirited and exhausting diversions. It was undoubtedly a god-send that we drank so little, or we could never have stood the pace, and it is significant that all the surviving members of the gang have become successful painters, professionals all. We represented a reaction against the priggishness, posturing, and posing, which had been left as a legacy to the Slade from John's generation, and we must have been a sore trial to poor virgin Tonks. We had little or nothing to do with the girl students, a completely new state of affairs, as I understand that in John's day there was great camaraderie between the sexes. The woman's movement was in full swing, however, and we were tremendously manly and thought ourselves vastly superior beings and lords of creation.

As usual women found a way in the end; and before I left the Slade, affairs of the heart already existed between the gang and the girl students, ultimately breaking up the gang. I coquetted with a girl with whom Gertler was violently in love. Poor girl, she killed herself on the death of Lytton Strachey, years later. Brett, who eventually joined D. H. Lawrence, was another, while Ann Somebody was pursued by both Allinson and Wadsworth, although she adored Wadsworth. They were grand girls, junior in years, but really much too old for us. In some things we were so very young and stupid, and we never hesitated to indulge in every form of dalliance which roused the jealousy of our best friends.

A model caused a good deal of trouble by producing a child which was put down not only to me but to seventeen other men, including Professor Tonks! Ian Strang always swore it was my child because he said it resembled me. I offered to marry the girl and got a very rude refusal.

By now my work was being noticed. Through the Friday Club, a remarkable little clique which was eventually ruined by the amateurish dilettantism of Roger Fry, I was given opportunities for exhibiting pictures. Robert Ross praised

29

me as ‘ an old-fashioned gentleman ’ in the *Morning Post*;
Frank Rutter, whom I had known in the Women's Suffrage
movement, wrote a column on my industrial pictures of
East Ham and Liverpool Street, and of the gasometers and
power stations painted in the impressionist manner. I had
become a visitor to the Camden Town Group; Sickert
had encouraged me in my work, which I was selling; I had
formed with Gilman and Gore a friendship which was to
last till their deaths; and I had made the acquaintance of
Percy Wyndham Lewis. It seemed I was making progress.
Then Tonks advised me to abandon art as a career.

It is in my experience that most men surprise themselves
by their ability to stand shocks. When Tonks gave me
his opinion I remained calm; and with the debonair
nonchalance which was a peculiarity of mine in those days,
I decided to go to Switzerland where I could get some ski-ing
and think things over. A man is as irresponsible as he feels;
and although I might be accused justly of taking some things
lightly, it must always be said that art means everything to
me. There is also another point of view. If a young man
of twenty-one is worth anything at all, he has opinions about
his master just as his master has opinions about him. Had
Gertler, for instance, told me seriously that I was wasting
my time I should have been heart-broken, but as things
were I managed to bear up.

I enjoyed myself on my holiday and decided that my
future could not yet be arranged on other lines. It would
be interesting, I thought, to experiment with journalism,
and to that end I returned and looked up Philippa Preston,
who promised to help me. Some bright newspaper lad had
thought of a new angle. Famous people were to be interviewed and asked all about their besetting sins, and she
would take me round and show me how it was done.

Journalism seemed a great lark to me. We started off to
see Little Tich at the old Tivoli and found him standing
on the steps that led from Adelphi arches to the music-hall
door. Nobody had told us he was a vain little man, so
when he climbed five steps before turning round to address
us we naturally tried to get a little nearer. But each time

we mounted a step he went higher and backwards, in order that he might remain eye to eye. So engrossed was I in this game that I quite forgot about the interview. With each question put to him by Philippa I went forward and upward, but I didn't catch up with him until we reached the top of the building.

After that we had to see Marie Lloyd, the queen of variety. Marie had no use for publicity. She pleased herself, saw you only if she thought she would, when she gave you a tumblerful of champagne, refused to answer questions, told you a funny story, then ordered you out as she was going to change and was much too old for *that* sort of thing. On this occasion she had given us the slip. Like the other top-liners she was working three houses a night in different parts of London, sometimes appearing twice nightly at each of them, and using an old theatre bus-and-pair as the most reliable form of transport. Fast, fool-proof cars had not been invented, yet it was possible to move without a stop between Oxford Circus and Piccadilly and to do the journey in five minutes, too, instead of half an hour. But that was, as I say, in the bad old days before the internal-combustion engine had slowed everything up. We set off after Marie in a Fiat taxi—a wild extravagance which was not paid for by the newspaper—and we ran her to earth at Brixton, where she told us that her besetting sins were smoking and, of all things, singing at matinées in the cause of Votes for Women. At first we thought she was pulling our legs, but we discovered her confession to be true, and never shall I forget the enthusiasm she once caused at the Caxton Hall by singing an outrageous song entitled ' There's Nothing Really Shocking About a Stocking ' to an audience composed almost entirely of women determined to break down the ancient tradition that there should be one law for a woman and none for a man and that men should in future be as virginal as themselves. Her gestures were sublime and proved a knowledge of men which denoted that smoking was not her only weakness.

In due course a newspaper gave me some interviewing to do myself, and as I appeared to know something about art

I was sent off to see some Royal Academicians. Already artists were pretending to hate publicity and to despise journalism. The younger generation was accused by these old gentlemen of having no idealism and of merely desiring to see their names in print. Suffragettes were accused of going to prison for the same reason. But what humbugs these Academicians were ! Some of them are still living, so I will not mention their names. They usually refused to see me until I sent up a message that I quite understood, as I had been an artist myself, and that I would return to my editor and see that their names were removed, so that they would never be bothered again by ' mere journalists'. This always brought them dashing down the stairs, and they would pour out the most amazing copy and the most vituperative attacks upon their more successful brothers of the brush. I often wonder now if these dear old gentlemen realized how completely they exposed themselves to a rather shy young man. I felt, and still feel, contempt for the whole convention which even to this day is given lip-service at all banquets and discussions where artists are gathered together professing a contempt for journalism. Journalism as I saw it gave me a horrible knowledge of backstage, and of the impudence of people who live on the public and who are therefore dependent upon the Press as the means of informing the world of their doings. I prefer the frankness of the Film and the Stage to the methods of the artistic and literary professions, though it must be remembered that the literary man is probably the greatest humbug because he shelters behind his publisher, who pays thousands of pounds for advertisements. However, I stayed only a short time in Fleet Street; and although I went there because I had been told I was wasting my time in trying to paint, I have often had those few months of my life thrown in my face.

I went up to Bradford to join the Beldon family, with the idea of becoming librarian to a wealthy wool-merchant collector. The scheme, thank heaven, fell through; but I painted the mills and moors of Yorkshire and met a very talented family. Eileen Beldon, who was then a child, was destined to become one of Bernard Shaw's favourite actresses.

The Rothensteins were there, Priestley was sometimes spoken of, and I heard about Humbert Woolf. Wadsworth and Allinson arrived, too, if I remember rightly.

On my return, the gang had more or less formed up again and we called ourselves the Neo-Primitives. A portrait of us by Curry was hung in the place of honour at the New English Arts Club, and I suppose still exists somewhere. By this time I was largely under the influence of Gertler and was doing highly finished heads in the Botticelli manner. We had all previously visited Paris, but the gang now went in force, with David Sassoon in addition. It was a ghastly trip, as we travelled steerage via Dieppe, and poor Gertler nearly died from sea-sickness, being revived only by French sailors hosing him in the early dawn. However, the Primitive Room at the Louvre compensated us for much and our enthusiasm was terrific. But how we despised Rubens !

Returning to England, I spent an enchanted time with the Beldons at Port Erin in the Isle of Man, where I became engaged to the lovely daughter of a fabulously rich mill-owner; but she caught me exerting my charms on somebody else, as usual, and that romance went the way of others. Disappointed and disgusted with myself, I returned to London. Everything was flat. I was lonely, disillusioned, and unable to decide for myself what my future was to be. My Mother advised me to live abroad for a while, and I jumped at the suggestion. The Nevinsons never have any other solution for human ills but travel.

4

Soon after I had left Uppingham it had been suggested that Paris was the proper place for me to study art, and in my immature state I was lucky to avoid going. Now things were different. I was ripe for Paris and all it could teach me. For company I had a man called Baldwin, an old friend of St. John's Wood, and I could have had no better companion. His real name was Rudhall and he was a retired South African miner, a man of varied experience and great flair. He was a born dilettante, a hypochondriac who never exploited his gift of painting, but who had the most independent taste and an unfailing faculty for spotting an artist, whether embryonic or not. With him I quickly forgot the Tonks' nonsense about abandoning art.

For years my Mother and I had known the Post-Impressionists, although Roger Fry had just given his exhibition at the Grafton Galleries of such men as Cézanne, Van Gogh, Manet, and Gauguin; but it was Rudhall who first pointed out to me the paintings of Matisse at the Salon des Indépendents. He showed me the strange landscapes of Rousseau —almost amateurish they appeared to me then—and he took me to the Saturday Salons of Gertrude Stein, where I first heard the name of Picasso. I used to walk in and out of the place, taking their hospitality very much for granted. Only the other day I was apologizing to Gertrude Stein for my behaviour. She assured me the Germans were ruder than I. It was there I met Matisse, who looked like a sturdy man of the *bourgeois* type, with gold spectacles and a beard. He was at times rebuked by his wife for his obvious interest in the gastronomic rather than aesthetic.

At six o'clock in the morning I used to go round to

Julian's in the rue du Dragon. Segonzac had just left the school, but I saw some of his paintings, which were not quite so heavy in technique as his later work. In the evenings I went to the other Julian's, in Montmartre, and there I had more success. Through a misunderstanding, the half *crétin* concièrge wrote my name down as Nevinski; and, what with that and my good French, I found myself treated with respect. A Russian was accorded deference, while a mere English artist was not worth consideration. How I wish I had clung to that name, although such a course has its dangers. When Basil Cameron, the conductor, was starting on his musical career he looked round for a good name and decided on Von Hindenburg. And a good name it was, up to the beginning of August 1914, when Von Hindenburg quietly disappeared like so many Germans of the period. In his case, however, the public was astounded to hear that the brilliant young conductor they had admired was commanding the German Army. Fortunately, a young man named Basil Cameron was there to carry on in his place. Basil was a young man and so able to survive the curse of an English name.

Matisse's School was called the Circle Russe when I joined it. It was somewhere at the back of Montparnasse station, behind that terrible apache district that was round rue de la Gaité, the most sordid brothel café-chantant street in Europe in those days : not that I minded that. A great deal of my time was spent on the Fortifications, in La Villette, and on the Buttes Chaumont. The bleak poverty of Paris and the desperados were mere colourful grist for my mill. I was obsessed by Goya, Daumier, and Toulouse Lautrec. William Rothenstein and Calvert had both published books on Goya, and I always had a copy of one or other of them under my arm.

Through being a student at Montmartre, and a Russian at that—for Nevinski stuck—I was at last familiar with the apéritifs at the Moulin Rouge, where several of ' Les Girls ' remembered Lautrec, and where all manner of people would assemble. It was there I met Whistler's friends, the Pennells. But it would be useless to attempt to give a catalogue of names. It is enough to say that this was the meeting-place for the aristocrats of Austria and Russia, the intellectuals and artists of all the other countries, and the snobs of England. The orchestra, which was Tyrolean, wore uniforms of green knickers, embroidered shirts, and little felt hats, and the rhythm was often accentuated not only by Germanic shouts and yodels but by the firing of revolvers, an alarming custom to the novitiate. The can-can was reserved for the evening. One curious feature of Montmartre was that people never troubled to change their clothes. The can-can girls would stand about in their befrilled and bepetticoated dresses, though the gamin was the fashion, with tight skirts, bobbed hair, long black stockings and no underclothes, a fact which was often displayed. The Tyrolean band when off duty would walk about Clichy in their strange get-up; the tango orchestra would be dressed *à la* Sud-Americaine; and the Hungarian tzigane would stroll in their befrogged uniforms of brilliant blue, with shakos and top boots. Cyrano's next door looked like the wings at an opera, and all this at half-past five in the afternoon. On the other side of the Butte was the Lapin Agile, which was then a meeting-place for real cut-throats and a number of first-rate French artists. Picasso was particularly fond of this *auberge*.

Usually I dined at the Elephant, in rue Blanche, a restaurant with food *de luxe* and theatrical motley. There I met Harry Fragson, the man-at-the-piano who amused Paris and London with equal facility. Lots of French artistes dined there, and I remember being struck by the beauty of Alice Delysia. Music was most beautifully played by two Spanish guitarists, who always read the *Paris Sport* instead of the music sheets, and turned the page to follow ' Les courses' while they caressed the strings in some lovely cadenza. Madame, ever ready, sat at the *caisse,* and delivered various messages, *pneumatiques* and *bleus* to the right wife, lover, or mistress. Her knowledge of the love intrigues of Paris was accurate and complete, and she had never been known to make a mistake when a slip might have been catastrophic. She wore the most marvellous diamonds and had difficulty in writing on account of them, though every order was entered

36

in her book in that bewildering method of French triple entry. She also sang, she joined all the tables, had a *petit verre* with the majority, bullied the chef, hounded the waiters, looked after her canaries, and remained open until six in the morning, when she went to the market to do her own buying. She never looked tired, although her husband did. He was always polite, and sometimes he would arouse his wife's jealousy by being a little too gallant to the exquisite exotics who came out at nightfall. Madame was highly respected when she died at the age of seventy-two.

After dinner we usually went to Medrano's Circus, where we had drinks with the clowns and sat among the horses. The café was in the stables and the performers acted as waiters and waitresses for *rendezvous, pourboire,* or *ballons*. It was there I met Titi, a Cockney-Italian clown, with whom I formed a friendship. Picasso, Asselin, and Marx were often there, too. To me it was almost a holy place because of the drawings that Degas and Louis Legrand had done of it. We would stroll on to the Tabarin, the Royal, or the Monico, where I first saw Severini. Sometimes we caught the Nord-Sud home, but generally we walked all the way across Paris, sometimes in the green dawn, tired out and with feet splitting. I would sleep for what seemed a few minutes, then *café complet* would arrive and drive me off to work again.

Inevitably some nights would be spent quietly in Montparnasse, at the restaurant Le Duc, with a drink later at the Dôme or the Closerie des Lilas, and endless, endless discussions on art. The intellectuals of to-day ought to realize that all their chatter of aesthetics and pure art was already stale a quarter of a century ago. One can look with benevolence on youth's rediscovery of truth, but when the same ideas inspire men of middle age I am reminded of elderly women who coquette with gigolos. How we used to hammer out the solution of things in those days! Sometimes tone would settle the matter for good and all, but the next night it might be harmony, and sometimes colour, sometimes drawing, sometimes imagination, sometimes fantasy, sometimes spiritualism, sometimes the subconscious,

37

sometimes the liver, sometimes absinthe, sometimes continence in the very young, sometimes religion, and sometimes the lack of it. I am not sure that my own love for the theatre did not come into it : it surely must have done, for I was there so often.

Gravely I used to sit through over-elocuted performances at the Odéon and listen to Sarah Bernhardt at her theatre declaiming away so that she might keep her son in affluence. Poor Sarah, she was none too popular at this time, as her lifelong habit of refusing to pay for anything roused the furious envy of the entire French *bourgeoisie*. My Mother remembered her in Paris when she was persuaded with much difficulty to go to that barbarous country England, that land of fog, roast beef, and red flannel. It was about the time when Frenchmen pointed to an Englishman's turned-up trousers and said : ' See, it is raining in London.' Sarah Bernhardt feared the worst, for it was notorious—so notorious that it was untrue—that no great artist was ever recognized on our inhospitable shores. But Sarah needed money, and the guarantee was good, so she took the plunge. Continental trains in those days always arrived at Charing Cross. It was indisputable that the sun was shining from a blue sky and that the eyes of the people sparkled as the train drew in. Sarah drew herself up. England was about to do homage to France's greatest artist. And of all things, of all the lovely gestures, here was a red carpet for her proud feet to walk on. Sarah sailed through the station to the gasps of the crowd, and she bowed and waved her hand. It was all splendid. England was not ' *barbare* ', and she was wonderfully happy until a London policeman seized her by the arm.

' Here ! off that,' he commanded.

Sarah's eyes opened wide as she annihilated him in French.

' Oh,' said the policeman. ' A foreigner, eh ? Well you ought to know better when there's Royalty about.'

And with that he pulled her on to the plain asphalt and back to the cold truth.

I was often busy copying at the Louvre, where Matisse and Picasso came to do the same thing. In my humble opinion this was a useless form of training, as most of the time was spent in trying to imitate a patina which nothing but age can give. To this day I feel furious when contemporary art critics discuss quality of paint, and I assert with emphasis that all oil painting that is not directly handled and applied without much impasto will deteriorate, and that the scrumbles and glazings and other tricks adopted by many moderns in order to make their work look pleasant to-day will look most unpleasant to-morrow. Quality of paint cannot be judged under twenty years, and even then it depends on the treatment it has suffered during that period.

Feeling better about life, I returned for a while to London, where I purchased a motor-cycle, the act of a pioneer. At the New English I exhibited two works of which I was proud. One which created comment was of some men hauling a barge along the canal of La Villette. This was bought by a judge. Another, a self-portrait, found a purchaser in Horace de Vere Cole, the famous practical joker, although on this occasion his intentions were serious, acting upon John's advice. It is now in the Tate Gallery.

I was now earning my living by painting; and as I was mad on Art, I think I had taken a right decision after Tonks' advice. The Chenil Gallery, which was largely advised by Augustus John, took any picture I sent them. Newstub was a remarkable salesman and he got rid of most of my work, although he often took an unconscionable time paying me. He was also selling Gertler's and Curry's work well, but John and Orpen were the star turns of the gallery. Orpen married one of the Newstub sisters and Rothenstein the other. I do not seem to remember any of the Rothenstein paintings there, but I cherish the most charming letter from William Rothenstein on my self-portrait. What a kind man Rothenstein was and is to the young; how different from many artists. He asked me to go and see him, and I did. He was living then in Oakhill Park, and was a friend of H. G. Wells, who was then not popular through some book, *Ann Veronica,* if I remember rightly. Then Albert Rothenstein asked me to breakfast, carrying on the Whistler tradition. I was very self-conscious after mixing with the professionalism of Paris, where not only the artists but the actors lived in a most Bohemian atmosphere—I can find no better word—quite cut off from the *bourgeoisie,* or the *grand monde*, selling their pictures through an entrepreneur, or a dealer, or an exhibition. Only a few daring connoisseurs ever visited their *ateliers*. In Albert Rothenstein's studio, in Thurloe Square, I was once more back in the atmosphere not only of a cultured gentleman, but of an exquisite who showed me a poem, I think by Rupert Brooke, before breakfast, a fan before coffee, and we were discussing Granville Barker by the marmalade. He took me on to Harrods' to buy some silk he wished to paint on, and there I left him, slightly bewildered and wondering what to do with myself.

A bus took me somewhere down to Barking, and there I wandered among my factory chimneys and docks, where I purchased a workman's scarf down Sailor Alley and felt much better. Much as actresses take to country cottages, I, who was brought up for Oxford and the Army in a hotbed of intellectualism, religion, and the classics, found refreshment in ugliness and the uncouth.

My home was at that time obsessed by politics, chiefly Poor Law and Home Rule. My sister was practising and practising her music, my Mother was writing sketches for the *Westminster Gazette* and becoming quite famous, and she was also translating Juvenal and making his satire tally with the conditions of the British Empire while my Father, a little aloof, was writing for the *Daily News,* the *Manchester Guardian*, and the newly formed *Nation*. What an atmosphere ! Professionals one and all, shouting and arguing ; and if any one misquoted, meals would be abandoned while we hunted the library or the drawing-room for our proofs. My Father had reacted against the purely literary coteries of London and worshipped the Man of Action. I myself have this hereditary trait, and the conflict is always within me ; although it is easier now for me to see, after the behaviour of the men of action, that the most useless picture is better than the most useful bomb, and that contemplation is better than manoeuvre.

I gave myself up to my new toy, the motor-bike, and went all over the country. Never shall I forget the look of icy disdain when I turned up on my mount, most un-aesthetic, to a general meeting of the New English. I had lost touch with most of the Slade students, but now and then I would see somebody and hear the news. Lightfoot had committed suicide because of unrequited love for a model. He had been one of the most talented men at the Slade and was an undoubted loss. I was shocked when I was told; and blasé as I was, I felt bewildered when I witnessed the natural pride of the woman because a man had died for her. Gertler and Curry were good friends until Curry murdered a beautiful girl named Henry and tried to kill himself. For a while he lingered on, then in spite of all medical efforts to get him fit enough for the gallows he cheated them, poor fellow, and died. He was an Irishman from the Potteries, with a Napoleonic complex, and non-moral because of an over-reading of Nietzsche, a philosopher who profoundly influenced many of us.

My contact with the art world was through the dances and revels held at Covent Garden, the Botanical Gardens, and the Assembly Rooms of the Eyre Arms at St. John's Wood. It was at one of those I met Madame Strindberg, the origin, or shall we say one of the inspirations of Strindberg's tirades against women in general and married women in particular. She was in love with an artist who, in order to escape from her, had climbed down the drain-pipe of the Savoy when she had locked him in her suite. She was an interesting woman and the originator of night clubs in London, starting first, I think, with a supper club in Percy Street, and later, with the aid of the Arts and Dramatic, moving to Hanover Square. Many of us appeared, at her invitation, overdressed *à l'apache* for the opening night, at which all the distinguished people in London were present. We were supposed to eat a gipsy meal, and I spent an educational evening watching the dismay, disgust, and chagrin of the rich and well-fed guests when the feast did not arrive. It seemed that owing to some slight difficulty of a financial nature Madame had not given the necessary deposit for the caterers. She assured us that quantities of food were being prepared by the gipsies, but nothing appeared except the photograph of a hedgehog, and this did little to assuage the pangs of those sleek men and women who had dined fully two hours before. They listened to the singing, then by twos and threes went empty away.

At this time I was painting hard and showing my work at the Friday Club, the Chenil Gallery, and through the Camden Town Group, where we met every Saturday, each member in rotation acting as host and looking after the tea in a room in Fitzroy Street. Here I got on terms with Sickert, Ross, Manson, and Ginner. I was enlivened by the conversation of P. Wyndham Lewis—I must use the P. because of that very nice fellow D. B. Wyndham Lewis, the humorous writer, and I should hate anybody to confuse the two. Old Pissarro used occasionally to come in with Frank Rutter. Konody came, too, and Hume, who was later to play an important part in my life; also Lady Ottoline Morrell, sometimes with John or Lamb. The New English held two exhibitions a year, and I was usually hung, though sometimes rejected, treatment which caused me the blackest fits of depression.

I returned to Paris alone, to live in rue Lepic and begin the strangest epoch of my life. The work of Picasso, Matisse, Derain, and Vlaminck were by now well known to me if to no one else. The Fauviste school, through the influence of Gauguin, was reacting against the prettiness and technical accomplishment of French art. They were trying to introduce into their work a harsher or wilder note, a more intense expression, although, of course, Picasso was still swayed by Toulouse Lautrec and was only just leaving his blue period, mostly doing sketches at the Lapin Agile, or drypoints of acrobats, *sautabanques,* beggars, and children.

One day I was going through rue Lafitte when I saw a strange still-life, very much simplified, of a plate, a banana, and a mask, or what I thought was a mask. I went in to Sagot and he was enormously interested at my having remarked it. He showed me a great number of paintings, many of them geometric; and one by Marchand, of the roofs of Montmartre with an Indian-red factory chimney, made an astonishing impression on me. I was dissatisfied with representational painting, and already through Van Gogh I was using an outline simplifying form to accentuate my planes.

Cubism was only one step farther, but it was long before Picasso began splitting up his forms into almost incomprehensible pieces. After all these years it is impossible to describe the worry, the doubts, which this form of technique gave rise to. I felt the power of this first phase of Cubism and there was a desire in me to reach that dignity which can be conveyed pictorially by the abstract rather than by the particular. So often I had spoiled pictures by elaborating them. The form seemed to lose its vigour and its statement by my attempts at exactness, and my brushwork would follow suit. The heads of Marie Laurencin and Picasso, through the elimination of high lights and the accidental glitter in the eyes, seemed more like the work of the early masters. Wyndham Lewis had talked to me a great deal about the African mask and the curious earth colours and brick-reds of the early Derains. The austerity of Cézanne had thrilled me, and I never felt sympathy with the highbrows of those days who dismissed Van Gogh as a literary painter. Like many others I was attracted by abstract art, and the colour harmonies of Kandinsky seemed to me to be more important than they were.

It cannot be denied that the whole of this movement was opening out a new direction of aesthetic intention. Photographic art had never appealed to me, and for years I did not attempt to paint pictures just like life. I had accepted various conventions as being pictorially more satisfying, whether expressed in outline, spots, or streaks, or by any other technique which was non-representational yet conveyed the impression more strongly. It was a period of intense study, and I must have examined literally hundreds and hundreds of pictures. I was like a man in any other walk in life who is struck suddenly by a truth which he has always known to be at the back of his mind, and I was altering my standards accordingly.

I did not paint much from nature then, but hung round the Gare St. Lazare, the Gare du Nord, the Seine, and the outskirts of Paris, working on quick sketches and inventing a new formula for myself. It would be of great interest to me now if I could see some of my work of that period, but everything seems to be sold—to whom I know not.

5

Most evenings saw me at the Moulin Rouge, which
was burnt down a few years ago, and here an old Russian
woman who sold chocolates and kept an eye on ' the girls '
took a fancy to me because I resembled her son, who had
been killed by the Russian police. Through her I encountered one of the strangest sides of Paris. She used to
ask me to her flat, which was actually lined with pink silk,
filled with bric-à-brac, and frequented by the most extraordinary riff-raff it is possible to conceive.

Here I met a weird collection of Russian refugees—terrorists,
anarchists, men hiding from the police of the world, and
mild professors with blood on the brain. They were endless
talkers about Life and the social system; practical, logical,
horrifying. The women were either of the most degraded
and vicious type, or mistresses of journalists, doctors, and
deputies, some of them brilliant, all of them interesting. I
learned a great deal from them; and I, for one, was in no
way surprised at some of the things that happened during
the Russian Revolution.

There were also Frenchwomen who had revolted against
the appalling tyranny of the average French home life. It is
not even now realized in England how dull and miserable
the existence of a woman can be in the Latin countries.
My Mother and I once met a young girl who was studying
at the Sorbonne. Greatly daring, she had dispensed with
her *bonne* and was trying to live a life *à l'Anglaise*; and the
treatment she experienced and the insults which were heaped
on her would simply be disbelieved in England. She had
ventured down Boulevard St. Michel alone and on foot,
and as a result of what was said and done she cried the

whole way. It is not so long ago that a woman who was alone was compelled to travel by *fiacre,* and even this was often boarded by one of her gallant countrymen. To-day France has not changed much in correct circles. No 'nice' girl can sit on a *café terrasse,* even with her own mother, and how relations spy on them! Girls of this country should be thankful for their freedom.

Through Titi, the clown, I had now formed a friendship with Severini and was moving among people of high intellectual achievement. Picasso had joined up with Kleingweiler, '*un de ces Juifs*', as Sagot used to say, and was doing fairly well. His period of acute poverty was over, but he did not change his way of living and sought the company of clowns, a thing he always longed to be himself. He struck me as a man who rather relished persecution, but this of course was in keeping with the clown complex. Titi was never happy until he was laughed at, and he did not consider it a good evening unless he had been booted out of a *boîte,* or ejected for his impudence from a swagger dance place in rue Blanche or rue La Fontaine. Zelli's was not in existence, and the same building was used as a South American rendezvous and was full of Spanish dancers. Here I first saw the tango danced to the strains of Paloma.

In the Latin Quarter, the Closerie des Lilas was the meeting-place, especially on Wednesday nights, when the *avant garde* of the painters and poets turned up. Paul Fort used to come along with his wife and his daughter, who was to become Madame Severini. I was always being asked about Turner and Constable and Bonnington. Those three artists seemed to fascinate the French intellectuals. Turner was held responsible for the change in French painting and the Impressionist movement. There were ceaseless discussions, too, as to the influence over Michel, Boudin, and the *plein air* school exercised by Constable when he exhibited at the Salon. One old man told me that he remembered Michel's paintings hanging next to Constable's. I still wonder if he spoke the truth. For sentimental reasons I have always been interested in Michel. My Mother used to describe Montmartre to me just as he painted it, with,

46

stone quarries and windmills, with dance halls attached, which were opened on Sundays and on fête days. My Mother used to go there sometimes from Asnières, where she was at school.

Severini had painted his 'Danse de Pompom' at the Monico, and through him I came to know Boccioni, Sofficci, and, later, Modigliani. I was also on nodding terms with Kisling. Most of these painters were desperately poor, but I was certainly in the *milieu*, and we used to sit and listen to Appolinaire. Zoborowski was often about, mostly gambling, but sometimes buying pictures for trivial sums whenever he had had a good day or night, another kind of gambling too, for that matter, as most of the artists were looked down upon by public opinion, connoisseurs, and critics.

In rue Delambre, Augustus John taught Euphemia Lamb to ride a bicycle. I am ashamed to say I giggled at the sight of Lamb (or was it Innes ?) exquisitely dressed, with a yellow French novel under his arm, watching while Euphemia, lovely and ash blonde, in black velvet, a yellow-scarlet muffler, and a great display of black silk stocking, curvetted and staggered down the road, with John, in corduroy trousers, jersey, golden ear-rings, and carroty beard and hair, dashing after her.

Through my Russian friends, who used to frequent the Rotonde, then a small *bistro*, I met a man now known as Lenin. He was a smallish, yellowish man with a good head, a revolutionary of some sort, and I understood he had already been in trouble with the police of his own country, although, of course, nobody thought any the worse of him for that.

Most of us, the Russians included, regarded Lenin as a cranky extremist, and he was thought little of by the serious revolutionaries. We had discussions at different times, but he was a one-minded man for all his obvious intelligence.

There were Russian meetings held just round the corner from the Rotonde, and we used to go to hear the speakers. Lenin, I am afraid, was listened to in a spirit of irreverence, particularly by the Russians. He was not counted one of the leaders at that time, and we used to hear him with an amused toleration. That he was in deadly earnest nobody

47

doubted. He used to froth at the mouth in his excitement. But that only made him the more amusing. Little did anybody imagine that one day this man would be the creator of the U.S.S.R. So many people are hysterical in frustration and blossom when the time for action comes, although it is given to few men to do what Lenin did.

I have often wondered who was the German genius who marked Lenin down either as a leader of men or as a mischief-maker powerful enough to wreck Russia and put her out of the War. He must have been a trusted spy, for his word was sufficient to make Germany provide the famous sealed train from Geneva to the Russian frontier. I probably met that man, yet none of the many Germans in Montparnasse seemed to have any gift of understanding. Undoubtedly Germany had hundreds of her agents in Paris then, for war was already being spoken of seriously. In London the hit of the day was Pelissier's song in the Follies, ' There ain't going to be no war so long as we've a king like good King Edward,' and that seemed pretty well to sum up the British attitude. Those who, like Lord Roberts, had spent the last few years of their lives in warning us of the dangers just over the horizon, were dismissed as cranks or axe-grinders. Governments do not take the people into their confidence. We were told as much as was good for us. Nowadays it is supposed to be different. I suppose that is why the whole Press of the world, *except our own,* discussed the crisis in 1936 when our entire Navy and the greater parts of our Army and Air Force were concentrated in the Mediterranean because Mussolini had shaken his fist at the British Empire.

Rumours of war were abroad long before King George V came to the throne. Journalists and officers used to discuss the matter openly at the Closerie, and they all vowed that Germany's plan was to attack France through Belgium at Liège, as the railway system demanded it. It is a mystery to me that the whole world should have been so surprised when Germany did come through Belgium. All the soldiers expected it; Hilaire Belloc wrote a brilliant article about it in the *London Magazine*; even my Mother, who knew

48

nothing about railway systems or strategy, told me that Belgium would once again become the cockpit of Europe.

All sorts of people were, of course, coming and going in Paris, and I was in touch with most of those who came over, often meeting Joseph Simpson, Ferguson, Roger Fry, Clive Bell, the Gordons, Everett, and various students of the Slade. I was exhibiting in Berlin at Der Sturm through my *entrée* from Severini, and in Munich I also had a canvas or two at old Sagot's. At the Salon des Indépendants I was unlucky. Although there was no hanging committee I was always badly placed, but what could I say when all the positions were drawn by ballot ? In my cynical old age I am not surprised that the artists with the biggest names invariably drew the best positions. Even now I know of a respectable club where the older or more famous members are always successful when a ballot has to be held for a dinner or coronation.

One day Severini and I called to see a Russian sculptor, and when we arrived he and Derain were standing before wide-open windows on a cold day and breathing deeply. I asked if there had been an escape of gas.

Derain turned and shouted at the top of his voice:

' Une fois j'étais Fauviste.'

Severini and I were mystified until he explained that Roger Fry had been there with another milord, obviously some *New Statesman* aesthetic Cambridge critic. These two tame and highly civilized experts, with their exquisite chatter, had thoroughly upset the Russian and Derain, who were infuriated that such precious dilettantes should appreciate their work, in which they tried to introduce a harsh and wild note. I was somewhat shocked at the time, although I understand that with the professionalism which is so essentially French they treated their visitors with the utmost gravity and attention. Poor Bloomsburies ! It is easier to mix oil and water than an amateur and a professional, although in England, of course, the gentleman is more reverenced than the player.

Then there is another side of the question. Neither the intellectual nor the general public has any idea of the ruthless commercialism which at times goes on behind the amateur façade in the exploitation or the sale of works of art. The average person believes that people do not buy pictures, that there is not much trade in them, entirely forgetting that business men do not take large premises at fantastic rentals in Bond Street and in London squares for cultural reasons. Vast sums are paid each year for pictures and not by any means for Old Masters only. Indeed, some dealers have assured me that when contemporary pictures are included in a show they sell better than Old Masters and give a better turnover. The Old Master business naturally has more headlines because it usually deals in what the newspapers call "sensational sums."

Dealers trade in the ordinary way of business, but a good many amateurs who profess their status too much could no more afford to turn professionals than their brothers in certain other forms of sport. Some of those much-prized letters, for instance, when one amateur writes to another amateur and congratulates him on the discovery of 'a fine example'—are they written for the pure love of art? It is difficult to believe this when in due course we find both amateurs *and* the letter in the same auction room.

But quite apart from any dubious dabbling in profession-alism, it is extraordinary how the Royal Society of Amateur Painters will attract a much larger, more fashionable, and more influential crowd than a better exhibition by pro-fessionals. The cry of some artists that people don't buy is made for one of three reasons; it arises from envy, it is an attempt to get in among 'the gentlemen', or it is in order to announce that they are pure artists painting for love and therefore commercially more valuable.

I have never considered it a sin to earn my living by painting, and I cannot understand the mentality of a man who con-fuses professionalism with prostitution. Sometimes when the money would have been welcome I have had to refuse work because it clashed with my ideals in art. Sometimes I have been incapable of adapting myself to the sort of standard demanded. Is it not obvious that a professional is as free as anybody else? The term 'commercial artist' is one I will never admit. The portrait painter or mural decorator who accepts commissions to enhance the drawing-room of a rich man is every bit as commercial as the man who accepts a commission to do a girl's head for a magazine cover or a decoration for a hoarding. I consider such men as Mac-Knight Kauffer and Colin to be fine artists. The distinction between a statue on the Underground and a poster on the same railway is beyond me.

For some time I shared a studio with Modigliani. He was a quiet man of charming manners and I knew him as well as, if not better than, most men. His pictures, which I sometimes bought for £5 and have, alas! let go, since sold for over four figures. Since his leap into fame the most utter nonsense has been written about him—how he drove his mistress to her death; how he begged for food; how he died of dissipation and poverty, and how is that possible in Paris? Modigliani should have been the father of a family. He was kind, constant, correct and considerate: a *bourgeois* Jew.

I first met him in 1911 and we were friends till his death in 1920. Latterly his lungs were weak, not because of dissipation but through German gas. He had been discharged from the French Foreign Legion for this very thing.

It is true he was often hard up, like so many other men whose value to the world is incomparably greater than their richer and non-creative fellows, but he never starved. Zoborowski the Pole, a man of taste and foresight, saw the worth of the young Italian and supplied him with a little money when it was necessary and worked to build up the artist's reputation. When Modigliani died in the influenza scourge that swept the city soon after the War, his mistress (who was a *rentier*) killed herself in her grief, poor girl—a gesture of love which will give some clue to the character of the man. His death was a great blow to all of us and especially to Zoborowski. It is true he made a fortune out of the artist's paintings, but somebody was bound to do that, and who better than the benefactor who had treated him with such generosity?

Modigliani's paintings are mostly heads of people in Montparnasse, while his nudes are nearly all of his charming *camarade,* as he always described her. He had nothing to do with the Italian Futurists, although he was friendly with Severini and Boccioni. One could trace the influence of Picasso and his negro mask period. He was rightly associated with the Fauvistes and started as a sculptor. His work was more Byzantine than Italian, or perhaps it would be more accurate to say that his work was nearer the Italian primitives of the arbitrary forms of Byzantine art, before they became more humanized by the Gothic. His colour was of great beauty, rich in the harmonies of earths, ochres and reds. His draughtsmanship was fine, and he had that gift of deformation which achieves a likeness out of characterization without the comic element which necessarily cheapens the art of caricature.

His nudes are among the finest paintings of women the world has seen. They have the decorative qualities of all that is best in Persian and Chinese art, expressed in a technique which is ultra-modern. They have none of the cloying sweetness of Boucher, Watteau, Velasquez, and Rubens. A natural and a beautiful severity runs throughout his interpretations of nudes, giving to them a classicism which puts Modigliani among the greatest figure painters of all time.

He loved women and women loved him. They seemed to know instinctively that though he was poor they were in the presence of a great man. Painters were two a penny in Montparnasse, yet even the most mercenary of the girls would treat him as *le peintre et le prince*. They would look after him, scrub for him, cook for him, sit for him; and before they went away they would beg him to accept a little gift ' for art's sake '.

Like Picasso, to whom we owe a great deal of modern architecture, furniture and design, Modigliani influenced the fashions. The Parisienne does not only look in the women's shops. Painting is as much a part of her life as the theatre or the cinema is to her prototype in London; and when she saw those wonderful nudes, such a longing possessed her for a body like them that she started slimming, a craze which has spread all over the world. His paintings also inspired the sudden cry for sunburnt colourings, ochre powder and the orange-red rouge.

Poor Modigliani ! How surprised he would be and how happy at his fame. He would never have thought of himself as an intellectual. He was a poet and a painter, intermingling line and colour. Argument left him cold. He was a worker, and because he was a worker he would have loved appreciation without any desire to be misunderstood.

6

The next two years were busy ones for me, so busy that I can hardly recollect them. In 1912 I visited Belgium and Holland, and the rest of the time I about halved between Paris and England.

While in London, I studied lithography under Ernest Jackson at the London County Council schools in Southampton Row. Of all the men I have met who deal with the teaching of art, he is the finest and most erudite: a technician and an artist. No wonder he is now in charge of one of the best art schools in the world. Many letters reach me from parents asking my advice about art and art schools, and it is not irrelevant to say here that I always recommend the Byam Shaw School for young people who have any real talent. The others who have not will soon, I hope, get discouraged and so be spared much loss of time and heart-break.

In various autobiographies I have noticed that many pages are given up to accounts of ill health. Practically all my life I have suffered from illness, yet I hesitate to mention it except in so far as it altered the uneven tenor of my way. I always remember John's remark about Sir William Rothenstein's book. The author had devoted page after page to the genius of Augustus John, and all John said was: 'Who wants to know that William Rothenstein had jaundice?'

Nevertheless, it is necessary for me to say that following pericarditis and rheumatic fever I was now crippled completely. I began to think I should never walk again. Everything was tried on me while I lay helpless on my bed. But for all that I was able to be of some use to Frank Rutter, who was organizing an exhibition of Modern Art, by writing personally to artists of the various movements.

I was moved to Buxton and was put in the hands of a great specialist there. After a long time, I began to be able to move again and my spirits rose. They must have risen uncannily, for I used to sing American songs at the Hydro, ' Cowboy Joe' in particular, at the concerts arranged there, and was quite a star turn. Here also I met Kathleen Knowlman, the most lovely blonde, who had come to keep her father company while he took his cure. She was warned against me, and rightly so, because eventually, and possibly because of it, she became my wife. As may be gathered from past pages, falling in love was not exactly my *métier*. With ghastly egotism, combined with a ruthless desire to be a real artist, I had usually left the love game to the female of the species. For all I know, that may be a common experience with all men ; but nevertheless I am bewildered, and was still more so in those days, at the number of girls who have professed to adore me : poor girls, poor girls. I have met many since, some very rich, some very poor, some happy, some unhappy, most of them now married. Sooner or later they all told me that I was the love of their lives ! I give it up ; I cannot explain it. I was always fat, ugly, indifferent and promiscuous, with a terribly roving eye, more from force of habit than from real desire. A most unpleasant creature, but blessed or cursed with a real love of beauty, the effrontery of a shy man, and a mind more than half-feminine in seeing their point of view, either through intuition or through acute observation, I am never sure which. Later this was to develop more and more, till now I have an almost uncanny X-ray eye, which I can apply to both male and female. I can smell their secret desires and thoughts, and more often than not I can hear people thinking. These faculties naturally make me extremely unpopular amongst the intelligentsia, who put up so many barricades and façades and who drown with pretentious hypocrisy their sub-conscious yearnings, or shall I say the yearnings which they will not admit even to themselves.

Whilst at Buxton, I was fortunate enough to receive a

long-awaited cheque from the Chenil Gallery, and I returned
to London, no longer a cripple. Now began my life as a
rebel artist, discussed everywhere, laughed at and reviled by
all contemporary critics with the exception of P. G. Konody,
Robert Ross and Frank Rutter. Looking back, I think it
was Frank Rutter who put me on the map. I was exhibiting
at the Independents, as I had exhibited with the Independents
in Paris, although the London gallery, the Royal Albert
Hall, was most unsuitable. There was of course, no jury,
and a guinea subscription entitled us to exhibit three or
four pictures each, one of which was to be hung on the
line and all of which were to be hung in a group. Lavery,
Sickert, Spencer Gore, Ginner, Gilman, Pissarro, Manson,
and Wyndham Lewis were the backbone of the exhibition;
I a mere fin. But my work had attracted sufficient attention
to get me into the Dorée Gallery with Signac, Cézanne,
Picasso, Derain, Sofficci, Bala, Ernst, Marx, Gaudier-
Brzeska, Wyndham Lewis, Wadsworth, Gilman, Ginner,
Severini, Matisse, Vlaminck, Delaunay, and I think Utrillo.
Modigliani did not send, although I wrote to him. Frank
Rutter lectured in the evenings on Modern Art, and here
I met Lady Muriel Paget, Lady Grosvenor, Lady Lavery,
and through them pre-War Society.

In the meanwhile P. Wyndham Lewis and I had become
friendly, partly because he had asked me to join his party
against Fry and the Omega workshop. To quote his letter,
he felt Fry was ' a shark in aesthetic waters and in any case
only a survival of the greenery-yallery nineties '.

I found Lewis the most brilliant theorist I had ever met.
He was charming, and I shall always look back with gratitude
to the enchanted time I spent with him. I little knew that
he was to become my enemy. It is said that he suffers from
thinking he is unpopular, but this is not so. He is essentially
histrionic and enjoys playing a rôle; while being misunderstood is one of his pleasures. A good talker, to be
understood would mean, in his estimation, to be obvious.
He likes to keep himself to himself. If only he would.
However, I am anticipating. We were friendly then.

Marinetti, the Italian Futurist, thought of coming to England and told Severini, who wrote to me about him. I asked Severini to persuade him to come. My father had met him on one never-to-be-forgotten occasion in the Balkan Wars, when the Italian had found himself cooped up in a train full of journalists for a whole day, a golden opportunity for him. He made the most of it by reciting for hours on end various Italian poems and expounding the theory of Italian Futurism to an audience which could not get away. His idea was to make Italy a country with a future as well as a country with a past, and to attack the malady of passé-ism, which was the way he defined the intellectual curse of Europe and America.

Wyndham Lewis and I organized a dinner at the Florence to welcome him, and we gathered together about sixty of the intelligentsia, including Harold Monro, Laurence Housman, and Wilenski. It was an extraordinary affair. Marinetti recited a poem about the siege of Adrianople, with various kinds of onomatopoeic noises and crashes in free verse, while all the time a band downstairs played, ' You made me love you. I didn't want to do it.' It was grand if incoherent. I made a short speech in French and Lewis followed, then jealousy began to show its head. Marinetti knew of me through Severini and he understood my French better, so he paid more attention to me. He did not know, poor fellow, that he was wrecking a friendship that promised well. His French was good, having nothing of the Italian accent or phraseology I associated with Severini or Boccioni. It certainly was a funny meal. Most people had come to laugh, but there were few who were not overwhelmed by the dynamic personality and declamatory gifts of the Italian propagandist; while still the band downstairs tinkled on: ' You made me love you.' It seemed incapable of playing anything else. This was my first public appearance before the Press. It was also my first speech of any kind. The men who covered it for the papers knew little of what was said, but from a sensational point of view they got all they wanted, and for a time my name seemed always to be in print.

I was now lunching and dining with all the rich and great

of the land. It ought to have gone to my head. I met our old neighbour Asquith, who was, of course, Prime Minister, Sir Edward Grey, F. E. Smith (Lord Birkenhead), Sir John French, with a man named Moore and a host of others I cannot remember. Nancy Cunard was then about fifteen or sixteen, the brightest, prettiest and naughtiest little girl, with a vivid intelligence that often embarrassed her mother. It was at Lady Cunard's I met Eddie Marsh, Lady Diana Manners, and one hundred and one Guardees and Guinnesses. Lady Lavery was beautiful beyond dreams. The food and wines would have made old men cry for joy, but the curse of it was that I was on a strict diet and was almost a total abstainer. This was especially galling, as I was often at Lady Constance Hatch's and the cellar was the finest in London. For reasons best known to himself, P. Wyndham Lewis turned up to one of these dinners in ordinary clothes. This embarrassed nobody except himself, but my inoffensive white tie did much to increase his enmity towards me.

In the meanwhile I had issued the following with Marinetti:

A FUTURIST MANIFESTO

VITAL ENGLISH ART

F. T. Marinetti
C. R. W. Nevinson

I am an Italian Futurist poet, and a passionate admirer of England. I wish, however, to cure English Art of that most grave of all maladies— passé-ism. I have the right to speak plainly and without compromise, and together with my friend Nevinson, an English Futurist painter, to give the signal for battle.

AGAINST:

1.—The worship of tradition and the conservatism of Academies, the commercial acquiescence of English artists, the effeminacy of their art and their complete absorption towards a purely decorative sense.

2.—The pessimistic, sceptical and narrow views of the English public, who stupidly adore the pretty-pretty, the commonplace, the soft, sweet, and mediocre, the sickly revivals of mediaevalism, the Garden Cities with their curfews and artificial battlements, the Maypole Morris dances, Aestheticism, Oscar Wilde, the Pre-Raphaelites, Neo-primitives and Paris.

58

3.—The perverted snob who ignores or despises all English daring, originality and invention, but welcomes eagerly all foreign originality and daring. After all, England can boast of Pioneers in Poetry, such as Shakespeare and Swinburne; in Art, Turner and Constable (the original founders of the Impressionist and Barbizon School); in Science, Watts, Stephenson, Darwin, &c. &c.

4.—The sham revolutionaries of the New English Art Club, who, having destroyed the prestige of the Royal Academy, now show themselves grossly hostile to the later movements of the advance guard.

5.—The indifference of the King, the State, and the politicians towards all arts.

6.—The English notion that Art is a useless pastime, only fit for women and schoolgirls, that artists are poor deluded fools to be pitied and protected, and Art a ridiculous complaint, a mere topic for table-talk.

7.—The universal right of the ignorant to discuss and decide upon all questions of Art.

8.—The old grotesque idea of genius—drunken, filthy, ragged, outcast; drunkenness the synonym of Art, Chelsea the Montmarte of London: the Post Rossettis with long hair under the sombrero, and other passéist filth.

9.—The sentimentality with which you load your pictures—to compensate, perhaps, for your praiseworthy utter lack of sentimentality in life.

10.—Pioneers suffering from arrested development, from success or from despair, pioneers sitting snug on their tight little islands, or vegetating in their oases refusing to resume the march, the pioneers who say: 'We love Progress, but not yours'; the wearied pioneers who say: 'Post-impressionism is all right, but it must not go further than deliberate *naïveté*.' (Gauguin.) These pioneers show that not only has their development stopped, but that they have never really understood the evolution of Art. If it has been necessary in painting and sculpture to have *naïveté*, deformation and archaism, it was only because it was essential to break away violently from the academic and the graceful before going further towards the plastic dynamism of painting.

11.—The mania for immortality. A masterpiece must disappear with its author. Immortality in Art is a disgrace. The ancestors of our Italian Art, by their constructive power and their ideal of immortality, have built for us a prison of timidity, of imitation and of plagiarism. They sit there on grandfather chairs and for ever dominate our creative agonies with their marble frowns: 'Take care, children. Mind the motors. Don't go too quick. Wrap yourselves up well. Mind the draughts. Be careful of the lightning.'

'Forward! HURRAH for motors! HURRAH for speed! HURRAH for draughts! HURRAH for lightning!'

WE WANT:

1.—To have an English Art that is strong, virile and anti-sentimental.

2.—That English artists strengthen their Art by a recuperative optimism, a fearless desire of adventure, a heroic instinct of discovery, a worship of strength and a physical and moral courage, all sturdy virtues of the English race.

3.—Sport to be considered an essential element in Art.

4.—To create a powerful advance guard, which alone can save English Art, now threatened by the traditional conservatism of Academies and the habitual indifference of the public. This will be an exciting stimulant, a violent incentive for creative genius, a constant inducement to keep alive the fires of invention and of art, so as to obviate the monotonous labour and expense of perpetual raking out and relighting of the furnace.

5.—A rich and powerful country like England ought without question to support, defend and glorify its advance guard of artists, no matter how advanced or how extreme, if it intends to deliver its Art from inevitable death.

F. T. MARINETTI

C. R. W. NEVINSON

This was published in *The Times,* the *Observer* and the *Daily Mail,* but we were not content with that and I used to go to the galleries of theatres and shower the manifestos on the heads of the unsuspecting people in the stalls and the dress circle. When I was located I was escorted from the building by the largest commissionaire. It would be untrue to say that this joint effort shook England to its foundations, but certainly stirred the art world; and P. Wyndham Lewis, white hot, wrote to *The Times,* the *Observer* and the *Daily Mail,* dissociating himself from Marinetti, to the great satisfaction of all and the derision of Fleet Street.

Lewis was at that time anxious to produce a paper somewhat on the lines of the Futurist manifestos. He asked me to help him and I went so far as to suggest the title, which was *Blast.* We used to meet at Verrey's to discuss the first issues; and as I had more on my hands than I knew how to cope with, I was at the same time able to put work in his way. We were designing a tableau for the Albert Hall Picture Ball of the Futurists, while Lady Cunard had arranged for me to decorate the drawing-room of Mr. Moore, who was giving a dance to General Sir John French. I went fifty-fifty with Lewis.

The Countess of Drogheda was thinking of having a modern *décor* in her new drawing-room, but somehow or other he got the job entirely. Fortunately this made no difference to my friendship with Lady Drogheda.

At the same time Madame Strindberg had started in

Heddon Street the ' Cave of the Golden Calf ', with statuary by Epstein and decorations by P. Wyndham Lewis.

I gave my first lecture on Modern Art at the Dorée Gallery and was fiercely heckled by Gaudier-Brzeska. The comments on the occasion in the *New Age* by Bechoffer Roberts were galling, although no doubt some people enjoyed reading them. I don't think I was meant to. Many years later Bechoffer wrote the life of Lord Birkenhead. Brzeska was killed in the early part of the War, but not before he had done some lovely work, and I am proud to say I was one of his first patrons. He was the hero of that famous book, *Savage Messiah.*

Marinetti went to Berlin and Rome, then returned to London, where he lectured at the Dorée Gallery and declaimed his poems. On this occasion I was given a drum to bang in order to enhance the dynamic qualities of his verse, and under his direction I made a good deal of noise and enjoyed myself. Marinetti also brought with him on this visit two surprises. The first was a new model of his modern clothing with ' one dynamic button '; interesting but probably too practical. And I never got as far as wearing one, or even seeing one on anybody else. But the other surprise, his noise tuners, was heard of a good deal. It says a great deal for Marinetti that he was able to induce Oswald Stoll to put him on at the Coliseum. Nobody else could have done it. Naturally I went to see the first performance, and I must say it was one of the funniest shows ever put on in London, provided, of course, that one looked at things from the right angle. Marinetti swaggered on to that vast stage looking about the size of a house fly, and bowed. As he spoke no English, there was no time wasted in explanations or in the preparation of his audience. Had they spoken Italian, I do believe Marinetti could have magnetized them as he did everybody else. There was nothing for it, however, but to call upon his ten noise tuners to play, so they turned handles like those of a hurdy-gurdy. It must have sounded magnificent to him, for he beamed; but a little way back in the auditorium all one could hear was the faintest of buzzes. At first the audience did not understand that this was the performance offered them in return for their hard-earned cash, but when they did there was one vast, deep, and long-sustained, ' Boo ! '

George Graves came on immediately, and before he had time to say a word he was greeted by round after round, as much a sign of disapproval of Marinetti as of approval of George. When the tumult died Konody, the critic, rose and gave George one little ' Boo ' of his own, and how the audience cheered then !

When I went round to the back I found Marinetti in the best of spirits, dismissing the unanimous condemnation of the audience and calmly announcing to the Press, ' C' était un cabal.' For the next performance Stoll introduced a gramophone record by Elgar to bring a little melody into the act. It helped, and the effort was received in stony silence. Marinetti described it as a ' succés fou '. Since then some of his musical theories have been introduced into modern music, but with technical skill and the use of legitimate instruments.

Another club that started well was the Crab Tree, which was founded by Augustus John, Marchant of the Goupil Gallery, and Lord Howard de Walden, as an intellectual meeting-place. It rapidly became a mere night club, but certainly it was glamourous and full of actresses such as Lillian Shelly, and Betty May. There were artists, writers, poets, East-end Jews, men-about-town, dancers, *cocottes,* and all the rest of them. There was a fellow there, a strange, *fin de siècle,* who claimed to be ' the spirit son of Oscar Wilde and Aubrey Beardsley '. He was an artist just out of his time. He did some fine imaginative works illustrating *Gulliver's Travels,* and I have often wondered what became of him. Years afterwards I met him in Paris, married. In the Crab Tree days he had long golden hair and burning eyes, was always exquisitely dressed and wore marvellous dancing pumps. A splendid poseur, often in dire poverty, but fortunate in having an old landlady who was fond of him. He walked everywhere, and what a walker he was ! At the Crab Tree he was fond of offering a pinch of white powder to all and sundry, it was menthol snuff, of course; I know, because whenever he said, 'Have a pinch, old chap,' I invariably did and it never had the slightest effect. Cocaine was then unknown to the average person and could be legally purchased, but he would never have had the money to buy the stuff even if he wanted to, while menthol snuff cost only sixpence a box. But it gave an air. Decadence, and the 'naughty nineties' were still reverenced in 1913.

I was busily experimenting on, but not exhibiting, many pictures of a purely abstract nature, and I was attempting to convey movement: the dynamic rather than the static, as it was pedantically called. Those experiments were of real value to me when I did my war painting later on. About this time Hume, a brilliant mathematician and philosopher, who had, I understand, done little while he was at Cambridge, was gathering round him a remarkable *salon*, the equal of which I have never seen, at Mrs. Kipplewhite's place in Frith Street. Hume had the most wonderful gift of knowing every one and mixing every one. The refreshment when we met was chiefly beer, and it was seldom that any one had more than his share of it. Here I used to meet Epstein, Squire, Gaudier-Brzeska, W. L. George, Douglas Ainslie, Rupert Brooke—something of a dandy— Ashley Dukes, Orage, Mrs. Hastings, Eddie Marsh, Bevan, Harold Monro, and Flint; Germans, Frenchmen, Italians and Spaniards, including the philosopher Maestro, who 'they say' was shot in the Spanish upheaval. There were journalists, writers, poets, painters, politicians of all sorts, from Conservatives to New Age Socialists, Fabians, Irish yaps, American bums, and Labour leaders such as Cook and Larkin. From this atmosphere originated the London Group.

Gilman was the motive force. Slowly but surely with the help of Hume he gathered all the warring elements of Impressionists, Post-Impressionists, Neo-Primitives, Vorticists, Cubists, and Futurists. At the first general meeting we had Sickert in the chair, and Marchant consented to let us have the Goupil Gallery on the usual commission basis, provided that he dissociated himself from the Group. We did not realize at the time that this proviso was a blunder, as I shall show. I was elected secretary, Gore treasurer, and Gilman eventually accepted the presidency because Sickert, with his usual modesty, refused the honour. Since then he has been president, I think, two or three times, but as I write I hear he has resigned again.

We then proceeded to offend half the art world by rejecting half the established painters of the day. Roger Fry succeeded in getting elected after a second shot, a mistake. The first exhibition was magnificent in its failure. Nobody came. We hardly knew enough people in London to fill one room with an audience, much less three. But the Press loved it. Terry, who was writing in collaboration with Low, the cartoonist, made every one laugh by a most facetious article about the highbrows looking at the pictures. A girl, it seemed, had looked at a statue of mine and announced loudly that it looked better at a distance, so Low and Terry took a bus to Ludgate Circus to be sure. But that was not all. The ridicule attracted an audience; and as Marchant had dissociated himself from us, he led likely buyers gently but firmly to view his own pictures on the ground floor. We were not only baited but used as a bait, and we got precious little out of it.

Then the Allied Artists, or Independents, took a great plunge. They left the Albert Hall and rented Holland Park Skating Rink for an exhibition. In conjunction with Ethelbert White I did a very large picture of Hampstead Heath which I exhibited there. Another picture, painted mostly with sand to make a contrast with the shining, metallic guns, I called 'War'; and Wyndham Lewis had a large one entitled 'Plan of War'. None were good pictures, but they were interesting inasmuch as they prove what Sir Michael Sadler has stated, that some modern artists had a curious pre-sense of the catastrophe which was to come. In retrospection it certainly would seem that some of us were already preparing our technique to express the horror, the cruelty, and the violence which were to be our destiny. The show, needless to say, was a fiasco, though a splendid one.

My legs had been troubling me again. Walking was difficult, and soon afterwards I left Tilbury for Marseilles—a young man who was to return to England to face an entirely different life. My pre-War epoch was almost ended. How would I have developed if Germany had not invaded Belgium ? A useless surmise. I was respected as a draughtsman. My experiments in the newer forms of art were looked on as such by those who knew me and I was given every form of encouragement by most people, with the exception of Tonks, Roger Fry and Clive Bell, who despised me chiefly because I was English and a professional of artistic integrity, with a knowledge of draughtsmanship and technique, and not an incompetent amateur addicted to aestheticism, cocoa, puritanism or jabbering about ' sincerity '. As far as I knew, I had aroused neither the animosity nor the jealousy of any brother artist save Wyndham Lewis.

It might be imagined that my life had been all fun, associating as I was on the one hand with actors, clowns, dancers, ' Society people ', men-about-town, and on the other with extremists who were reacting against puffy vulgarians stagnating in complacency and commercial expediency. Actually I was a serious, and even a grim, hard-worker, often doing eighteen hours on end and sometimes painting as many as three pictures a day. I studied all kinds of art, materials, techniques, and mediums, swotting away at theory besides practice. I dabbled in things medical and scientific, had a knowledge of mechanics, was well informed about the political conditions, and aware of the crash that was to come.

Socially, it is true, I had come to know nearly every one who mattered in London life, yet work has always been my lodestar. In Paris I was well known, no matter where I went, and I even had a bar named after me, for in Montmartre they called me Charlie or Charlot, and sometimes *L'apache qui rit*. I was high-spirited and bursting with energy; but I combined my fun with an idealism which I hope I shall never lose.

I have always been intensely interested in other men's work, with no great opinion of my own. Indeed, of that I am

65

at times apt to be despondent. But I get real pleasure from art and am not ashamed to say it. Brought up as I was in a professional family, I was always convinced that a good picture would find an outlet, and that the public, and especially the intelligent or picture-buying public, would appreciate achievement and more or less respect failure if the aim was high and the intention genuine. I still think I was right. Fear, apprehension, Americanism, commercialism, exploitation, masochism and sensationalism were not the ruling emotions as they are to-day. But of this opinion I must beware, lest people say I am extolling the 'good old days' and growing aged. Perhaps we have not changed so very much, yet my youthful idealism made me believe humanity to be a little better before the War.

To one approaching his half-century, the world to-day seems more vulgar and cheap-minded than it was. Edwardianism—by which, of course, I mean the years after the Boer War—was bad enough, but the national feeling suggested depth. The tolerance shown to me by more experienced elders is seldom extended to youth with the same symptoms to-day. Maybe publicity has killed something. The venom of current writers and the personal vindictiveness now displayed was then almost unknown, while the kindness of such men as Robert Ross, Frank Rutter, Clutton Brock, P. G. Konody, Lewis Hind and Hume, is bewildering to me. Perhaps poverty and the struggle for existence was not so great in general, yet the poverty among my contemporaries was terrible. Against that, there was a stronger feeling that achievement would receive its reward. There was far more *esprit de corps,* far more culture, more cosmopolitanism, more liberalism; and there was little of the mass production and regimentation we now know, and race worship had not usurped the place of ethics and religion. Above all, propaganda was practically unknown.

It is a black thought for me to look back and see that I was associated with Italian Futurism, which ended in Fascism much as Christianity was quenched by the Spanish Inquisition or charity by angelic Bishops. Mussolini seized on it and worked his thug will. What a fate for an intellectual idea!

In passing, it is interesting to note that just as the Russians thought little of Lenin in the old days, the Italians were in no way impressed by Mussolini, whom I met when he came to Paris. He was then the representative of a Communist or Socialist newspaper. It is curious that three of the most outstanding men I have ever met should have given no hint of their powers to come. Lenin, Mussolini and Chaplin were all blown to the top by some sort of revolution. Let us admit that Lenin was the greatest of the three, and the worst actor.

Futurism was but the candlelight for Fascism. Marinetti the fiery was made an Academician after he had been described by his Duce as the John the Baptist of the movement, and regimentation had blackened out Italy. Needless to remark, Marinetti is now more anti-British than d'Annunzio.

The Cubist movement which promised so much has ended in sterility, a dehumanized geometrical formula, producing little except incomprehensible articles by Herbert Read, Grigson, Sevier, Clive Bell, Marriot, Popoffski and Wilenski. Their writings have alienated many thinking people, and their Literary theories have done much to lessen public interest in 'modern' methods and the understanding and enjoyment of all kinds of pictorial work.

Had I but known it, I had looked on pre-War England for the last time. We steamed south, and when we arrived at Gibraltar we became conscious that there was grave trouble underground in Europe. There had been flying competitions at Algeciras, but all the French airmen and their wives had suddenly been recalled and they boarded our boat for Marseilles. What was happening was beyond them and us, for this was *before* the murder of Sarajevo; a significant fact of some historical interest.

However, I painted away at Marseilles, then visited Aix en Provence, the home of Cézanne and Zola. My Mother told me an amusing story about Zola while we were there. When he had written ' J'accuse ', which had helped to secure the release of Dreyfus, Zola was in consequence covered with glory. He went to stay in his native town of Aix, and on his return to Paris some artist friends of my Mother asked him if he had called on 'Le Mâitre' as they called Cézanne. Now it was Zola who first introduced his school friend Cézanne to Manet and the Impressionists. But on this occasion he turned to the artists and in reply to their question he said, 'No. I am a little tired of failure.' That is a strange thought to-day, with Cézanne ranking almost with Raphael in the auction rooms, and Zola forgotten.

On our return to Marseilles we found a state of excitement extraordinary even for that extraordinary city. Crowds surged through the streets under the hot afternoon sun; white men, yellow men, brown men, black men, in all kinds of weird costumes that varied from Bond Street to Basra. The brothels which then formed one of the main industries of the city were overflowing with 'artistes' and complete theatrical companies who had been abandoned by their managers, and these were to be seen in their stage costumes —no use asking why in Marseilles—not only in the Vieux Port but in the cafés of the Cannebière. I loved it, in spite of that sensing of thunder in the east. Then crash! came the news. War! Wild demonstrations up and down the streets made life impossible. The anti-wars seemed as strong as the patriots, and trouble was expected. My Mother had no delusions about the Germans after her experiences in Paris in 1870, and, describing them as a frustrated people even in victory, she thought it high time for us to go home.

By the time we reached Paris the mobilization order had gone out in France and Russia, and everything was just about as abnormal as the French can manage when they really try. Mobs were queueing up at the banks to withdraw their savings; and although we had more than enough ready cash, nobody would change it into francs. If you were prepared to wait in a queue all night you might be lucky and get fifteen francs for the golden sovereign, but our five-pound notes were indeed scraps of paper. Fortunately I was well enough known to obtain credit at the restaurants, so that we managed to get food, but they resolutely refused to take ready money. It is difficult to under-

stand such an attitude. Nobody ever questioned the value
of gold in those days, and the matter could have been put
right in five minutes by any one in authority. The truth
is that those people who were making fantastic profits out
of the disaster had no wish for the facts to become known,
and the French shopkeeper naturally believed that the money-
changers were right and that the bottom was dropping out
of the whole international exchange.

When the panic subsided we were able to get some paper
money at Lloyds' Bank, and we felt more comfortable. I
called in to see Madame Sagot and found her almost delirious
with fear. Every one in Paris knew what war was. France
had never been able, like us, to do all her fighting beyond
her frontiers. Madame told me how Picasso had stood for
hours until he had got all his savings back in his hands, and
that he was off to Barcelona. I bought a Gauguin from her,
but I never saw it again.

I had read so much of Guy de Maupassant that I seemed
always to have known what it was like in Paris in 1870.
And here we were with the same enemy on the march; all
my family life I had lived in an atmosphere of war somewhere
or other.

The next day we caught a train which was leaving for
the coast, perhaps England ? We were lucky to get a seat,
for it was packed with Americans, some of them weeping
and many of them behaving as though the Germans were
already at Port St. Denis. In the midst of a great panic
My mother and I were very calm. I had the curious feeling
that the experience was not new to me.

7

Our household in London took the outbreak of war with the utmost calm. There was no hysterical talk, no wild ideas about God, cricket, and democracy. My Father had been for years a war-correspondent, and my Mother had always expected the Germans to make another attack on France. I regarded myself as having no patriotism, although I preferred the English. This state of mind, and this preference, I put down entirely to my travels abroad. A man who lives and works in a foreign country begins to understand its people, and surely understanding is the enemy of all such folly as patriotism and insularity. Preference, on the other hand, is quite another matter. The longer I live and the more I travel, the more strongly do I believe that the British are the best and the only 'grown-up' nation.

Brass bands, union jacks, and even 'Kitchener Wants you' had no power to move me. I am sure I could even have listened to that old rascal Bottomley without shedding a single tear. And yet, this long-expected outrage on the Belgians; was there not something I could do? The thought of general service was far from my mind owing to my limp, as I was well aware that I should pass no doctor. This was when only the very fittest men were taken by the Army. Thousands used to queue up all night at the recruiting stations and by daybreak the line would be miles long. Then a sergeant would stroll along, and when he came to any smallish man, or any fellow who didn't look up to scratch because he wore glasses or was tired through waiting, he stopped and said, 'Sorry, lad. I don't think they'll pass you.' Tears of chagrin used to well in the eyes of those rugby players and boxers who were turned away. My own doctor said the Army was out of the question for me.

Still, I was pursued by the urge to do something, to be 'in' the War; and although I succeeded in the end and was 'in' it, I was never 'of' it. I was under contract to give a one-man show at the Dorée Gallery, but a feeling of futility overwhelmed me and at my request the dealer released me. Next I gave myself a course in motor engineering. I became a proficient mechanic and could drive well. Through my Father I heard of the shortage of ambulance drivers in France. There was no need to pass any doctor, as I would be working for the Red Cross instead of the Army, and I could go out straight away to Dunkirk. This was excellent. I was accepted as a driver and found myself attached to a unit which consisted almost entirely of Quakers.

I travelled down to Dover immediately, put on uniform there—it was the same as the Army, with different badges—and spent the night at the Y.M.C.A. The next day we crossed, and by the evening we were in Dunkirk and working in a shed full of dead, wounded and dying. It was a sudden transition from peaceful England, and I thought then that the people at home could never be expected to realize what war was. A few hours from London, with its theatres playing to crowded houses and a kind of mock heroism abroad, with its few weeping women and its few long faces— just an hour or two away, and here we were working in a shed that was nicknamed 'The Shambles'.

The French medical service had completely collapsed, and some poor devils had been left wounded in railway sidings for three weeks with no medical attention except that given by a French *infirmier*. The railways were disorganized, all the rolling-stock was required to rush reinforcements to the front, and the wounded were for the moment forgotten. These soldiers had been wounded during the retreat on to the frontier at Furnes just before the battle of Ypres. They had been roughly bandaged and packed into the cattle trucks which were to carry them to hospital. Here they lay, men with every form of horrible wound, swelling and festering, watching their comrades die. For three weeks

71

they lay there until only a tortured half of them were alive; and then, a staff officer happening to pass that way, there were protests because the train should have been used for other and more important things, and the men were dumped out of the way in a shed outside Dunkirk.

There we found them. They lay on dirty straw, foul with old bandages and filth, those gaunt, bearded men, some white and still with only a faint movement of their chests to distinguish them from the dead by their side. Those who had the strength to moan wailed incessantly.

'Ma mère—ma mère!'

'Oh—la, la!'

'Que je souffre, ma mère!'

The sound of those broken men crying for their mothers is something I shall always have in my ears.

It was dark when we arrived. There was a strong smell of gangrene, urine and French cigarettes, although a spark on the straw would have turned the place into a crematorium. Our doctors took charge, and in five minutes I was nurse, water-carrier, stretcher-bearer, driver, and interpreter. Gradually the shed was cleansed, disinfected and made habitable, and by working all night we managed to dress most of the patients' wounds.

The gratitude of the men was pathetic. They were certainly not so sure of the priests, who drifted about with a strange sense of being able to tell when a man was about to die. They would rush to him with the last sacrament and often be heartily cursed for their pains, for most of the soldiers disliked and distrusted them. As soon as a man died, the priests would try to collect all the walking wounded and then harangue their little audience, using the corpse as a sure sign that God was angry with France because she had disestablished the Church. When I came to talk with those priests I discovered most of them to be ignorant men, peasants by birth and Breton in origin. In their outlook they were pro-Vatican and anti-French, and that is saying the best of them, for some were actually pro-Germany because she was punishing France.

Our unit got into trouble with the French authorities

because the doctors and dressers attended to some German prisoners whose bandages had become agonizingly tight over their swollen wounds. It seemed that we were permitted to be in France on the understanding that we looked after the Allies, and that the Bosche might be attended to only when there was no other case needing attention. This attitude did not please our doctors, who did not hesitate to reply that the Red Cross was there to succour the wounded and that they would never demand to know the nationality of a patient.

As one of the cooks put it, with the quaint Cockney belief that all foreigners must regard themselves as being not quite like other men: 'They're all bastards, so wot's the odds?'

The Germans could blame only themselves for being unpopular, but was it always necessary to put them in charge of black men—'colonials' of the French army to watch over their endless job of cleaning out French latrines? The black with his cigarette and his long bayonet always seemed to me to be a direct inducement to mutiny.

Shortly after the row over the German prisoners, our Red Cross unit nearly caused friction between the Allies, or so it seemed from the expostulatory terms in which we were addressed. A French soldier was brought in with a bad wound in his leg. Like many other cases at that time, it had been neglected and gangrene had set in. Our doctors did what any doctor would have done: they amputated the leg. The man's life was saved, but such a thunder-clap of protest descended on our unit. Did we not realize that limbs could be amputated only by special official permission? Our doctors smiled as though they had no interest in any such authority, and they were shaken out of their 'phlegm' only when they learned the facts. The French had a definite and fixed rate of compensation and pension for the loss of a limb, and with true Gallic logic the Government preferred to risk a man's life rather than have the certainty of paying a pension to a disabled man. A Red Cross doctor could do what he liked to a man so long as he left him whole. Later on, I understand, this regulation was changed when

France realized that many a legless man had the makings of a father. But it certainly shook my hopes for civilization when first I heard of it.

By the time I had been at the Shambles a week my former life seemed to be years away. When a month had passed I felt I had been born in the nightmare. I had seen sights so revolting that man seldom conceives them in his mind and there was no shrinking even among the more sensitive of us. We could only help, and ignore shrieks, puss, gangrene and the disembowelled.

The War was now settling down for the winter into some sort of trenches, and at our end of the line at any rate things began to sort themselves out. Gradually we received more help from the French authorities, and I must say they were grateful for what the Red Cross had done. A hospital had been started by the Red Cross and the Quakers at Malo-les-Bains, and I was given the job of driving the worst cases from the Shambles at Dunkirk to this point. Mostly we travelled by night; but as the French and British armies had the same idea, the journey was often difficult.

From Dunkirk I was sent on to Woosten to work in a convent which had been converted into a field dressing-station. The nuns were working there as nurses, and they seemed to me to be literally without fear and prepared without a murmur to lay down their lives in the service of mankind. I should not like to think they had to share Heaven with those fat little priests I had met at Dunkirk. In the end the Army had to insist that they move to a place of greater safety, and they consented to go as far back as Poperinghe. We had another dressing-station at Ypres itself, which was shelled a good deal during the first battle of Ypres. On one occasion, as on others which have been recounted throughout the War, a tremendous attack was expected, and we were all turned out, Red Cross men as we were, to resist it, even to the cook with a long knife. Could we have claimed immunity because we were Red Cross men? No, we should probably have rightly been shot as non-combatants and I should have been saved a lot of trouble.

It was at Woosten that I had a shell go clean through the

74

back of my ambulance. To say I was impressed does not meet the case. I was amazed, and a trifle indignant. Certainly I was not as frightened as I ought to have been, for a shell is a shell, and if my van had not been a flimsy affair it would have exploded. Instead I had a nervous indigestion, but I slept like a log. Of this I am inordinately proud. I was nothing of a soldier, and considered my work as being something that applied to both sides. Looking back, I now know very well I was too vain to show much fear. It was only after a succession of events that men's nerves cracked, and I am thankful indeed that I escaped the strain unimpaired. Later, I became a driver from Dunkirk to Furnes and from Furnes to Ypres. When, at a still later period in the War, I saw that road during the Passchendaele battle, there was no sign of our convent at Woosten. It had been entirely demolished.

My leg started to give me trouble and I was put on indoor work in the hospital at Malo, where I was turned into a male nurse and expected to give a hand in the operating theatre. I quickly adapted myself to the aseptic surroundings and was soon handing instruments to the doctors with the deftness of an experienced nurse. Through my knowledge of the language I was in a short time on terms with the motley crowd which came our way. There were French soldiers, marines, Algerians, Zouaves, Turcos, and Spahilis; there were anarchists from Paris and miners from Marseilles, many of whom had revolver and knife wounds received in civilian life before the War. Cynical Parisians from La Villette and soldiers from Boulogne-sur-Seine would discuss English food, and in two minutes we would be talking about Bonnard and his famous gang of apaches who, back in the summer, had raided a bank and shot a few *flics*.

It seemed trivial with so much shelling around.

Those Frenchmen often spoke about the extraordinary drunken condition of the German troops outside Rheims, and they declared that their victory had been made more certain because of champagne. Both German officers and men, they vowed, had been brought to a complete standstill in an alcoholic stupor, and one desperado boasted that he had bayoneted hundreds as they lay drunk, a statement not necessarily accepted by the others, since he came from the Midi. Perhaps Von Kluck had more difficulties to contend with than are generally recognized. As a comment I may add that only in 1936 I read how General Ludendorf in writing on military tactics insists that an advancing column must be kept strictly teetotal, 'from head to tail'. Was he thinking of the advance from Rheims to the Marne?

My worst case was that of a dignified, bearded Frenchman of culture, who had twenty-seven wounds. He lingered between life and death for weeks, and I gave him nearly all my attention. Eventually he began to show signs of life under saline injections, and after a struggle the doctors saved him. He was a schoolmaster in Tunis, and years afterwards he wrote to me. His letters are treasures of mine, as the love of fellow men should be, and I felt humbled, embarrassed, and grateful. Of him and of those others I shall always cherish a memory. What citizens of the world they were! I still possess some extraordinary mementoes of many of them, some of whom died—letters, trinkets, photographs. One devil-worshipper gave me his charms.

The whole atmosphere was unlike that of any English hospitals I was to see later. Religious discussion was of the frankest nature, especially after the visit of a foxy-faced cardinal who arrived with gifts for the wounded. Many of the men handed them back, saying he had got them out of old women by terrifying them with threats of hell. It was as well that the majority of the English staff did not understand much of the French conversation that went on, for it was impregnated with French realism, for all the idealism and camaraderie that peeped through because of the national trait which enables the French to be democratic without familiarity.

Dunkirk was one of the first towns to suffer aerial bombardment, and I was one of the first men to see a child who had been killed by it. There the small body lay before me, a symbol of all that was to come. Another time a Zeppelin loomed over us, guided by the treachery of a station-master, who lit a fire in the Dock. He was shot. It was said that a telephone wire had been laid before the War to Ostend. As I was working a great deal about the railway sheds which were being used as dressing-stations, I heard all kinds of stories about this man, but what impressed me most was the sense of outrage felt by the railwaymen when they realized they had for years been touching their caps to an ' *espion* '. At this time spy fever was sweeping Europe, and many a peasant was executed for lighting his pipe at the wrong moment; but even if a Dunkirk *chef-de-gare* were innocent— a thing I doubt—it was not the moment to start lighting a fire.

It was during this Zeppelin raid that I had a narrow shave. Fires broke out in the docks and were spreading to the Shambles. We had orders to evacuate all the helpless cases immediately. I dashed along with my ambulance. There were no lights anywhere and I had nothing but the fires to guide me, and as a result I had no sooner filled the ambulance and started than I jammed a wheel in the railway points that ran beside the shed. About a dozen men came to my rescue, and we pulled and lifted and hammered and levered. Nobody noticed an enormous engine of a troop train slide out of the darkness towards us, but by a miracle the driver spotted us in time and pulled up three feet from the bonnet. Another few seconds would have seen the end of all of us, to say nothing of the wounded, who were shrieking piteously every time we banged at the wheels of the ambulance. With French adaptability the engine-driver climbed down, tied an old rope to the ambulance, and backed the entire troop train to get us out, with nothing worse than my front wheels out of alignment. Congratulations on all sides became so voluble that it was difficult to hear what was being said and impossible to believe that the Battle of the Dunes was at its height only a few miles off.

I was there for that famous first Christmas which was to see the end of the War, when the snow gave everything a Christmas-card look and men sank to death in the mud. In early 1915 organization was better and the War seemed to have settled down. But it was alarming to hear what some of the new men were beginning to say about the old codgers who were running the War.

By now the wounded were well looked after, and in some ways they were treated even better than they were later on. I was working between Boulogne, Dunkirk, and Ypres, and I watched the Belgian Army re-forming in the north. Air raids were becoming increasingly effective, and Commander Samson had his headquarters at Malo with the Naval Division. Then I crocked up and was sent home

Back I went to London, to see life still unshaken, with bands playing, drums banging, the New Armies marching, and the papers telling us nothing at all. A man is all the sadder for seeing war; but I grew better, and painted. Then Pond, the lecture agent, came to see me and discussed my going to America. I was tempted and I worried on, working hard and turning things over in my mind. Soon I heard that the 3rd London General Hospital had made an appeal to the Chelsea Arts Club (of which I was not a member) for men of intelligence. With an impulsiveness that afterwards made me ponder, I threw up everything and joined the Army.

When I presented myself I had only to enlarge on my experiences with the Red Cross in France, remain silent about my rheumatism, and I was through. I had presumed that life in the R.A.M.C. would be very like life in the Red Cross. It was and it was not. I had as much work to do, and more bedpans. But whereas in the Red Cross it was presumed I had been born with a head, I quickly found that even to imagine I possessed such a thing was a handicap. I complained to a fellow slave. He asked me a few questions, and when he heard that I could have returned to the Red Cross instead of joining the Army his solution of the problem was no compliment to my intelligence.

'You 'ad a soul in the Red Cross,' he explained to me. 'But don't you think you're going to come that nonsense 'ere. You ain't got nothink of your own now, and there's only one thing the Army can't do with yer—that's put you in the fam'ly way.'

Then came a queer period when I did all kinds of things. I helped to make roads, to equip huge new wards, and to cook; I met hospital trains, and I helped in the operating theatres. After a time we got a rush of wounded, and because I was an artist the sergeant-major put me in charge of the 'balmy ones' in the observation ward and the detention cases. This is the worst job I have ever tackled in my life. Lots of the balmy ones were indeed balmy and needed every attention, while the detention cases were made up of malingerers and ne'er-do-wells whose patriotism had outrun their caution and who now wished to be quit of the Army by pretending to have every disease under the sun. I had a good deal of power with the mental cases, who themselves were a mixed lot. Some were mad, some were shell-shocked, and some were nit-wits. The change of environment and breaking of routine, or a dreadful experience in 'the line', or for some the proximity day and night of other men in the same plight, sent them completely into a world of hallucination and persecution, especially the latter. There would be strange grievances against the man in the next bed, or the sergeant-major, or the nurses, and particularly against their wives. I began to have an uneasy feeling that I was catching their complaint, and had it not been for the observation of one of the doctors I believe I should have become one of the balmy ones myself. Scientific or not, I am convinced that mental instability is infectious. I was moved into the blind-and-deaf ward, the deaf being terribly morose and the blind extremely gay. For some months this went on; then we were informed that we were to be part of a draft for Mesopotamia.

In the meanwhile I had formed a great friendship with Ward Muir, a writer, journalist, and photographer. He suffered from T.B. and he was continually volunteering for dangerous service and being turned down. His lungs had collapsed, his heart had moved from his left side to his right, yet he was a man of indomitable courage. He became the editor of the hospital magazine and in this my war drawings were reproduced.

The London Group was still in existence, and my people arranged for me to exhibit 'La Patrie', 'The Road to Ypres', and 'The First Bombardment of Ypres', three pictures which created a tremendous stir at the time. The intellectuals made violent attacks on them, and I remember Harold Monro saying, 'What on earth are you doing journalistic clippings for?' Of course, the Clive Bell Group dismissed them as being 'merely melodramatic'. *The Times* was horrified and said the pictures were not a bit like cricket, an interesting comment on England in 1915, when war was still considered a sport which received the support of the clerics because it brought out the finest forms of self-sacrifice, Christian virtues, and all the other nonsense. I had painted what I had seen, without a thought for exhibition. To me the soldier was going to be dominated by the machine. Nobody thinks otherwise to-day, but because I was the first man to express this feeling on canvas I was treated as though I had committed a crime. The public, however, as usual, showed more intelligence than the intelligentsia, and I was also well treated by the general Press.

The very fact that I was a private in the Army made a good story for the newspapers, and I had one of the boosts of my life. In the ordinary way any artist would have been grateful for such praise, but in the circumstances I felt a little embarrassed. My intuition was right; for in the hospital this 'notoriety', as it was called by some of the Chelsea Arts Club, was something to be deplored, and several people did what they could to make my life miserable. Against this, men like Murdoch and old Pirrie, who is now president of the Royal Scottish Academy, were above this type of meanness.

Since those days I have known triumph and wretchedness, but I still look back with horror on my life at the 3rd London General, not because of the War or its work, its dullness and squalor, but partly because this was my first real taste of the jealousy of artists and the nastiness of the intellectuals, and partly because I was under Army nurses. With very great exceptions they were the most repulsive bosses, thinking of little but currying favour with the doctors and, with a magnificent indifference to truth and justice, blaming the soldiers under them for every conceivable thing that went wrong. The V.A.D.s were altogether different, and they themselves were often reduced to tears in the wash-places by the cruelty of their sisters or ministering angels, as the sergeant-major so cynically described them.

Winter came early, and still we were kept in readiness for foreign service. Sometimes we would have medical boards and I would be passed for the draft, and the next time I would be declared unfit for service in the East. Doctors did not worry about the bedside manner in those days, and I am sure they upset a lot of people by looking puzzled. My own faith in the medical profession was sadly shaken then by their inability to decide what sort of a man I was, but perhaps Army privates are not considered ordinary human beings, and don't count. Being quite sure that when it came to the final test I should be pronounced fit—everybody could count on that now—I applied for leave to get married.

This was granted. I reached the train on a milk cart, arrived home for breakfast, when I cut my hand badly—reached the Town Hall in 213 Haverstock Hill and was shown to Room 13, where the registrar was to be found, and waited for my bride. She was late and I was nervous. Ward Muir had managed to come and he was the only cheerful member of the party. At length the bride arrived and I felt tremendously proud of marrying such a beautiful girl. The handful of relations behaved as though they were at a funeral, but my father-in-law gave us a car with an enormous gas balloon on its roof to get over the petrol difficulty, and my spirits rose somewhat. My own father, of course, was in Gallipoli. In a downpour of rain we departed for the Gobelins, the Old Cave of Harmony, then a restaurant and now a post office.

We travelled third class to Ramsgate. No firsts for privates, of course. We had for company on the train a drunken journalist with a bottle of whisky, and a touring actress who burst into tears when he finished the bottle and sang Tosti's 'Good-bye'. She nearly threw herself out of the door because the song was an unlucky one and she was on her way to open at Folkestone. That wedding day certainly had all the omens against us: two thirteens, a cut hand, a downpour of rain on the bride, and Tosti's 'Good-bye'.

We were to stay in an hotel which was run by a Frenchman,

but here again it was very awkward because I was a private. Some of the officers looked as though I had no right to be seen in the company of one so lovely, and I hope I looked duly contrite. Anyhow, we stayed. In the morning, through Ward Muir, photographs appeared of the artist private who had now married ' the most beautiful woman in London ', and the position eased. My presence in the hotel was ignored, if not forgiven, as I was obviously a Somebody, and a private merely with a view to getting a commission.

On our return to London I still had two days' leave, and I painted ' La Mitrailleuse ' and ' The Deserted Trench on the Yser '. It was a queer honeymoon and typical of my wife that she put up with it. Again I was feeling ill and when I returned to the hospital I reported sick.

When I saw the orderly officer I felt like death, so he put me on light duty. This meant that I had to spend the next few hours in carrying sacks of coal from the lorries to the furnaces, and of course I had to try. Doctors had no idea what light duty meant: the sergeants saw to that. I collapsed, was taken to the Receiving Ward and ordered to take a cold bath. Eventually, by the grace of God, I was examined by the famous Dr. Humphreys. He took one look at me, checked my temperature, and ordered me to be put to bed immediately. This I was just able to do myself. My temperature went up and up, and for weeks I was on the danger list with acute rheumatic fever.

After a time I began to recover, but my hands were in an appalling state, scarcely human, and my wife and my Mother were terribly worried. My Mother saw Sir Bruce Porter about me, and through his kind offices I was examined by a medical board, whose president, Sir Alfred Gould, recommended my total discharge. The thought that I was to ' get my ticket ' went to my head. I was the envy of the ward.

Very soon there came the word that the wards were to be cleared for a sudden influx of wounded from Gallipoli. Round went the doctors and every man who could hobble from his bed was passed on. My time had come. I was bundled into a chair and rolled away to another medical board with a caricature of a War Office martinet in charge. When I came before the old fire-eater I fainted and annoyed him, as he wanted to get to lunch. I came round to hear him addressing a broken-looking man with a shattered face and one eye.

'No reason at all for leaving the Army,' he was saying. 'You can make yourself useful by cleaning out latrines and that sort of thing.'

At that my spirits fell so low that I fainted again; and this, combined with the fact that my medical report had a knight's name on it, seemed to impress him. He gave me a baleful look, and told me in petulant tones that I was unfit for further service. With those magic words I was rolled from his presence, a free man again.

It is true I was shortly to discover that during my illness everything I possessed in hospital had been stolen, but then the Army always insisted that the letters R.A.M.C. stood for Rob All My Comrades. The Paymaster handed me quantities of back pay and a gratuity which he described as blood money. I accepted everything: I queried nothing. In a daze I reached home, and to this day I have not the vaguest idea if I travelled by cab, ambulance, or train.

8

When I had regarded my trip to Mesopotamia as a certainty I had given up my studio, so my Mother, who was unlike most mothers-in-law and extremely fond of my wife, invited us to live with her. My Father was then with the forces in Egypt, and I don't think had even heard of my marriage.

This attack of rheumatic fever was even worse than the previous one, but I became better in time and was able to hobble on crutches, a form of support I have often had to rely on. In fact, I have lately met an old Russian friend who declared he had never seen me without them before. Yet in spite of this suffering I had a glimpse, later on, during the campaign against my methods of painting, of the vindictiveness which lies deep in small minds. In the course of an alleged criticism of my work, the curator of a midland museum considered it a pity I survived the War. Unfortunately, he hinted, I kept out of danger as an official war artist. When I wrote and protested against this form of art criticism, he replied: ' Be a man.' I detest the way curators dare to lie about private life and to cause prejudice against the artist's work.

After I left the Army I felt so ill even when I could walk, that I went nowhere. ' Troops on the March' and ' Flooded Yser' were exhibited and sold at the London Group, but I was too weak to attend. It was the same with the Allied Artists exhibition at the Grafton Galleries, where I sent my ' Mitrailleuse '. I did not go near the place. This picture was bought anonymously and presented to the Contemporary Art Society. As far as I can recollect, these are the only two London exhibitions of mine I have failed to attend when

I was in England. Yet when I found a measure of success, the Bloomsburies accused me of every form of pushfulness and publicity. I suppose it was extremely artful of me to lie in my Mother's home and wonder if I ever should be free from pain again, but I have always failed to see why such conduct should be termed pushful. There are still those, of course, who think the Great War was a 'stunt' of mine !

My success I owe to Frank Rutter, Lewis Hind, P. G. Konody, and the Allied Artists. Art critics were not only powerful in those days, but constructive and helpful. I was unable to do anything for myself, and Lewis Hind, who himself was recovering from a grave illness, asked for some reproductions of my work. He took these without my knowledge to Brown and Phillips, of the Leicester Galleries, and I was astounded and delighted when I was offered a one-man show on a date which had been reserved by Munnings and cancelled by him. As usual, the Galleries did not hold out much hope of success. Brown was quite charming and assured me they would do their best, but he warned me I must not expect to benefit financially.

My blood had begun to course in normal fashion, my joints were loosening and my hands were gradually beginning to look human. I was fired with the opportunity which had come my way, and I painted and painted and painted. Those pictures which had been sold I borrowed, and we did everything to help the show. Every one we knew was asked to the private view, but the times were abnormal, many of our friends fell by the wayside, and it was sparsely attended. The Press had little to say about it and things were beginning to look black when, somehow or other, the clientele of the Leicester Galleries began to come along. I had a letter from Professor Sir Michael Sadler to say he would be at the Galleries at eleven o'clock one Tuesday morning. Knowing his punctilious habits, I was there to the minute, and so was he. He bought my ' Marching Men ' and three other war pictures. This was grand. Then Arnold Bennett bought ' La Patrie ', and slowly but surely the exhibition sold right out. According to the advertisements of Brown and Phillips, I became the talk of London.

General Sir Ian Hamilton honoured me with the following preface :

The appeal made to a soldier by these works lies in their quality of truth. They bring him closer to the heart of his experiences than his own eyes could have carried him.

In France, that flesh and blood column marching into the grey dawn seemed simply—a column of march. Seen on this canvas it becomes the symbol of a world tragedy—a glimpse given to us of Destiny crossing the bloodiest page in History.

Look at that star shell! To the soldier crouching in a mine crater, or crawling from cover to cover to cut barbed wire, the sudden ball of fire that fills his dark hiding-place with ghostly light is a murderous eye betraying him to enemies in ambush. Here, truer to the truth, it takes on a mystic semblance of the Holy Grail, poised over the trenches, bearing its mystic message to the souls of our happy warriors.

Then those aeroplanes! We take some linen and wood and make what, when all is said and done, seems a very poor imitation of an insect. Into its body we thrust a small steel heart; feed it with a drop of petrol; turn a handle, and lo! rapturously, it scales the rainbow skies and rides the stars. And yet we know it is a machine—a poor imitation of a grasshopper trying to look at a distance like a gilded butterfly. But war spiritualizes, magnifies, intensifies. The artist lets us glance a moment through his magic lens; we see what he sees: we see, instead of the Taube, Satan flying meteor-like from Paradise, chased by the swords of the Seraphim. Is this an illusion! No, it is a symbol.

The spirit of war is very present with us to-day. Nowhere does it display itself in clearer colours than in the picture wherein we admire the clarions, the brave clarions, leading a battalion into the unknown. When, once upon a time, a Queen of Spain saw the Grenadier Guards, she remarked they were strapping fellows; as the 92nd Highlanders went by she said, ' The battalion marches well '; but, at the aspect of the Royal Irish, the words, ' Bloody war! ' were wrung from her reluctant lips. Here, too, seeing this picture of the French battalion on the march, the Pacifist himself is compelled to cry, ' Bravo! ' Force in full cry after Adventure; energy can be carried no further. And so we come away feeling that the Cup of War is filled not only with blood and tears, but also with the elixir of Life.

Owing to the interest shown, the exhibition was extended for a further week, and when it was closed I received a flood of publicity. The newspapers had heard about my success, a little late perhaps, and they proceeded to make up for lost time. I became ' news ' in Fleet Street. Clutton Brock's leading article in *The Times Literary Supplement* a few days before the exhibition closed was of enormous help to me, although the general trend of the article was entirely antagonistic. My obvious belief was that war was now dominated by machines and that men were mere cogs in the mechanism. Brock voiced the opinion of a great many people, particularly of the old Army type, that the human element, bravery, the Union Jack, and justice, were all that mattered.

Nowadays, of course, everybody takes the mechanized Army for granted, but in those early days I got into hot water simply because I was the first to paint it. I, who had seen more of human anguish than the majority of artists, was accused of being dehumanized. It was said I believed man no longer counted. They were wrong. Man did count. Man will always count. But the man in the tank will, in war, count for more than the man outside. It was the essential difference between the civilian and the soldier, and not unnaturally the public agreed with the civilian. What was a joy to me was that my work was taken seriously and my point of view debated.

All manner of people had attended the exhibition. Bernard Shaw and Galsworthy were there. Conrad came, and told me incidentally that I had written some of the finest prose he had read in the younger generation: Heaven knows why, for he vowed he was not confusing me with my father. William Archer cried: an exquisite compliment. Officers of high rank came, and terrified me so much that I nearly stood at attention. Ramsay MacDonald, Philip Snowden, Balfour, Mrs. Asquith, Winston Churchill, Lady Diana Manners, and Garvin were to be seen arguing before my pictures. It happened that I was the first artist to paint war pictures without pageantry, without glory, and without the over-coloured heroic that had made up the tradition of all war paintings up to this time. I had done this unconsciously. No man saw pageantry in the trenches. My attempt at creating beauty was merely by the statement of reality, emotionally expressed, as one who had seen something of warfare and was caught up in a force over which he had no control.

Indignation amongst the older men was therefore intense, and the clerical opposition was voluble. It is strange to say it to-day, but I am proud to think that three canons actually preached against me and my pictures. Now, of course, the entire English-speaking world, including America, and most people in France and Russia, would never dream of saying my outlook was wrong. It is, indeed, opposed only by the extremists of Italy, the paranoiacs of Germany, and the Fascists of Spain. In the whole world, Japan is the only nation which still whole-heartedly regards war as man's finest achievement.

While the discussion raged on about me and my work I was away in Falmouth, trying to regain my health, and unaware of the excitement I was causing, although thankful for the money my pictures had brought me in. About this time I came to know the Sitwells through having met darling Edith with Mrs. Chandos Pole at P. G. Konody's. I had been rather rude to Osbert, who had written to me, merely thanking him for his praise and making no attempt to meet him, although I now realize his letter was an invitation to do so. With my usual stupidity I thought he was just a Guardsman. However, he wrote again when I returned to London and asked us to dinner. He was then living in Viola Tree's flat, which was owned by da Costa, the artist, in Mallord Street. My wife distinguished herself by fainting, a thing that not only proved the stress under which we were all living at that time, but brought out the beautiful human side of the Sitwells. They behaved with kindness itself, and when Kath recovered we all seemed friends of years' standing, linked by the misery around us. It was one of the most memorable nights I have ever spent. Here at last were some wonderful English people, not only of great culture, but of understanding, in love with all the finer achievements of man, yet full of wit and diabolical cynicism. Withal, they were tolerant, and they had a real knowledge of professionalism. Osbert had been wounded at La Bassée, Sache was still at Eton, and Edith was writing hard. That night was the beginning of a friendship which was to develop into an oasis in the desert of war-weariness and cheap heroics outside.

Here I met again Robert Ross, Guevara, Robert Nichols, and Sassoon, and through them I met Colonel Chandos Pole, who bought some of my pictures which did not deal with the War. He was a remarkable old man, perhaps the finest gentleman by birth and privilege I was ever to know; a survival of the great landed gentry, who accepted artists without question as an essential to civilization, and liked them to be men of the world. Puritanism with its twisted judgements was unknown to him. The Sitwells cemented my friendship with P. G. Konody, who wrote an essay for my first book of the reproductions of war paintings which Grant Richards wished to publish.

Through Grant Richards I met Ronald Firbank, that weird writer who was the originator of so much in modern literature. He was hostile to me when Richards first introduced us at lunch at the Café Royal; hostile and peevish. But he told us how a medical board at Oxford had discovered he was tubercular in the presence of a number of nasty, rude, common men, and I roared with laughter. The precision of his words would have made any story funny, but the fact that I dared to laugh won his vanity, and he was flattered that I had spotted him beneath his pose not only as a knowledgeable fellow, but as one with a profound understanding of men; a fact of which he was extremely proud, and seldom credited with. He clung to me like a leech and we went on to the New English exhibition together. He was horrified at my painting of ' That Cursed Wood '; so horrified that he refused to express any emotion, but merely remarked that he had to go to Cox's to get some money. When I pointed out that the banks were closed he left me with the debonair farewell of a real exquisite, saying: 'In that case I must become militant and force Mr. Cox open with a crow-bar.' He coughed his way out with a hectic flush, but in complete control of his mind, body, and speech.

Grant Richards and I became very friendly, and from him I began to learn all manner of the niceties of life. He is a gourmet of distinction, a man who knows what food and wine can be, with the culture of Paris behind him and a love of the best in literature and in art. His Hungarian wife was a joy: beautiful and feminine. Occasionally she had to go away and cry secretly because of the sufferings of her people. With him I met A. E. Housman, and to watch the poet dressing a crab was a revelation. I never knew poets ate such food. Housman's knowledge of birds and flowers was also unexpected, as I have often noted that intellectuals babble of Nature but neither observe it nor know anything about it.

Another poet I met was John Masefield, who asked us to dinner. Owing to the air raids the street lighting was almost extinguished, and we had at times to grope our way in the dark. When we arrived we were shown up to the drawing-room by a maid who obviously expected guests. As there was nobody there, I looked at the pictures and was astonished to see 'The Monarch of the Glen' over the mantelpiece. There were also some hunting scenes which mystified me until I remembered my host's poem, 'Reynard the Fox.' But still, such pictures could not be. I rang the bell. I was right. We were in the wrong house. Let this be a lesson to those who neglect Art. It has always been a mystery to me why some people damn themselves by their pictures. A carefully dressed woman would never show that she was wearing a red flannel petticoat. However, every one has a skeleton in his cupboard. The Englishman hangs his on the wall.

I was now mixing with a recherché set, an entirely new experience for me; so that although the War was still dragging on, my love for things creative rather than destructive was stimulated. At the request of Sickert, who had praised my

'Mitrailleuse' in the *Burlington Magazine* as being the most significant utterance in the War, I resumed my secretaryship of the London Group, which was now almost defunct owing to the depletion of its membership. Then came the first real breach with Roger Fry and the precious artists who surrounded him. Hardly anybody had attended our previous private view except a few of the exhibitors and their relations; and in the course of my job as secretary, my wife and I, who hate this type of work, got a copy of *Who's Who* and circularized every likely person from A to Z. The result was a really big attendance at the next exhibition and quite a few sales, because at this time there was a reaction against the tightening of the purse strings and money was being freely spent. But the only thanks I got for this herculean labour was a priggish condemnation from Fry, who informed me at the next general meeting that I was trying to turn the London Group into a fashionable gathering, and that he felt it was not the right public to look at pictures. I rightly pointed out that if we exhibited in public it was our duty to get as many people to look at our pictures as possible, and that we should make no snobbish distinctions; especially as we were professional artists without cocoa behind us: a rude thing to say, considering his name and that he was a Socialist with no desire to be taken for the *rentier* that he was.

I resigned from my secretaryship, but not from the Group, my Father having told me as a rule of life never to resign because it only played into the enemy's hands, and I am proud to say I was a thorn in their flesh for many years. I knew my Quakers well enough to be sure that they would continue to use the lists I had drawn up, in spite of all their virtue and all their hatred of selling pictures. Even in those days intellectuals protested their sincerity too much, and I mocked them by flaunting my professionalism in their faces.

It is unnecessary to say that I had the support of many good men, such as Gilman, Ginner, Nash, and Sickert. Here I may mention that my Futurist training, with all its Latin logic, had convinced me that a man who lives by the public should make his appeal to that public and meet that public, and that all hole-and-corner cliques, and scratch-aback societies are disastrous to the artist and his output. A coterie becomes a tyrant, falsifying a man's standards. Consciously or unconsciously he trims. When he is dealing with a wider and perhaps a more undiscriminating public there is always the chance that his point of view may appeal to an unknown individual. In the past it has been the expert, the critic, and the ' artistic ' who have been wrong, and stray members of the public always right.

No wonder the Bloomsburies revolted against me.

9

We were now in the middle of the War, which seemed to have become a permanent and public-school affair. I was told that Amery was introducing a bill to Parliament which provided for the re-examination of all discharged men. Conscription obviously had to be on the way; in spite of the decoy duck of the 'Derby' scheme.

My hands were still swollen and painful, and I limped; but I was better than I had been, and after my experience in hospital no one knew better than I what Army doctors were.

By the time Amery thought of his scheme for harrying those who had escaped once, recruiting for war had become a serious problem. A man had only to put his nose inside the door of a recruiting office and when he 'came to' he was in uniform, or so they said.

I thought I would apply for a commission before the rush came. Like all men who have been privates, I was determined never to be again. I knew that any recurrence of my illness might this time be final. My outlook was that the War was a loathsome job from which there was no escape; but if I must go back, I was this time going as an officer. After all, I was a public-school man, and things were being run as though it were a public-school war.

I wrote to Eddie Marsh, who could do nothing for me. I then travelled up to Grantham with a view to joining the Machine Gun Corps, where I had heard they had vacancies for draughtsmen, map drawers, and modellers, jobs I felt very fitted for. Captain Reid, who had also done some war paintings, did his utmost for me, but the doctors did not like my physical condition and I was turned down.

I then wrote to Douglas Ainslie, who was a very influential man, having been in various Embassies and places of that kind. He was, I knew, extremely interested in my work and particularly in my war paintings, some of which he had bought. He wrote straight to his friend, the Quartermaster General. I had no idea what he had written, as he merely informed me he had done so. Imagine the nervous state I was thrown into when I was suddenly rung up by the War Office and asked if I would be good enough to call upon General Cowan. Only those who have been privates will understand my feelings. I would certainly have been no more surprised if Kitchener had rung me personally and invited me to lunch. It must be remembered that I had been humiliated and bullied by the sergeants, I had been under hard-bitten women nurses. No wonder I was terrified.

I polished up my silver badge with ' Services Rendered ' on it, and, queasy with fear, sidled into the War Office. Here a sergeant-major made me jump by springing to attention when I mentioned General Cowan's name. An appointment with the Quartermaster General ! Before I knew what was happening I had been whisked up in a lift, propelled down a corridor, and pushed into a room—all very respectfully, of course. Here I was greeted by a charming Etonian with a lovely florid face that matched the scarlet on his uniform. I started to salute, then shook the hand he offered me. Would I sit down ? I did so. I have that temperament which suffers agonies before an event and becomes calm at the time of the crisis, and now I listened judicially.

The officer made me a graceful little speech. He hoped I would excuse the Quartermaster General for being unable to see me personally, but I would understand that he was terribly busy.

' Now,' he went on, ' about this letter from Mr. Douglas Ainslie. You will understand that this is not quite the right department for dealing with such matters. It really concerns the Intelligence, so we will go along and see General Blank.'

Off we went down the corridors, and on the way I explained that I was a public-school man (what a dreadful description for any grown man !), that I had already seen service twice, and that I thought this time I would prefer a commission.

At that he stopped.

' But I understand you want an artist's commission,' he said.

' All right,' I agreed in my innocence. ' I should be happy to join the Artists' Rifles.'

He referred again to the letter, then glanced at me.

' But Douglas Ainslie says you ought to be made an Official War Painter.'

I had just enough presence of mind to give him the right answer.

' Of course,' I said. ' If it could be arranged it would be ideal.'

So on we went to General Blank, who was most pleasant and even knew my name and work. He passed me on to another General who neither knew my name nor wished to know it. Now I had three Generals on the list, but he passed me on to a fourth to make sure. Now, with four Generals behind me, we crossed to the Foreign Office, where we saw Buchan, who sent us on to Buckingham Gate to see Masterman. I knew him and the interesting game stopped. He told me with that queer wit of his that as he could not possibly disobey all the Generals in the British Army he must see about making me an Official Artist at once. There was, however, one great difficulty.

' What's that ? ' I asked with sinking heart.

' There are no funds to pay you.'

My spirits rose. Was that all ?

' Well, if you can't pay me, you can't,' I told him. ' But I'd like to do some more war pictures.'

' Indeed ? ' He seemed surprised. ' Well, you are a discharged man and I see no reason why you should not join our Bureau of Information. I can then send you abroad to our Press Chateau.'

It was agreed that all my work should belong to his Bureau for reproduction purposes, while I retained the right to sell the pictures and arrange exhibitions. He promised to help me in every way. At that time all manner of intellectuals, artists, and what not, were being officially or unofficially employed to spread the culture of Britain to the Allies and neutrals, Germany having stolen a march over us in this connexion.

Within two days I was sent to do some drawings of the making of aircraft and of aeroplanes in flight. I visited all kinds of factories as a privileged person, and then took my first flight in an aeroplane with General Sir Sefton Brancker. A first flight must always be a momentous occasion, and it was even more momentous in those days than it is now; but apart from that I had always understood as a private that a General could do nothing like an ordinary man, and I was filled with the gravest doubts about trusting myself to him. However, there was no way out of it, and I went. Afterwards I was told that Brancker was not a very good pilot, but he seemed all right to me and rather on the cautious side, a feature for which I was thankful. If his landings were bumpy I did not realize it. I was always glad to get one foot back on the ground. This dapper little man with an eye-glass became a great friend of mine. He did much for me, arranging all sorts of flights with all sorts of pilots, some of whom were too good to be put in uniform and were kept at Hendon and such places where their expert knowledge was made full use of.

Through Elizabeth Asquith and Lady Parsons I had the extraordinary experience of going up over London among the searchlights in a balloon. What a strange sight it was. The twinkle of the street lamps, the dark patches which looked like the parks and probably were not, the groping, sliding searchlights, and now and then the moving lights of a train. It looked strangely unlike that dear old London of mine and I felt very lonely up in the heavens. As C. F. Montague pointed out later, I was the first man to paint in the air, and in all modesty I still think my aeroplane pictures are the finest work I have done. The whole newness of vision, and the excitement of it, infected my work and gave it an enthusiasm which can be felt. The pictures were exhibited at the Fine Arts Society, with Muirhead Bone's marvellous lithographs of the 'Dockyards of the Clyde', and Sir George Clausen's symbolic drawings of Aims and Ideals of War. Ernest Jackson did all the printing and proving of the lithographs. Brancker came along and did his best for me. Years later, on the night of his death I had a telegram from him regretting he would not be able to come to us as he was just off on the R. 101.

Masterman arranged for me to go to France, carrying a magnificent passport, which described me as the King's guest; and just before I went out I met Will Dyson, the cartoonist, who had been made an Official Artist for the Australian Forces. He gave me a tip worth knowing. He had accepted a commission with the rank of major, and he told me I was on no account to take one. I pointed out that so far nobody had suggested such a thing.

'Never mind,' he said. 'One day somebody may come along and put it up to you. You'll think you'll be better off with a commission, but you won't. Dressed as an officer as you are and with a Press brassard on your arm, you can meet any one. Generals included, and you can go direct to them. I have to apply to a colonel and so on. Keep out of the machine.'

At Boulogne I was met by a car, with a chauffeur, an orderly, and a conducting officer, who turned out to be Good-hart-Rendel, the great architect, who was doing that job because of ill health. I was driven rapidly away to the north to the famous Chateau d'Harcourt, where the visitors were received. Here I was met by a magnificent gentleman, all over blue facings, white hair, and white dogs and I am sure, a white castle in Scotland. An orderly in white gloves showed me to my room, where he unpacked my wretched kit, told me it was not necessary to change for dinner, and apologized for the lack of baths. I could not have been so many miles from that old shed the Shambles, and I pinched myself to make sure I was awake. Yes, there were the guns thudding distantly. This was a new sort of war to me. I began to realize how I had hitherto missed *The Times* point of view.

In the circumstances it is only natural that I felt somewhat embarrassed. The War Office had been bad enough, but now the discharged private was preparing to have dinner with all manner of Generals in France. But when I went down at last and joined the group I found them most perturbed because their expert cocktail-shaker has gone to G.H.Q. for the night, and here I was able to help. At different periods of my life I have been pleased at my ability to do certain things. When I was very young I was inordinately proud because I could stand on the saddle and the handlebars of a bicycle. When I attained the age of appreciation I had a tinge of vanity because of my ability to mix cocktails. As a result of my training in Paris, I was able to mix a drink from most ingredients; and here, in this chateau, was a plethora indeed. I offered to do my best, I mixed one, and after the first few sips there was a visible thawing, even a warmth, in the atmosphere. It is not often one is permitted to work one's will on government property, and I am not ashamed to say I mixed a great many; so many that in the words of one colonel I was 'a very fine fella'. It is possible to be an artist in more things than one, and by some dispensation of Providence I can always mix the right amount and fill the glasses, be they twelve or three, just to the brim, with not a drop to spare. As Mark Hambourg says: 'Cocktails are like music; the same notes, but oh, such different music.'

It is only fair to say that the relief and the warmth I have spoken of was largely due to the fact that those officers of high rank had been depressed by the belief that they were about to entertain yet another intellectual bore of ascetic habits. G. Bernard Shaw had just left. I was the only guest that evening, and owing to my knack of being able to remember masses of useless information, I was able to discuss dogs with a colonel, Shanghai with a lieutenant, the Anglo-Indian branch of my family with a major, the general health of all, my preference for pipe smoking, the delights of beer after physical exertion, and port as an hereditary taste. I could see that suggestion of a commission looming in the background.

The next day was spent mostly in the Somme, arranging where it would be possible for me to be put up, and the necessary permits for sketching. I returned to dinner after miles and miles of motoring, to find that James Barrie and a very shy yet talkative attaché from Pekin had arrived, in the company of some surly and contemptuous French journalists, genial American bankers, fanatical New York preachers, and a few American newspapermen, one of whom I knew as a London correspondent. Then there appeared the Mother of Matrons, who was inspecting the accommodation for nurses in the zone. It was a bewildering dinner, and my sympathy went out to the officers who had been detailed to entertain such a company. Once when there came one of the many pauses it would be bridged by the treble of the attaché, who asked the Matron urgently if she found drawers opened and shut easily—we assumed he was talking Hospital equipment. Barrie grew increasingly nervous and kept tilting his chair backwards and clutching the tablecloth to save himself from tipping backwards. It made my heart jump to watch him. After they had been well dined, they were given a lecture by an Intelligence officer on the position of the Allies. Fortunately, I did not have to attend.

Next morning they were aroused at dawn, formed up, drilled by a sergeant, and marched off to the gas chamber in the stables, where actually only a sulphur candle was burning. This greatly impressed the distinguished visitors, one of whom was overcome by gas, taken out with apologies, fitted with another gas mask and conducted back to the sulphur candle to prove that nothing was defective. They were then rushed off to Vimy Ridge, where batteries were instructed to fire so that they might have their baptism. They returned full of awe.

One of the American correspondents had spotted the sulphur candle, and he whispered these words to me:

' Half these guys take your officers for fools. I'm with you in this fooling business and am saying nix. I know you Britishers, and it sure does me good to see a Chicago wheat manipulator look wise and sad when he has no need to worry.'

Phillips Oppenheim arrived soon after this. He was magnificent, and I rejoiced to see how he swallowed not only the dinner but all the theatricalities which were arranged for his benefit. You could not blame him, for it all looked real enough and would have deceived most men. His lurid account of the hot, passionate breath of the shells which hurtled past his neck greatly impressed the censors.

My great difficulty lay in doing the work I was appointed to do, as my car was incessantly borrowed, courteously I admit, for the use of the distinguished guests. This took me all over the place behind the lines and I saw a great deal, as naturally I did not want to hang about the Chateau alone with nothing to do. I used to sit in the car which was supposed to be mine in the seat meant for the orderly, and I went to such places as Etaples, G.H.Q. at Montreux, Calais, Abbeville, and even Paris. Eventually I wrote to Masterman about it, and through the influence of Rendel he had me attached to the 4th Division at St. Nicholas, between the old Hindenburg line and Arras, with General Sir Charles Lambton in command. And very charming company they were. This released the car and the chauffeur from the taxi business and I was able to get down to work.

I was now living with the Divisional Staff, and they seemed impressed, much like the lunatics in the London General Hospital when told I had been a private. General Armstrong, a gunner, helped me in all possible ways to maintain touch with Brigade Headquarters and the front line at Monchy. One day he came to my tent after we had been machine-gunned by a Bosche aeroplane to see if everything was all right with me. He was astounded at my lack of kit. I only had a razor, some shirts, and a green canvas flea-bag, besides some sketch books. Looking round, he asked where my bath was. I said I always went down by car to the Officers' Club, I did not, of course, but I always respect the religions of others, he lent me one of his own, and I was grateful. He knew General Nevinson, a gunner, I believe, in India, whom I had never met. All the same I tried to look and talk like a very near relation.

That morning in mess I admitted to the fact that I had been at Uppingham. This impressed another General who came from Yorkshire. He was wondering whether to send his son aged five to Eton or Uppingham, and when it was said that Uppingham was the more expensive—it may be—my prestige was enormously enhanced, and I was accepted as an officer and a gentleman. In spite of the fact I had been a private and was now 'an artist-chap'. At night I was often urged to tell stories of the Latin Quarter, a spot which seemed to cause much yearning among the middle-aged.

However, I was working at last, and from here I did such paintings as the 'Road from Arras to Bapaume', the 'Survivors at Arras', the 'Very Lights at Monchy', the 'Roads of France', the 'Destroyed Canal at Ypres', the 'Hindenburg Line', and 'Brigade Headquarters', pictures which were destined to be distributed throughout the world, the last one being in Tokio.

One day I received a note:

'I understand you know Robert Ross. Do come and dine with me. I am in the sausage balloons next to you at St. Nicholas.

RICHMOND TEMPLE'

I went, to have a dinner and to meet a truly remarkable man. We had many things in common, and in the circumstances I was more than delighted to meet him. He is now an organizing genius of the Savoy, Claridges, the Berkeley and such places. After dinner we saw a concert-party performance of outstanding vulgarity. The lewd enjoyment of the audience, most of whom were back from the line for a short time only, made me sorry I did not see the end of it. An order was brought in for Temple. He was to go up in his balloon immediately, and he asked me to go with him.

Slightly bewildered, I demanded to know what he could see in the dark, and he explained that this was the best time for spotting gun flashes. Like ourselves, the Germans were continually altering the position of their guns. I was strapped to a parachute, given a knife to cut myself out of trees and up we went.

It was a weird experience. After the aeroplanes I had been accustomed to, the silence was painful. I cannot say how far up we went, but it was a long way. The movement was like that of a small boat, an illusion which was heightened when I heard the sighing of the wind through our ropes. Above, the stars were blotted out by our sausage. Gradually the various sounds came to me from below; the hooves of the horses and mules, the engines of cars and lorries, the regimental band in Arras, and innumerable gramophones making an orchestra of the wildest modernism. Then came the crashes of the heavies behind us, the sharper banging of the Field Artillery ahead, and the stealthy sound of hostile shells slipping their way through the night to Arras, where they fell with a flash and then came the roar.

I was enthralled until a German 'plane saw us and zoomed down with a hail of bullets from his machine gun. So far my life had been varied, but never before had I been hung up in the sky for a foreign gentleman to exercise his skill on me. Fortunately he proved to be no crack shot, and after the first few bursts from his gun the anti-aircraft, or Archies, took up the cudgels on our behalf. Those well-meaning people brought me no consolation whatever. It was kind of them to put a barrage round us, but they seemed to forget that their shrapnel whistled all round us as well as the foreign gentleman's and I expected the balloon to go up in flames.

Richmond Temple seemed to regard this state of imminent disaster as an incident comparable with a cut from a safety razor, but I was glad to realize that we were being hauled down. The barrage had its effect on the Bosche, who turned away, but unaccountably he suddenly appeared from another quarter. That machine gun of his was wasted in his hands. Back came the Bosche bungler and nearly got a bull's-eye; and at the same moment I was horrified to hear Temple telephone below to stop the descent. I inquired if he was partial to being used as live bait, but he only grinned and told me it would be unwise to drop lower as we should probably have to jump and we must leave a safety margin for the parachute to open.

Jump! Jump from that basket. I told Temple I couldn't jump, it was bad enough jumping into a swimming bath. But out into the void—well! However, all the world knows that the English are famous for compromise, and it was arranged that I should sit on the edge of the basket and

Temple would push me over. While we were arguing we suddenly noticed that things had become quiet. The foreign gentleman had gone home to supper. The Archies ceased fire. Down we went, so very slowly that I was convinced they were not really trying below.

After this, I was able to spend a good deal of time in the balloons, and I did some drawings from the air. I also did a sketch for my lithograph, 'Hauling Down a Sausage at Night'.

I was still sleeping in my tent with the 4th Division, and a most unhealthy spot I found it at dawn. German 'planes would always be worrying Arras and various railheads, and on their way back to their lines they usually gave us a morning greeting as they passed.

One thing troubled me a good deal, my uniform. It was a bastard affair. In the distance I looked like any other officer, but I had no badge for my cap or lapels, and no pips or crowns to show what my rank was. On my arm I had a brassard with the letter 'P' on it, but otherwise I was an object of suspicion to any vigilant sentry. I became tired of being taken for a spy. I used to wear motor goggles round my cap so that the absence of a badge would be missed, but when I was challenged and this was noticed, it was usually taken for granted that my number was up. Of course, it must have seemed suspicious to some when I sat down and began sketching a gun emplacement, but as I once peevishly pointed out, if I had been a real spy I should have taken care to have my regimental badges on. I would be hauled off to appear before some old town major, where I would hand him my papers, grin politely, and walk out again.

The rumour had gone round that there was likely to be some real fighting at Passchendaele, and when I heard that an officer in the Balloons was anxious to collect his kit, which he had left at Ypres, I suggested that we should both go there, as a real officer made it easier for me and my car. He was delighted and off we went. We arrived at Ypres, and while he went to the Officers' Club I wandered on up towards the Salient and obtained notes and rough sketches for my painting, 'Harvest of Battle'. On my return I found the car had been damaged by a shell. This meant we had to stay in Ypres for some time while the car was dragged away for repair in a field repair shop, so I had time to obtain more rough sketches for my Passchendaele picture, 'Harvest of Battle' and also for 'Shell Holes' now in the Imperial War Museum. When the car was ready we returned straight to Arras. There I found a telegram from Masterman instructing me to go to Paris, where I was to meet a dealer and arrange an exhibition of the works of the various artists and photographers. I said good-bye to my Generals and left for the capital immediately.

Once there, I arranged matters with the dealer, who in the best French manner promised everything and did nothing. I also settled my debts with the *restauranteurs* who had given my Mother and myself free meals at the outbreak of war, and what a greeting I got. Dinner parties and kisses. It never occurred to me that I had to report to the Town Major of Paris, as I heard afterwards I should have done. It was with a clear conscience that I returned to G.H.Q. calling at the Press Chateau on the way, where Montague wanted to see me about an article he was writing for an official publication. Philip Gibbs was walking about like a lost wraith; Perceval Phillipps was as calm and stoic as ever; and several other journalists were present.

But when I got to Montreaux I found stacks of telegrams awaiting me. 'Report at once.' 'Where are you?' 'Address unknown; return at once.' In some trepidation I went to see Major Lee, of Intelligence F, and hastily began to explain to him what I had done and where I had been. He listened rather grimly as I told him of my flights, my ballooning, and my sketching. I spoke of Passchendaele, I showed him some of my rough work and mentioned 'Shell Holes', which was the last picture I had completed. I even produced Masterman's telegram ordering me to Paris.

'Do I understand,' was all he said, 'that you have been to Passchendaele?'

'Oh yes,' I assured him, and I showed him some more sketches and told him how I had wandered all over the place and seen everything.

' Aren't you aware that you are forbidden to go to that section of the line ? ' he demanded.

I said, ' No. Nobody ever instructed me to keep away from it.'

' Of course not,' he snapped. ' We were forbidden to tell you.'

I am certain I did not laugh, but something of my thoughts must have got through to my eyes.

I had broken a rule which was never on any account to be told to me. Rank insubordination !

I saw it coming. In a few days I was back in London.

10

The fact that my presence had been found necessary in London did not in the least disturb me. I had rough sketches enough for many pictures.

I set to work in a large studio I had taken in a slum off the Hampstead Road, in Robert Street. It had once been Whistler's; Sickert had, of course, used it; and it suited me very well. It was also next door to old Robert Winter, a sculptor for Albert the Good who was then secretary of the New English Art Club. Here I did my pictures for my second exhibition of War Paintings at the Leicester Galleries. It proved to be a most difficult exhibition. As I was an Official War Artist, anything I produced about the War must have the approval of the British Empire. In other words, my work was censored. This meant that all sorts of young men in khaki with red tabs, green tabs, blue tabs, and no tabs at all, had to signify their pleasure or displeasure. The Bureau of Information had blossomed into the Ministry of Information; and hundreds of young girls, bent upon doing their bit towards the winning of the War, used to write to me for information about all sorts of curious matters. True, I never answered their letters, but their misapplied energy appalled me. In time I fully expected the order to produce my pictures in triplicate, according to the Army fashion. But they stopped just short of that.

Robert Ross was in charge of the Imperial War Museum, and before the exhibition opened he bought some of my pictures: the 'Arras-Bapaume Road', 'Gun in Elevation', 'Shell Holes', the 'Group of Soldiers' and 'The Paths of Glory'. Unfortunately the last two were censored: one on the ground that the men were not sufficiently good-looking, and the other because no photographs of the dead were allowed. Photographs, mark you ! With the help of Arnold Bennett, who agreed with me that this was hardly the time to try to reach an understanding as to what constituted manly beauty, Masterman was able to have the ban removed from the ' Group of Soldiers '. But ' The Paths of Glory' remained censored. In company with another picture which I called ' The Doctor ', it is now in the Imperial War Museum, hidden from the public eye : a state of affairs which sheds a curious light on the official mind when one remembers the grim films that have been exhibited and the books of horrible photographs that have been published. What I had painted in ' The Paths of Glory ' was reality. I showed dead men caught in wire.

Lord Derby had been approached about opening my exhibition. He agreed to do so, then heard of the trouble I was having with the censors and very rightly wrote saying he would be unable to come. I then asked Lord Beaverbrook personally. He was now Minister of Propaganda, and he made his first public appearance as a Cabinet Minister in opening my Exhibition, for which I wrote the following preface :

This collection of pictures represents the work of the last seven months. Most of them were completed at home after my return from the Western Front where in my capacity as one of the Official Artists I was attached to various divisions and given every facility for sketching and recording the ordinary every-day life and work of the Imperial Forces.

This exhibition differs entirely from my last in which I dealt largely with the horrors of War as a motive. I have now attempted to synthesize all the human activity and to record the prodigious organization of our Army, which was all the more overwhelming to me when I contrasted it with what I remembered on the Belgian front 1914–15.

All of my work had to be done from rapid short-hand sketches made often under trying conditions in the front line, behind the lines, above the lines in observation balloons, over the lines in aeroplanes and beyond them even to the country at present held by the enemy.

*I relied chiefly on memory, a method I learnt as a student in
Paris and for which I am ever grateful : nature is far too confusing
and anarchic to be merely copied on the spot. Although the followers
of the ' plein air ' school always laid great stress on working directly
from nature, their work is none the less pure invention marred by all
manner of nature's accessories. An artist's business is to create,
not to copy or abstract, and to my mind creation can only be
achieved when, after a close and continuous observation and study of
nature, this visual knowledge of realities is used emotionally and
mentally.*

*Every form of art must be and has always been a creation worked
out within definite unrealistic conventions or formulas which should
never be judged by what they represent. It may even be that
they represent nothing at all. Most of the finest works of art
of the world express some visual realities, but many absolutely
none.*

*In England most of our so-called ' Advanced Painters ' are not
artists but literary men or women : so obsessed are their minds by
literary or journalistic association that they cannot paint any human
being or human activity or even landscape without some literary
subject being conveyed to their journalistic minds.*

*Hence they seek ' Pure Form ' through nothing but still-life—
endless green apples, saucepans and oranges, ' Picasized ' and
' Cezanned ' with a learned, ponderous and self-conscious sub-
consciousness. The whole thing has a false naïvete for all the
world as though a gawky English old maid were trying to be a
Marie Antoinette posing as an Arcadian Shepherdess.*

*Some years ago ' Le Rire ' had an amusing cartoon of some
talented enthusiast, who had previously been a ' fin-de-sièclist ' and
' decadent ', suddenly taking to child-like antics and gamboling about
an exhibition expounding the beauties of his ' sub-conscious ' work.
But for the ' Elect ' of Bloomsbury to do so just now is pathetic and
out of date—even in London, that ' Intellectual back-water of
Europe '.*

*Fortunately I have no literary or journalistic tastes, and I can
paint in consequence without any prejudice or association a man in a
tin-hat or a man in a bowler, being merely interested in plastic form.
Only by this happy fortune of having an unjournalistic mind am I
enabled to paint war at all.*

Some time I wish to be able to create a work of art out of this aspect of human activity which up to the present time and through all the ages has unhappily been the most serious occupation of man. Peace is too often a mere interlude of growing stronger numerically or nationally, however much many of us may hope that by very gradual and painful evolution men—and even journalists—will cease to be destructive and scientific animals and become constructive human beings governed by a finer sense than that of fear and self-protection. But that is a hope no Englishman dare seriously to conceive until military autocracy in Germany and its secret admirers in this and other countries are overthrown.

Since my last exhibition I have experimented with various styles of painting : I wished to create a distinct method in harmony with each new picture. I do not believe the same technique can be used to express a quiet static moonlight night, the dynamic force of a bomber and the restless rhythm of mechanical transport. Many painters to-day try to find some particular style of mannerism, and when found they never vary it, hoping always to hall-mark their canvases and deceive their public (the Intellectuals especially) into the idea they have individuality. The truth is that the personality of a painter—if he has any personality, of course—enables him to withstand the test of any technical method.

Ever since I left off wasting time at a Public School I have associated with the ' Intellectuals ' and with the Art circles of London, Paris and Milan, and it is chiefly because I have learnt to know them that I now prefer to exhibit my work to the largest possible general public.

I have no illusions about the public for, owing chiefly to our Press, our loathsome tradition-loving Public Schools and our antiquity-stinking Universities, the average Englishman is not merely suspicious of the new in all intellectual and artistic experiment, but he is mentally trained to be so unsportsman-like as to try to kill every new endeavour in embryo, especially if it shows signs of developing a future health and strength.

Being by nature a democrat, I prefer even this form of opposition, which after all is only due to British kainophobia, to the lip service of the self-satisfied cliques, the petty groups and the jealous causeries of the superior ' Intellectuals '.

I also feel convinced that it is the duty of every sincere artist to *have the courage of this bellicose ideal, giving his finest, singing his song from the roof-tops, even using a megaphone if necessary to overcome protesting howls, in order thoroughly to counteract the effect of that powerful section which can always be depended upon to give the public what it wants, and so, deliberately and cynically, to supply and cater for every low, mean instinct of the mob, blighting all hopes for democracy, and compelling decent-thinking persons utterly to despair.*

C. R. W. NEVINSON.

March, 1918

The exhibition sold out. My one regret now is that I did not ask more money for my pictures. My prices were ridiculous, but I still had the pre-War French standard in my mind.

The one fly in the amber was ' The Paths of Glory '. Under the belief that the censors would pass it at the last moment I had it hung, and when permission was finally refused I pasted brown paper over it rather than leave a hole on the wall, and wrote ' Censored ' across it in the manner of French newspapers. At the Press show, Hannen Swaffer, with the knowingness peculiar to Swaffer, who is ' always right because he knows ', refused to believe there was a picture behind the brown paper. He felt perfectly certain, as Swaffer always feels perfectly certain, that it was ' a stunt '. No words of mine, nor of Ross, or of the official representing the Ministry of Information, could convince him that the thing had been done at the last minute when permission to show the picture in question had been finally refused. Off he went, to write up his suspicions. I was in headlines again. The result was that I was summoned to the War office and severely reprimanded for using the word ' Censored ', which appeared to be a word forbidden by the Defence of the Realms Act (D.O.R.A.).

By now I was all in the wrong with the military authorities. I insisted on putting my point of view, and I was thankful that I held no commission and could talk to those brass hats as man to man. But it was getting increasingly difficult for me to hold my own against the hundreds of little official minds that delighted to feel themselves in some authority in a commandeered hotel around the Strand. I was being grossly overworked, and was doing from eighteen to twenty hours a day, when I ran into Paul Konody again.

Konody had been put in charge of the Canadian War Memorials, and he was interested in all I had to tell him about my work and my difficulties. The first thing he did was to come along to my Exhibition and buy four pictures of the ' Roads of France ' and most of my Lithographs. The next thing he did was to have me transferred to the Canadians, and I escaped from the ghastly petty tyrannies of Intelligence F, G.H.Q., the British Censor at the War Office, and the various Ministries of Propaganda in Norfolk Street and Arundel Street. I was now in a new world. The Canadian officers with whom I came in contact showed a readiness to help and an understanding of my job which made life possible for me.

Soon I was off again to France, where I was housed at the American Chateau and later transferred to an aerodrome near St. Quentin. Unfortunately for me, I was set a subject by Konody which was not really suitable for me. He wanted me to illustrate or reconstruct an aerial battle of the great Canadian airman W. A. Bishop, who won two V.C.'s, the M.C., the D.S.O. with bar, and the D.F.C. I was given all manner of descriptions of the fight and two or three photographs of the machine used, and was granted every facility for flying about in the clouds, where the fight took place. But I had not actually witnessed the fight; and although I had seen a good deal of aerial warfare and had myself been attacked by hostile 'planes, I found the task a terribly difficult one. What with flying, ill-health and overwork, I broke down under the strain. Through Robert Nicholls, the War poet, I was put in the care of Henry Head, the great neurologist, who was in charge of all men suffering from what was then called air nerves. Head wrote to Lord Beaverbrook and advised that I should be sent right away for a holiday, as I was in the awful condition of feeling that I was falling through the air, just as I was about to go to sleep, and of waking up with an imaginary crash.

III

Like many sensitive men, I can honestly say that I have never felt fear at the moment of danger. In emergencies I can always be counted upon to act as quickly as the average man, if not more quickly; and I have a calm and decision and detachment that always amaze me. But some hours afterwards, and when in complete safety, I suffer intensely from delayed shock, starting with a terrible elation, followed by uncontrollable tremblings, and ending with vomiting, with all forms of anticipation of evil and with eventual prostration. Actually this always happens to me after a public speech, or when artists have indulged in some form of personal spite or vulgar attack on me. I am perfectly good-natured and calm at the time, and then a few days afterwards I go through every hell of rage, frustration, or mere pique.

When he received the letter from Henry Head, Lord Beaverbrook sent for me and was extremely kind. He said that in future I need paint only tiny sketches, and that he would have them photographed and enlarged. I was to go away and get well, and then he would make a regular circus out of me (I quote his words) as I seemed to have the qualifications of genius and the knack of pleasing the public. By now I was almost too exhausted to argue; but I did point out that I could see the War would not last much longer, that obviously I had my artistic career to consider, and that his suggestion would probably ruin my future as an artist. Beaverbrook is a very understanding man. He dismissed me good-naturedly as another damn-fool artist who failed to appreciate what he was offering, and he told me that Orpen was the only artist who understood business.

Away I went to Cornwall, to paint anything but the War and to be taught aquatint and etching by that master of the medium, Hartley. Sickert had already advised me to try etching and had assured me it was the easiest medium in the world. On my protesting that this could not be so and saying that I had read a great deal about etching and the difficulties of the technique, he explained that all one did was to get a prepared plate on which your drawing had been photographed; or, if you preferred to be a purist, you merely wetted your pencil drawing, had it pressed and therefore reversed on the wax and then kept the plate in your pocket, and did a bit of drawing with a needle while you were waiting for a girl. If you wanted your lines to be darker you cut into the copper, as the Old Masters did, and dipped the plate in nitric acid as soon as you felt you had done enough. That was all. It was a thoroughly inaccurate description of etching, but a very helpful one in those days when the art was so clouded by the mumbo-jumbo of the experts and the writings of connoisseurs who knew little about it.

It has always been my habit to go to the best teacher when I wanted to learn something. I was initiated by Fulleylove into the art of water-colours; an academic school had taught me the use of oils, and the Slade the use of pencil and charcoal; I had gone to Paris for gouache, pastel, and tempera; to Ernest Jackson for lithography; to Hartley, Everett and Strang for etching and aquatint. My motoring, even to the complete reassembling of an engine, I had learned from Thompson, one of the best teachers of the day; and my cooking I had gathered from a German, an Army cook, and a French waiter. I like to know the real technique of my subject before I exercise my talents on it, and I have always been impatient of 'picking it up as I went along'.

Hartley taught me many things, and I returned from Cornwall with a fresh interest, if not much better in health. We travelled back to London in the train with William Jowett, K.C.; and, like the rest of us, he was most pessimistic about the progress of the War. The Germans had nearly broken through, Russia had collapsed, and everybody felt that a terrible blow to the Allies was perilously near. I got back to find that a bomb had fallen on the printing works where my lithographs were kept, and that my stones were damaged. The reason for the extra ridge in my lithograph of the 'Arras-Bapaume Road' is because I had to put it in to cover the injury done to my original stone.

I worked again on my Passchendaele picture, 'Harvest of Battle', and on 'War in the Air', for which I paid another short visit to France to do some more flying. My recollections of this period are indistinct. The future seemed black for England, for although America had come in, Russia had gone out, and the War looked like lasting till eternity, with nothing but death as a release from it. I remember attending a dinner given at the Ritz by Lord Rothermere and Lord Beaverbrook in honour of the artists employed by the Canadians. I was sitting next to Winston Churchill, upon whom I fainted. He looked after me, but I was carted away to recover and returned to find he had explained to everybody that I was ill, not drunk, as some might have thought. But the seats had been changed round, and this time I sat next to Lord Beaverbrook, and when I fainted again, I fell on *him*. I am afraid I did not add to the festivities, and eventually Churchill sent me home in his car. Konody told me later that one result of my display of unfitness was to stop the mud-slinging of some of the older artists who thought they had been unnecessarily overlooked in the making of records of the War.

At this stage, there were several dinners arranged by the Army and Propaganda authorities; gloomy affairs, not only because every one was exhausted by the War and nerves were all awry, but also because artists are generally very bad company in the presence of other artists.

It is difficult to suggest in words the despair and monotony that immediately preceded the Armistice. I shall never forget seeing poor John Nash—still in the ranks—one day at the Sitwells. He was just back from the front line; and, almost unaware of where he was, he yet mechanically behaved as though he were accustomed to dine with intellectuals night after night.

Although we all knew now that the morale of Jerry had broken we could not believe that the end was in sight; and when Kathleen and I heard the maroons explode at eleven o'clock on the morning of 11 November, while I was working on my Passchendaele painting, all we said was, ' Good God! Another air raid.' We ought to have known better, for Harry Preston had told us three days previously it was possible the Germans would ask for peace. Trust dear old Harry for getting advance information.

For me, Armistice Day will always remain the most remarkable day of emotion in my life. When we heard the cheers outside I dropped my brushes and rushed out with Kathleen into the Hampstead Road, where we jumped on a lorry which took us down to Whitehall. Here we saw Winston Churchill beaming on a mob that was yelling itself hoarse. With a thousand others in Trafalgar Square we danced, ' Knees Up, Mother Brown '; then to the Café Royal for food, where we were joined by a gang of officers, and drank a good deal of champagne, and raided the kitchens because the staff had knocked off work. After that, I must needs go round to rejoice with my dealers, Brown and Phillips, and at their galleries I met one of my patrons who was quite shocked at my excitement. Then on to the Studio Club, to find a crowd of demi-intellectuals terribly calm and indifferent to the noise of the multitude, and some of them even apprehensive as they saw the end of their well-paid jobs. Back into the streets, to rejoice with human beings; and back again to the Café Royal, to find yet more friends gathered to do homage to the day; poor Kathleen with an American *cocotte* lying over her knees, crying; and another girl sobbing because nobody cheered for Serbia, although she herself came from Birmingham; a crowd of journalists, with Scott of the *Manchester Guardian*, who for no reason at all was bitten by a French girl, who then bit me; and, realizing that bites from promiscuous women might have unpleasant effects, chasing round between the yelling mobs in Piccadilly to a chemist, where we showed our wounds and explained our predicament, but could not spare the time for prophylactic treatment, and parted from him, ten shillings the poorer and with nothing but cold water on our wounds. Back in the Café Royal, we were joined by generals, subalterns, and grave literary men who wished to discuss the peace terms with Scott, but I could not bear to listen, and with some others I climbed the pillars of the old café instead. Often I marvel how this was done.

We finished the evening by going round to Van Leer's place in Regent's Park. He was not then a famous dealer in the rue de la Seine. But we crept away from the place with Scott in the early hours because Betty May suddenly armed herself with the fire-irons and tried to start a new war; we had seen enough of war.

Never did I imagine that I would live to see another generation come up and face a condition similar to 1914.

11

At the time I did not notice it, but actually I finished my war paintings with the end of the War. I may have varnished one of them and framed another, but after the Armistice I did not do a stroke of painting which dealt with the War. It was a period I wished to put behind me, and I immediately fixed up a contract with Brown and Phillips and began painting my peace show.

The relief that the War was over was tremendous, yet this turned out to be for me the most repulsive time in my life. At one of the many dinners given by the Canadian Memorials, Sims had asked me if I would care to put my name down for the Royal Academy; and he asked also Kennington, Nash and Augustus John. Afterwards he wrote and informed me that he had got Sir John Lavery and Solomon J. Solomon of the Camouflage to second me, and that he did not think my name would be long on the Book, especially as he considered my Passchendaele picture to be the best painting of modern times. This recognition of me naturally upset the intellectuals and the superior people, who seemed always to mistake modern artists for public agitators destined ever to fight a losing battle. To be misunderstood and to be amongst the unappreciated was, and I dare say still is, the only aesthetic criterion for a great many artists and certainly for the majority of critics. This aesthetic standpoint comes from the satisfaction of three emotions always dominant in the English intellectual: superiority, self-pity, and a sadistic pleasure that an artist is being ' put through it '.

While I was painting for my one-man show, the Canadian War Memorials hired Burlington House for the exhibition of the paintings of their Official Artists; and it was here that I first encountered the hostility of the intellectuals, who ferociously attacked my work. It is interesting to note that nowadays the same breed cannot speak too well of my war paintings, and wisely shake their heads over my deterioration. They forget that twenty years ago they were doing the same thing over the works they now praise. When I was twenty-one I painted my self-portrait which is now in the Tate Gallery, and when it was exhibited at the New English Claude Phillips remarked in his criticism that he had been much struck for some years by the deterioration of my work. This was a little hard on a student. What fools these critics be. So Claude Phillips was knighted. One grows a little tired of the same note.

My aeroplane pictures particularly annoyed the critics, and one of them headed his column ' Exit Nevinson '. This caused the wildest pleasure among the artistic coterie, the boozers and the hangers-on whom I used to know in the Café Royal. It was a clique very much in touch with Fleet Street then, and in return for a few drinks it would supply the critical matter for any poor journalist who had been sent to cover an art exhibition. It is amusing to look back upon, although it was painful at the time. A great deal of nonsense about Art, a great deal of criticism, and all sorts of chatter about artists originated from the quasi-artists and the Chelsea ' Bohemians ', who seldom painted and were successful only in the art of borrowing money. Thank Heaven that has changed and the pernicious environment engendered by the Café Royal gossip no longer finds its way into print for millions to read.

I was conscious of hostility on all sides. On the suggestion of Alvaro Guevara I joined the Chelsea Arts Club, but I was a member for one night only. I had dinner there with Guevara and his guest, Lord Berners, but I cannot honestly say that any of us enjoyed it. Derwent Wood was present. He regarded himself as an old enemy of mine, and resented having seen me a good deal with Epstein, whom, of course, I knew before the War, and whose company I had enjoyed in Paris and at the Café Royal. Wood turned to me during the meal, and, addressing me as Nevinstein, asked me in a loud voice who my German friend was. At that time to be called German was derogatory and provocative. Wood meant to be nasty. We tried to ignore him, but he became increasingly offensive and eventually Guevara and Berners left. I saw them off, and an Australian painter came up to me and said, ' Come back and face the bullock.' So I went. With drunken repetition he demanded again to know the name of my German friend, and when I informed him that Guevara's guest was Lord Berners the shock almost sobered him. Never have I seen a Bohemian so horrified. He was simply overwhelmed by the thought that he had insulted an English peer. White and shaky, he asked me to bring Berners back, but it was impossible to do so, as they had gone on to see a real professional fight elsewhere. I must say some of the Chelsea artists were grimly amused, and the attitude of hostility was by no means so great as when I entered; but I resigned next day, pointing out that I had no need to pay for such insults, as I could get them in the artistic world for nothing.

It is difficult to define the misery I felt at this time. If I came across any one connected with art, or even interested in it, I was at once the victim of cheap sneers. So I packed up and made, as usual, for Paris. It was a terrible trip via Southampton, with no proper connexions between the trains and the boats, and hours of waiting in the passport sheds. I was still carrying my diplomatic passport and was given certain privileges; but there was such an extraordinary crowd of the flotsam and jetsam of all nations, either leaving Europe or flocking back to it, that the delay was wearisome. I had travelled so often across the Channel that the detectives knew me well, and they put me in the train with the King's Messengers and Sidney Dark, who was then a journalist covering the Peace Conference for the *Daily Express*. If I recollect rightly the journey took sixteen hours, and I arrived at St. Lazare to find hardly any trains running on the Nord-Sud and such as were doing so crammed inside *and* out. I had a hard job to get to Severini's studio at Denfert-Rochereau, but I reached him at last and he put me up in the gallery.

Few Englishmen have been privileged to see Paris under

so many conditions as I have; I had known it in the days of the fiacre and the three-horse bus, in the grandeur of the immediate pre-War days, at the outbreak of war, and during the War; but never have I seen a more dismal city than it looked to me soon after the Armistice. London is always the same. Paris is a city of moods, and its unchanging architectural appearance and the habits of French life seem to accentuate the feelings of the people. Military conditions still existed at this time, and there were all manner of regulations as to food and drink, the opening and closing of cafés, art galleries, and many of the shops *de luxe*. But, as is usual when the French are down, every one was most amiable and polite. Good times have a bad effect on the French character, and I know no people more wonderful when it comes to tightening the belt and making the best of bad conditions. I was heartily welcomed not only in Montmartre but in Montparnasse. Montmartre had sadly fallen away. The Tabarin was a roller-skating rink, and American officers and soldiers dominated—I am afraid I can use no other word—the music halls. But Montparnasse had not become a wet suburb of America.

I spent wonderful evenings with Kisling, Zadkin, Modigliani—who was suffering from gas—Asselin, and Severini. Sometimes I dined with Mme. Paul Fort, but M. Paul Fort, the ' Prince des Poètes ' was not much in evidence, as he was in love with a girl of sixteen.

This caused some acrimonious comments and much discussion from *Grandmère*. Of this I knew nothing at first, but I soon learned. She had gone to some trouble in preparing meals for me, and one day in winter I took her a bouquet of flowers, an offering which she received with extreme coldness. I was crestfallen and a little puzzled until Severini enlightened me. It seems that the old lady had been a flower vendor before Verlaine cast an eye upon her, and with the suspicion of old age she believed my gesture to have been a reminder of her past. A most unfortunate business.

Picasso had abandoned Cubism, and was doing realistic work based on a form of Neo-Classicism of Ingres. He was even studying the more traditional methods of Gainsborough. Once Paul Rosenberg, the dealer, showed me a portrait done in the manner of the English master and asked me to guess who had painted it. Being versed in the discussions of Montparnasse, I knew all about the latest change in Picasso's methods and was able to name the right artist. Rosenberg was so impressed that he took me aside and showed me his entire collection: a very rare privilege, only at times extended to millionaires. For hours I was permitted to study Ingres, Delacroix, Daumier, early Corot, Cézanne, Gauguin, and Sisley. There were also strange collections of early Victorian jewellery, for which he had taken a craze. In those hours I received a more liberal art education than I had ever had in my life. To-day, French art dealers are often held up to scorn because of their business acumen, but I learned their almost superhuman knowledge of aesthetics which must be the foundation for those men.

Picasso was living in a flat above Rosenberg, but I never met him there. He was sent for by the concièrge on two occasions without result; but, as Rosenberg put it, he was being very difficult at the time. Probably he thought it was another fool of an Englishman, and I have since learned that he was very worried at the turn of his own artistic conscience. The tyranny of abstraction was fully upon him and he was seeking all avenues of escape, a process which many artists have suffered since.

Besides, Severini was none too popular at that moment with Picasso, who was envious of his bewildering manual dexterity. In a fit of exasperation with himself Picasso had told Severini how much he envied him his skill, and Severini, with his Italian arrogance, had rubbed it in. It is interesting to look back on that episode to-day. Severini never had the inventive genius of Picasso, and his manual dexterity has always interfered, in a sense, with his individual creative qualities. Although his work is obviously the work of Severini, it is nevertheless based upon the theories or discoveries of others. He was a sick man at that time, and compelled to rest for hours during the day, but with the optimism of the consumptive he had married the daughter of Paul Fort and produced a darling little girl called Gina.

My stay in Paris was curtailed, as I had once more become a cripple. Public locomotion was practically impossible, there were no taxis, and there was nothing left for me but to return to London. Once there, I began painting for my Peace exhibition, more convinced than ever that abstraction was a cul-de-sac from which there was no escape : a dangerous thought, as the advanced Bloomsburies in particular and critics in general had decided that abstraction was now the only recipe for good painting. Representational painting was airily dismissed as *vieux jeu,* or *trompe d'oeil,* the favourite catchword of the art circles.

The Imperial War Museum was organizing an exhibition at the Royal Academy of the works of the British War Artists. Ross had died and I had attended the funeral, where I met again with Ramsay MacDonald and Philip Snowden. I was unhappy about many things. In none of my war paintings had I attempted to glorify war on the one hand, or use its horrors as pacifist propaganda on the other; and although I have always been influenced by Goya, I attempted to keep the balance as a detached spectator and as an artist. Yet officialdom hated me, and already I had suffered all kinds of humiliation from those gentlemen who, even at that time, regarded war as a glorious adventure, vaguely confused with the rules of cricket and surrounded with a mock ambience of Lancelot and the days of chivalry. Because of my antagonism to this kind of stupidity, I was even regarded as defeatist, a thing I can honestly say I was not : though I regard peace and the maintenance of peace as something more noble and better for man's destiny than the waging of war. Strife may be a necessity for man, as some say ; but nevertheless I consider the struggle to tolerate a neighbour as something more heroic, and something more difficult of accomplishment, than his destruction. It is also better for both the defeated and the victorious. I could not glorify war, and immediately after the Armistice this attitude made me a pariah to the many who considered our sufferings to have been worth while.

This particularly applied to those in charge of the forth-coming exhibition of war pictures. I no longer had Ross to defend my case; Arnold Bennett had turned against me; Masterman had been submerged in the Ministry of Information; Beaverbrook and Konody were interested only in the Canadian War Memorials; and Orpen was in Paris. The result was that my works were thrown to the tender mercies of Muirhead Bone and Professor Tonks, who, as he wrote and told me, had always disliked my work almost as much as he disliked me. I did not begin to suspect the prejudice which existed against me until I went to Rottingdean, where my wife, as she was pregnant, had gone to stay. Here I found both William Nicholson and Ben Nicholson living practically next door to us, but they deliberately ignored our existence and passed us in the street. Ben had been a student with me at the Slade, and as far as I was aware the only possible reason for his rudeness was my success as a war painter.

However, I came up to London for varnishing day at Burlington House, and there I discovered that every trick known in hanging pictures had been tried on mine. With the exception of the ' Road from Arras to Bapaume,' which Tonks had professed to like, all my work was diffused and skied, and my big Passchendaele picture was hidden away in one of the smaller rooms. All the other artists' work had been more or less grouped and given a show. Then Muirhead Bone, of all people, came up to me and added insult to injury by saying he considered me a pot-boiler. I forget what I answered. Let us hope it was rude.

That was indeed a day of disillusionment. I had painted those pictures for practically no money: although I was no servant of the State I had put up with all kinds of insults from the officers at G.H.Q., from the Ministry of Information, and from the War Office, because I did not conform to their idea of public opinion, paint heroic pictures for the glorification of war, and present it as a splendid sentimental pageant. I had spent hours in the air, in the front-line trenches, even in front of the front-line trenches with the Lovat Scouts. I had undergone dangers unnecessary for a discharged man, often while I was in pain. And the sum total of it all was that I was informed by two self-ordained chargés d'affaires that I was lacking in artistic integrity.

Not unnaturally I was furious. I wrote to Tonks, Conway, and Yockney, and told them how deeply I resented their schoolmasterly treatment of an artist who had as much right to justice as any of the others, even though I had sold pictures and had publicity; especially as Muirhead Bone had written to me to say he wished the artists to work on an absolutely democratic basis. In a further attempt to keep me out of things Tonks had asked members of the Press not to mention my name. It showed how they combined prejudice with stupidity, for of course the Press sensed the trouble and pounced on me. I told them my side of the story and how strong my feelings were on the subject. Naturally they looked for my pictures, saw what had happened to them, and next morning my name and reproductions of my pictures were prominent in all the newspapers. The *Daily Mail* ran my Passchendaele painting right across the page. I have always wanted to thank that old woman Tonks for how his malice ended, though I discovered later in life that if there is one thing some artists resent more than the sale of another man's pictures, it is another artist's name in print, or the reproduction of his paintings in the Press which they affect so much to despise.

I refused to be drawn into the controversy and had the good sense to avoid everybody, even my own home, and lick my wounds in isolation. Muirhead Bone called that night at my studio to apologize; and when my wife inquired why they behaved in such a manner he informed her that it was because Tonks said I had such an aggressive face. A strange form of art criticism to make to a man's wife in his absence and under his roof, especially as I associated little with English artists at that time and did not inflict my ugly face upon their sensitive eyes. Never before had it been suggested that an artist must be good-looking in order to get his due, and if it comes to that . . . Tonks was no oil painting.

That finished me with the Imperial War Museum. I

have never since had anything to do with it, nor have I seen my pictures there, although I understand from friends that, with a change of management, I am now given a good show. For this I am grateful, but the very mention of war pictures revives such feelings in me that I prefer never to think of them. It was a curious position, for I had made my name with my war pictures, yet the meanness and pettiness of those in authority spoiled everything. However, time has in this as in other matters washed away much of the rancour, and I often sit on committees in complete harmony with my former detractors. We will let it go at that.

Then came my peace exhibition, and I am afraid this caused a hullabaloo. This is the preface I wrote for the catalogue:

> *I wish to be thoroughly disassociated from every ' new ' or ' advanced ' movement; every form of ' ist ', ' ism ', ' post ', ' neo ', ' academic ' or ' unacademic '. Also I refuse to use the same technical method to express such contradictory forms as a rock or a woman.*
>
> C. R. W. NEVINSON

I offended all sorts of people, and I admit that my pictures of ' Hampstead Heath ', ' Adam and Eve ', and the ' Inexperienced Witch ' reflected too strongly the spirit of the immediate post-War days. It was not much of a spirit to reflect. I did not see the storm that was gathering, because Matisse was holding his first exhibition of paintings in London in the next room to me at the Leicester Galleries. At first I was terrified that my efforts would look unusually futile in juxtaposition to his work, and I was more than delighted when he expressed his great admiration for one of my paintings of ' Clapham Common ', which had been bought by De Graffe. Matisse actually told the critics about it, a gesture of generosity possible only in a great artist.

I had, of course, met him previously at Gertrude Stein's in Paris, and when he was visiting teacher at the Circle Russe; he hardly remembered me, but we formed a real friendship while he was in London, and he often came round to my studio. I was more than ever struck by his calmness and detachment from all petty polemics which at that time were ruining the Parisian *avant garde*. That he had been terribly wounded in the past was obvious; and he told me how his wife used to hide the press cuttings from him, as the dirtiness of some of the art critics drove him to desperation. What would he have done if he had had to read the ignorant filth of English Art parasites?

He was somewhat overwhelmed by London and complained bitterly of its rush, but it was brought home to him that the sublime greatness of Turner could be understood only in this country of atmosphere. The mists of London seemed always to leave him marvelling; an interesting comment on some modern English painters who, in their efforts to copy the outlook of Cézanne, deliberately ignore atmosphere. Matisse kept on saying: 'How can they?' The light of the Midi and the clouds of England cannot be ignored and made similar by a sensitive artist.

One day he wanted to do a lithograph. I offered him all my chalks and stones, but he would have none of them. He got some lithographic paper, broke one of my lithographic chalks in half, and left himself with only about an inch and a quarter of grease to draw with. When I protested and pressed him to take a box, he assured me it was unnecessary and much too expensive a gift, a comment on the wonderful French economy and the appalling poverty he must have suffered in his early days.

There was something magnificent about Matisse, in his manner, in his intellectual outlook, and in his calm; something that makes him for me the finest of the great men I have met. He was delightfully human, and fond of his dinner, a thing I had noticed years before in Paris: the antithesis of all the nonsense that both his friends and his enemies had written about him. He pressed us to visit him at Issy, where he then had a house, and thought we might be interested in some of his more important decorations. The dear old man was positively self-conscious and apologetic because his exhibition showed only examples of his small work, and he was really delighted when I told him

I knew his decorations, such as 'Joie de Vivre'. I was very sorry to see Matisse go.

It was now I learned from an artist friend that Professor Tonks was getting up a secret petition to have my painting, 'La Mitrailleuse', removed from the Tate Gallery. To this day I have no reason to doubt my friend, who even told me he had refused to sign the petition. Whether they went on with it I know not, but I got my lawyer to write to the Curator, Charles Aitken, and he replied, obviously alarmed, that the matter had never come before his committee, though he had heard about it, but that in any case I must expect opposition. At this time the Tate Gallery was nicknamed the Slade Gallery, the Tête-à-tête, National Coterie of French Art and its Sladish Corridor, but that was small consolation to me. My success had offended too many people. Owing to Tonks, the New English and the Tate were against me; Roger Fry, who now dominated the London Group, was more than hostile; while Lewis was sending telegrams only occasionally signed. Yet I was still selling extraordinarily well and the public did not share the feeling shown to me in art circles. In fact, I held the record of having sold three one-man shows right out. That was a tangible consolation. But it was a nightmare of a time for me, and the vilest things were repeated to me as facts by comparatively well-meaning intelligentsia who had listened to the wave of tittle-tattle and gossip.

Through the introduction of Oliver Brown, of the Leicester Galleries, I met David Keppel, of New York, and when he saw some of my war etchings he offered me an exhibition of my prints in his gallery. Kathleen and I talked it over and we decided that I must go with them. It was an unfortunate moment for my wife, as not only were we still living in the unsuitable Robert Street studio, but in a short time we were expecting a child. The question of a new home was a difficult one at that time, as such enormous premiums were being asked for the few places available. It is necessary to remark how little the great and the wealthy care where an artist lives; and my studio, which was reached through a dingy passage of a tenement house reeking of cats and cabbage, was visited by such people as Lady Oxford, the Countess of Drogheda, Lady Grosvenor, Philip Snowden, Ramsay MacDonald, Sir Henry Wood, and a host of intellectuals. As Sickert said, they seemed rather to like it; and so did the inhabitants of Robert Street. Except for funerals, we provided the chief high-spots in their lives. The factory girls gaped at my visitors, children climbed over their cars, and sauced supercilious chauffeurs whose startled eyes and condescending behaviour made them splendid targets for Cockney jibes.

At last we discovered a flat in a new block of buildings; and leaving this in the hands of the decorators, my wife went to a nursing-home and I prepared for New York. Just before I left, Grant Richards organized a farewell dinner in my honour, upstairs in the Café Royal, with Sickert in the chair. It was a distinguished gathering. Sims wrote to say that he was too ill to come, but that I had a number of Academicians to wish me well. Among others, I remember Harold Monro, Ronald Firbank, Guevara, Laurence Housman, Garvin, C. E. Montague, and the keeper of the British Museum print room, Campbell Dodgson, who had described a lithograph of mine as one of the best of modern times. There were about a hundred people in all, including a number of American Pressmen.

Sickert made a very good speech, but mostly in Greek and therefore incomprehensible to the majority. I made a hopeless one, and I still go hot when I remember it. Garvin was fine; but unfortunately Ronald Firbank got schoolgirl giggles and had in the end to be silenced by Guevara, who jammed handkerchiefs down his throat. It was a strange send-off, but certainly an original dinner, and I still meet men who remember it vividly. The Pressmen present paid for their dinners, but curiously enough it got a remarkably good press, perhaps because the dinner was so good. But then Grant Richards and Chadwick Moore had seen to that, and bullied Mr. Judah into complete reverence.

12

Before I actually left these shores I heard an equivocal American comment on beauty. Chadwick Moore and I were crossing the Atlantic together, and the moment we left the train at Southampton he marched me straight to the purser and demanded that we be put at the captain's table. He then inquired whether there were any good-looking girls on board. The purser shook his head, and said there were only seven or eight women on the trip, mostly nurses, and they certainly were no beauties. ' Wall,' replied Chadwick Moore, ' they will be by the time we get to the other side.'

The *Mauretania* was then a troopship, and was taking back to America what seemed to be thousands of Canadian soldiers. There were only about thirty civilians aboard. For fear of trouble, not one drop of alcohol was shipped, and this caused a little bit of trouble to the gentleman in the next cabin to mine. The sudden change in his mode of life caused him to blow taxi whistles through most of the night in order that the women who were lying on his bunk should be sent home. Later the women changed to rats, animals which caused the wildest of yellings and his removal to sick bay.

As far as I could make out, none of the soldiers slept. All night and all day they played crap, making the ship echo to the yell of, ' Another little bet '. One hard-baked rancher banked three hundred pounds with the purser at the end of the second day. All he had when he came on board were a stolen Army blanket, a cigarette tin, and two dice; but he hired out these gambling accessories, took a sixpenny rake-off for every second win, and, needless to say, never gambled. They were the wildest set of men I ever met, and what they found to bet on and to fight over passes all understanding.

At the ship's concert I sang my inevitable ' Cowboy Joe ', and had the honour of being taken for an American professional singer by Al Woods, the musical comedy impresario of New York and Chicago.

At Halifax the troops disembarked, some of them to travel to Vancouver and then farther north. The poor English gentleman who was no drinker was landed on a stretcher, shaking horribly, to the wild cheering of the troops. It took longer to disembark than was anticipated and the *Mauretania* did a record run from Halifax to New York. Food and sleep were impossible, as the whole boat shook even worse than the " alcoholic."

Then came New York. It was a wonderful morning, with some of the skyline in mist and the higher towers jutting out of it in clear silhouette. Much as I love Venice, I was overjoyed by that glimpse of beauty New York gave me as we made our way up from Staten Island to the docks. My first day was a dismal one. Nobody met me and my club gave me the most cold welcome. I did not realize what the Arts Club was. Grammercy Park seemed more disheartening than Spittal Square. I walked and walked from Central Park to the Battery; came back by the Elevated, and suddenly felt I had seen all New York. A great city is a dreadful place to be alone in, and I felt unusually forlorn.

The one bright spot I had to look forward to that day was dinner in the evening with Chadwick Moore at the Ritz-Carlton. Naturally I dressed, and the excitement caused by my top-hat, white waistcoat, and tails had to be seen to be believed. Negroes bowed to the ground, bell-hops frantically pushed out their hands, and people stared at me in such open-eyed wonder that I was filled with embarrassment. It was only then I learned that America in those days wore the Tuxedo—dinner-jacket—and a straw hat. Not being aware that it was the custom to tip before and not after, with as much aplomb as I could muster I ordered a Manhattan in the lounge, and waited—and waited. Eventually I heard my name being paged, and I was taken to the 'phone to hear the agonized voice of Chadwick Moore explaining that he could not make it for another hour. By now I felt a complete fool.

It was most unpleasant to feel over-dressed in a place like the Ritz-Carlton, where the clientèle seemed aware it had all the money in the world and yet was not quite sure of itself. It was known, too, that many titled people were coming to New York, and the American idea then was that those of blue blood dressed differently from the common herd.

I did the only thing possible. I retired to that little oasis known in America as the Men's Rest Room, and I emerged only when Moore and his wife turned up. Mrs. Moore was beautifully gowned, and she did not seem to appreciate the overwhelming attention paid by everybody to my white waist-coat. Afterwards we drove round New York, and I saw it in the glory of its illuminations. To my amazement, I discovered in Washington Square that American officials were unaware the War was over. They were still recruiting, blowing bugles, and massed bands were playing the current American national anthem, ' Over There.' Later I discovered that the army clothing contractors were still making money, but I did not realize at that time the slowness of American officialdom and the quickness of commerce to take advantage of that lethargy.

The next day I went to Keppel's, to find the show already hung and the inevitable barrage of journalists. This was also my first meeting with a remarkable American gentleman named Mr. Grant, who, with Mrs. Grant, was connected with the British Bureau of Information under Louis Tracy. Those Grants were magnificent. They assured me not once, but a thousand times, that they just loved Britishers, and that they would do everything in their power to bring the grand ideals of England and the beautiful policy of the British Empire before the American public, which was liable to be prejudiced by the Hearst newspapers, which were taking a not too sympathetic line because Mr. Hearst had not been received at Court owing to ' some misunderstanding' that ' was, mind you, due to no fault of your great King ' !

They were in charge of all the lithographs I had done for the Stationery Office, and to my amazement they told me they had sold thousands and would shortly give me a statement. So far I have not received one, although time is getting on.

They were sure I would understand that this statement involved a great deal of checking up. I *was* sure of it. Then they said that owing to 'some misunderstanding' the Worcester Art Gallery had obtained many paintings by Orpen, John, and others, including myself, because some English colonel had signed away our pictures in the belief that they were propaganda films which could be duplicated, and not genuine, hand-painted oils which would take time to make replicas of.

On this information I acted immediately, and in spite of the 'misunderstanding' I succeeded in getting the original oils returned to England and myself into trouble with official America, who for some reason thought I was taking a high-horse attitude because I refused to let them get away with it. It was almost what is known as a thankless task, for although I saved a number of pictures, Orpen was the only artist to express his gratitude. Tracy wrote a long-winded letter to me explaining that the mistake was an easy one, as pictures in America meant films. My only comment can be that the English colonel learned the language with alacrity.

I was grateful to Mr. Grant for telling me about the pictures, and I was grateful to him because he was the first O. Henry character I had come across. I always enjoyed his company. Every morning he visited me at my club, where he made his legs comfortable on the radiator and began:

' Wall, Boy, who shall we do to-day, and what shall we do to-night ? Though I don't mind telling you this morning I need beer, as I'm kind o' rattled and I need steadying, and you would hardly believe it, but Mrs. Grant is a very remarkable woman who certainly can kid no horse-flies.'

Mr. Grant did much to brighten my visit, and if I had a spare half-hour he saw that it was filled.

David Keppel's was a dignified art gallery. He had no belief in the value of Press publicity, and he was probably right, for the pictures sold well to his clientèle, who rarely read the opinions of critics and never of American newspaper boys. I was asked everywhere and made a member of innumerable clubs: the Bankers, the Lawyers, the Players, the Salamangundy, and all the rest of them. There were dinners and lunches galore; speeches and lectures, up-town and down.

Curiously enough, I never saw any American women at those functions except at one Greek dealer's dinner. I was entirely taken up by the men, and he-men at that. They were courteous if talkative, and seemed to me to resemble the French because of their continual boasting of their dealings with the fair sex the night before. If they did not do that, they were excessively married men who protested their virtue too much, who spoke with adoration and veneration of their wives, and with undying affection of their offspring. It might have been confusing, but a French *cocotte* had told me never to trust an American who shows you photographs of his wife and family. But they all do it.

Joseph Pennell was extraordinarily kind to me. He was supposed to be a bitter, complaining old man, always fighting the wars of Whistler over again, but I never found him like that. He saw that I was given facilities for sketching in New York and Brooklyn, a generous thing for an artist to do, particularly as he himself was doing a series of etchings of New York and the Hudson from his home in Brooklyn Heights. He seemed to belong to another school and generation of artists, for his intellectual generosity was equalled only by his kindness of heart and a desire to give a helping hand. It must be remembered that I was English and he had a loathing of the English at this time, I could never discover why. Many American artists like Sargeant, Whistler, Mark Fisher, Epstein, and Pennell, who had the choice of Europe and America, seem to have preferred the culture of London to any other. I suppose it is because the English buy more pictures and talk less about it than any other nation. In passing, it should not be forgotten that without Pennell Whistler would never have become so established in England.

It was through Pennell I discovered a queer trait in the rich New Yorker. I was anxious to visit the night life of Broadway and see the great roof gardens which were popular in those days. Years before I had seen paintings of them at the Franco-British Exhibition at the White City and I had often wondered what they were actually like. Not wishing to spend my money in the wrong place, I consulted one of my salesmen. He was sympathetic, but he said he knew nothing at all about that side of New York. After work he just went straight home to his wife. Then I asked a down-town American lawyer. He also was sympathetic, but he told me he kind of reckoned that 'the Great White Way, as we Americans call it', was run for out-of-town people, and that though he often went up it in his car to join his wife after a busy day down-town, he knew nix about it.

It was looking pretty hopeless when Pennell introduced me to an Englishman, a man-about-town who could discuss nothing but tailors, although he could help me in this. Correctly dressed in a Tuxedo this time, off I went with him about midnight to see some roof gardens. It was most interesting and particularly so when I saw my salesman dancing happily about. I had the satisfaction of realizing I had not corrupted him by my tentative inquiry, or put wicked ideas into his head, because 'the girls' were calling him Charlie, and you are neither called Charlie on first acquaintance nor for nothing in New York. Fearing to embarrass him on what was obviously his native heath, I explained matters to my mentor, who promptly took me to another and more exclusive place.

Here everything was even more beautiful than in the previous one, and in the first half-minute I saw my down-town lawyer. Although I was growing accustomed to American caution and New York bull, I felt angry, and I went straight up to him and said I would tell his wife. Instead of indignation, a look of profound admiration penetrated his horn-rimmed spectacles, and he insisted on our joining him in a bottle and meeting some of the girls, and on expressing in loud tones his 'tre-men-dous' admiration for my exhibition. He then inquired the prices, and, on being told, assured me they were much too low and that he would go to the galleries the following day and buy a whole lot. We had an evening, and when we were leaving I thanked him and mentioned that of course I would say nothing to his wife. He was overcome by emotion and made an oration about the Britishers being the finest, whitest set of men that yet populated the earth. It seemed that I was just dandy, too. But the next day came, and the next, and no lawyer arrived at the galleries to buy 'a whole lot'. What a pity I destroyed the fence I had put around him, but for a limey to put it around a down-town lawyer is indeed a feat.

The whole time I was in New York I worked hard day and night, drawing the city, which in a moment of enthusiasm I had described to a Pressman as 'having been built for me'. Americans have no sense of humour, and as I was later to find out, they took this Shavian joke in dead earnest. I was glad to meet Lewis Hind, the English art critic who had done so much for me in London. He had made a startling recovery from cancer of the bowel and was living over the Anderson Galleries and doing a certain amount for the Bureau of Information in the British cause and preaching Christian Science. I saw a lot of Brodzky, too, a friend of Gaudier-Brzeska. He was living in Greenwich village and the Bronx, and he took me among the art circles and the vague flotsam and jetsam of the intelligentsia round Washington Square. It was a strange set, working all day at some job such as truck-driving, waiting, or free-lancing, and devoting the nights to the arts or drinking. One day Brodzky spoke to me seriously. 'You've made good here,' he said, 'and they seem to like you. Beat it and get away with it, and don't come back. I know these New Yorkers.' As I had been approached by Léon Bourgeois, a dealer, to return in about two years' time, I was in a bit of a quandary, so I consulted Lewis Hind. He asked the profession of Brodzky, and then that of Bourgeois, and he said, 'You do as the dealer wants you. Surely you never take an artist's advice on a matter like this?' So I fixed up with the dealer, but in my bones I somehow felt that Brodzky was the more sensitive and shrewder man. And wasn't he, as later on I shall tell.

The most amazing art connoisseur I met in New York was Eugene Gallatin, a man who is an authority on the works of the Yellow Book and Aubrey Beardsley in particular. He was then absorbed in Picasso. His brother had a palace in Fifth Avenue filled with decorations by Delacroix. His collection was one of the finest I have seen, and there I had my first opportunity of seeing what a great painter George Bellows was, although I still prefer his etchings and lithographs. I was introduced to him and I had the privilege of going about with this fine, open-minded, cultured American. He was completely uncontaminated by the cheap intellectual clap-trap and art talk of Paris and London, and he was especially welcome to me at that moment, when I had left Europe devouring itself with art recipes, art restrictions, art superiorities, and art clichés.

Another intellectual experience was in meeting Miss Bliss and seeing her collection of the French Impressionists, of Cézanne, and of the drawings of Davis, to whom she was a great patron. She had bought some of my work and I felt very honoured to be in such company. I came to know her well and she told me how as a young girl, the daughter of a banker, she had gone to Paris to be finished. Instead of doing this she had, in fact, started. She discovered an enthusiasm for Impressionist paintings, completely unsuspected when she left America, and from that time onward she devoted herself to art. She seemed to have lived among, if not actually shared, the hardships of these painters during their unpopular days, and she loved to talk about that time. It was a strange link for me to meet a woman who knew so well Monet, Sisley, Marie Cassatt, and Renoir. Cézanne she did not seem to have met, but I think she was the first to buy his work.

What a bewildering city New York can be. Never had I come across so few intellectual people, yet that tiny minority was more first-rate than any circle I have discovered in Europe. At the Metropolitan Museum I saw an exhibition of Courbet, which was entirely American-owned and was the finest one-man show I have seen. I saw also the Toledo landscape of Greco, which was owned by a woman, a contemporary of Miss Bliss. Then I called on Quin, the great American lawyer, who years and years before had bought some of my work at the Chenil Gallery. He showed me a collection of Picasso, Matisse, Derain, Kandinsky, Augustus John, Jack Yeats, Mark Gertler, such as I have never seen elsewhere under one roof. His Rodins, Epsteins, and Maillols, were away in his country place at Long Island; and in Washington he had a house full of early Corots, Daumiers, Rowlandsons,

Constables, Jongkinds, and Sisleys. A marvellous collection. Yet when Quin died, the Metropolitan Museum lost the collection, which was dispersed in the most stupid manner owing to mismanagement and lack of commercial acumen, or else too much of it: it is difficult to define which when auctions take place. I always suspect wickedness rather than stupidity.

I had now been in New York a month; probably the most extraordinary month ever lived by an artist. I had given dozens of interviews, made goodness knows how many speeches, met hundreds of people, done innumerable sketches, and attended countless lunches, dinners, and suppers. I had seen New York from every point of view open to me, I had made friends, and I had hardly slept. When at length I collapsed on to the Halifax train at the Grand Central, who should dash up the platform but the one and only Mr. Grant. He had come, he said, not only to wish me good-bye and God-speed, but to present me with a large wad of notes and greenbacks as something on account for my lithographs and provided that I would mention his name to Lord Beaverbrook for his great services rendered to Britain and the Empire upon which the sun never sets. I shook him warmly by the hand —it was 102 in the shade—and I assured him I would remember. And I did, too. But Beaverbrook only grinned and said, ' Where's the money ? '—' In *my* Bank,' I replied.

We had two days and a night of unspeakable travel in a typical noisy and slow American train before joining the *Aquitania*, which had been delayed while disembarking more Canadian troops and had not troubled to come on to New York. Owing to my passport, on which I was still described as the King's guest, I was given a millionaire's suite for the minimum first-class fare, and this put me in direct touch with all the swells on board: a mélange of financiers, bankers, Congressmen, and Pressmen of the first order, who for reasons best known to themselves were going to the Peace Conference or to lend Germany money. There were strange English peers and various officials homeward bound after all kinds of war duties in the U.S.A. Pond, the lecture agent with whom I had been in touch at the beginning of the War, was also on board and he was always asking me which British writers might be least offensive and condescending to American audiences. He was a hard-baked young fellow, who, I fear, did not take the English literary people with the same seriousness with which they regarded themselves. After travelling hundreds of thousands of miles as a lecture impresario, with all kinds and shapes of distinguished foreigners, he once asked a club-woman why she ever attended lectures. She answered that she kind of didn't know, but she reckoned she must do something. This was almost similar to a speech of Salvator Dalli, the Surrealist, who lately said there was only one fool greater than the lecturer and that was the listener.

The voyage back was lovely and so calm. At one auction on the day's run a hard-faced gentleman acted as auctioneer, and a wonderful auctioneer he was. The majority of those on board were extremely purse-proud and the tickets went for enormous sums. Then it came to his own ticket, which had no chance of winning as the weather could not interfere with the average run. He started to bid that up, every one calling extravagant figures in the certain knowledge that it was the established custom for the auctioneer to buy the ticket back or outbid all the other people. When this fellow got his figure high enough, however, he left some poor profiteer with it and seemed more than satisfied. I turned to Pond and remarked, 'That was very financial.' At which a double-breasted woman, smothered in diamonds, pouted at me and retorted: 'Financial! I should say he is financial! He's one of the biggest manipulators of the Chicago wheat pit, and that's a thing you'd better remember, young man. Etiquette is just nothing to him.' This remark caused a good deal of tittering, and was one of those unfortunate little things that sometimes spoil a pleasant journey. Up till now the voyage had been so quiet that somebody simply had to start a row. Definite cliques were formed and mixing came to an end. It was all most amusing and of course I didn't care, as I knew I should see nobody again.

Just as we were reaching Southampton Water, an American woman journalist, very intense, very young, and with the full burden of the Versailles Conference already heavy upon her, asked me to explain exactly the value of titles. She just could not get it, as she had always reckoned that every one came out in much the same way. In order to avoid obstetrics and blue blood, I pointed out that to have a title was to have the greatest advantage in the world, especially in a war which had been fought for democracy. It was useful, for instance, in travelling. Ignoring my flippancy, she exclaimed, ' Is that really so ? How, may I ask ? ' As any man would to a serious American lady, I enlarged on the theme and informed her that titles never paid fares, never had their passports examined, and were able to take large quantities of opium through the Customs unchallenged. I assured her that after one of them had made a philanthropic speech as the chairman of the ship's concert, he would usually be met by a pinnace which would take him ashore first in order that he might avoid the Customs and the common herd. By this time the earnest young woman was looking at me fixedly and burning with indignation. Her eyes glinted when she said, ' Is that so ? Gee ! '

It was only then I noticed a girl laughing near by. She was sitting next to a man I presumed to be her father, a walrus-moustached old gentleman who had spoken to nobody during the voyage. As I looked, he became galvanized, and with the popping blue eyes of old King Edward he exclaimed, ' Not too much opium,' and lapsed into silence. We looked him up in the passenger list. He was Lord de Somebody; he did take the chair at the concert, and later he went ashore in the pinnace. I was terrified to think of the articles that were syndicated throughout America by that intense young woman journalist.

But after the nonsense I was told in New York and expected to believe, I made myself President of giving wrong information to distinguished foreigners.

On my arrival in London I was met by my Mother, who told me that my son was dead.

13

When I was told my son was dead, though it may be thought unnatural of me, even now I am glad I have not been responsible for bringing any human life into this world. Possibly because of the power of regimentation and propaganda, and the War, I have a fundamental dread, and even a terror, of life, with its sufferings and disappointments. That may sound neurasthenic, but I still feel a relief that I have not brought into existence any being with my blood, my morbid temperament, and cursed as I am with apprehension of torments and degradations yet to come. I am not a gambler and I cannot believe in good luck. Yet, paradoxically, unlike most gamblers, whose mental outlook convinces them they are likely to have one chance in a million, I believe that the nature of man is seldom as loathsome as it appears.

Though actually a true-blue in politics I am yet a believer in communism, though I know that humanity as a whole has not yet developed that trait which will make it work for the common weal, without thought of gain or personal advancement. I have known this trait to exist in our Tory lords in particular and in criminals, capitalists, socialists, and soldiers; perhaps even politicians. The fundamental love of strife and competition is often strongest in those with altruistic intentions. Put simply, this lurking emotion, at present almost entirely undeveloped, makes us superior to the animals. Platitudinous, maybe, but true. My objection to Western religion is because of its promises of advantage in the next world rather than in this. I would like to see a good deed regarded as a gratification, as a self-indulgent release of emotion, and not as an arduous task to be achieved with self-complacency. The only catch in the theory is that whenever I have done a good deed I have lived to regret it.

When I returned my wife was still very ill. We managed to move into our new flat and then went to stay in the country with the Grant Richards. Here Kathleen recuperated. Poor Madeleine Grant Richards was terribly upset about this time and used to hide while she lamented the fate of her country Hungary, which, because it was the weakest of the defeated nations, was being given away in large hunks by the ' Idealist' politicians in Paris. Her sorrow did not prevent her from having a houseful of invalids, however, including the Baxes, who were all being restored to health on goats' milk. There were herds of these on the common outside, as Madeleine was too tender-hearted to have any of them killed, although meat was scarce and Grant was very partial to kid. He told me it went very well with a full Burgundy, but in the circumstances I was not permitted to taste it.

In the past I had learned much from Grant Richards, but during this stay at his house I began gradually to organize my taste for exquisite living in food and drink, good conversation, and a real appreciation of the best in the works of art. He was convinced that a bad picture could spoil your eye, much as a cocktail could ruin your palate for wine, and from him I learned the phrase: ' It was a picture you could not afford to look at.' Sunday evenings were always the occasions for great hilarity, as Grant had to compose that wonderful work of art, his advertisement for *The Times Literary Supplement*. He always put it off till the last moment, then worked it out in a babel of argument that covered the iniquity of the Peace Conference, the bad luck of pearls, the systems of Monte Carlo, the advantages of a Catholic education, O'Rosen's latest suit, the futility of English parsons, the unscrupulousness of America, and the nuisance of pets, with which the house swarmed.

My time was spent in etching and I did practically no painting at all. I know of no job more engrossing and, to be frank, I think that is its danger. I certainly remember little about my work of this time. The Leicester Galleries gave an exhibition of my etchings, and fortunately I did extremely well with them and made a contract with Lefèvre to distribute copies throughout England, America, and the Dominions. Though the dealers took 66⅔% in commission I did very well, and for a while I was financially free of having to give a one-man show. Still the intelligentsia were showing me every form of hostility and contempt, and when I returned to London I found social life impossible. Everywhere I went I was wounded or driven to fury through some cheap insult from a superior Bloomsbury or an artistic Bohemian. I began to associate only with people who had never heard of art and certainly never heard of me.

As soon as my wife was well enough, we returned to Paris. We put up once more at Severini's studio, and every day he announced ' Pas de charbon ', and promptly stacked his stove with an Italian gesture of despair and the explanation that it was better to be warm once than tepid all the time. Paris had now recovered her cosmopolitan appearance, but the French were not doing sufficiently well to be rude. It was really our honeymoon, and my wife was able to see Montmartre for the first time under a sprinkling of snow.

Place du Tertre was still a working quarter with only one café, Le Lapin, where grand meals were served on wooden tables, with pitchers of rough red wine from the wood, and with everything reeking of charcoal, fustian, and petrol. We called on a great many friends, and were chased by apaches down the cobbled streets behind the Sacré Coeur when we had with us a girl in such high heels that she could hardly walk, much less run.

We attended an At Home of Léonce Rosenberg, where we were overwhelmed by the undecorative quality of the Cubist paintings, especially when hung together in serried rows. Marie Laurencin was talking, as usual, Apollinaire was sulking, and Léonce was bowing. Metzinger was in a great state of excitement about nothing, Severini was clowning elegantly, and his wife was pouting and saying that with such a method it was impossible to paint a portrait that was a likeness. All then tried to explain that a likeness could be obtained only by reference to the particular and not by the statement in general. In fact, the usual Paris scene, where sheer banality is talked on one side, and answered with exquisite brilliance on the other. It was a reflection of the most highly civilized race in the world, the only people who understand the meaning of the word *Luxe*, yet invariably put up with sanitary arrangements which would disgrace a peasant. It was also an example of that strange mixture to be found in all Parisian professional artistic circles, which are able to combine at one and the same time the most exquisite or the most revolutionary intellectual ideas with the most *bourgeois* mode of living, commercialism, and security. But as Picasso once said, when asked why he was not a Bolshevik: 'Surely you cannot expect me to be revolutionary in everything. I am a *rentier*.'

We must have visited more art galleries on this occasion than the average art critic hears of in a lifetime. At night we were usually in Montmartre or the Circus, although once we horrified the Severini *ménage* by telling them we had spent the evening with Kisling at La Rotonde, a haunt, as Severini explained to us, of Bolsheviks, spies, and drunken Americans. It was not fit for any one's wife to visit. It was not *convenable*. Kisling was wearing a cap and work-man's clothes and refusing to ride in taxis because they were symbols of the *bourgeois*. Later, he began to make money, and sometimes he was forced to take taxis, so he drove with the chauffeurs outside. Not so long after, we found him inside; and presently he was driving his own car. In the end he employed a chauffeur. The last time I saw him was in the American bar of La Coupole, he was wearing the Legion of Honour. When I chaffed him about this and reminded him of his first compromise when he rode with the taxi-driver, he explained everything with the gravity always used by a Polish Parisian when he speaks of himself. He said he was no longer young, then decided to make the Biblical excuse, but now—the women insisted on it. Poor Kisling. Always the Lothario. When he saw I refused to be taken in by his Parisian, mock-Biblical excuse, and told him that fifteen years before he would never have been offered the honour, I thought he would never stop laughing.

We were rather swells in Montparnasse when it became known that I had bought a Modigliani, a Zadkin, and a Kisling. I had been inquiring about a picture by Vlaminck, when Zadkin burst in on us to say that the artist had been taken up by Bernheim. I immediately dashed round to the dealer to settle my purchase, but it was too late. Overnight his pictures were trebled in price. The art world in Paris was becoming something like the Stock Exchange. Before we left London we had inquired the price of an Archipenko statuette. Imagine our amazement when, on a *terrasse* in Paris, complete strangers would address us and offer us an Archipenko for a quarter of the price we were asked in London.

I began to get an inkling of the boom that was going to be worked in contemporary French paintings. One Modigliani I had bought for five pounds. I offered it to the Leicester Galleries for sixty pounds and the offer was refused. I took it to France with me and showed it to a dealer who had a little notice outside, ' *On achète Modigliani.*' He declared it was not quite the type he wanted; it was not sufficiently ' *dur* ', but he would like to study it, and if I could leave it for a while he would be grateful. As it was approaching the lunch hour I agreed, but I was a little bewildered by his desire. It was while I was eating that I suddenly realized what he was doing. Between twelve-noon and two is the fateful time when most business is done in Paris. The dealer was undoubtedly ringing up all his confrères and fixing a price which none of them would go beyond, and they would all share the profits afterwards.

I kicked myself. When I went round at two-thirty the dealer was most pleasant. He thanked me for letting him examine the picture and assured me it was a veritable Modigliani and a very fine one, but it was not the particular epoch he wanted. I behaved like the silly Englishman, and he advised me to go round to some of his confrères, mentioning all he had telephoned. So stupid and grateful did I appear that he further advised me not to go to Paul Guillaume.

He had nothing against him, of course, but he knew he would not be interested and it would be a waste of my time to go. He assured me he was only thinking of my convenience. I thanked him and hastened away.

Naturally I went straight to Guillaume, realizing that he had been out when the dealer had telephoned. I offered him the picture, and he immediately gave me one hundred and twenty pounds in cash for it, much more than I would have got out of the *téléphonique* ring. Later I heard that the picture was bought by an English dealer for one thousand pounds, which probably means that it was sold to a collector for fifteen hundred or two thousand pounds. Dealers are seldom content with less than one hundred per cent profit. With capital appreciation of that sort it is no wonder that modern art in Paris developed into a Bourse, if not a racket. The prices were all too high. German Fascism and the American depression have got the price of French modern pictures back to normal levels again.

On our return to London we were invited to represent English art on a Mission which was going to Czecho-Slovakia. We agreed to go. The Mission consisted of H. G. Wells, Lord Dunsany, Robert Nichols, Ward Muir, Philip Page, Sir Henry Wood, Clifford Sharp, Ward Price, some disagreeable French newspapermen, some star American journalists like Webb Miller and Arthur Mann, and a host of ignorant ones, both British and American. There was a musical contingent, chiefly composed of agents and critics, and P. G. Konody, Hungarian by birth and full of contempt for the Czechs. From start to finish it was a strange affair.

We travelled down by special train from Ostend to Cologne, from Cologne to Nuremberg, and then we crawled slowly through Bavaria, stopping at every station for an hour or so, until we reached Eiger, the frontier town of Czecho-Slovakia. Here the train was met by peasants who cheered us heartily, a pleasing sensation which did us all good. H. G. Wells was to be extremely popular, and at every station delegations would shout loudly for him and yell ' Nazdas '. We reached Prague earlier than was anticipated by some of the passengers.

Dunsany had not even dressed when we were all turned out on to the platform, where we were received with musical honours by massed military bands. Somebody then delivered an address and we were presented with bouquets.

My wife, Bob Nichols, and I, none of us feeling or looking our best, were hustled into the British Embassy car with Sir George Clark, the British Ambassador at Prague. Frantic crowds, in national costume and carrying flowers, lined the roads from the railway station to the hotel and waved and cheered us all the way. Never did I feel so inadequate. Then came a round of delirious festivities and banquets, and visits to the Stadium to see the Sokol. Night and day, thousands of Czechs and Slovaks kept marching into Prague to attend the carnival. Whole villages came; each village had a band; and every villager sang. Such a medley of music, song, and cheering; it is difficult now to believe I was ever there. The whole city was delirious with national pride, and the British and American Missions were their most honoured guests.

We heard nothing but speeches and music, and although the population was obviously hard-pressed for food we were given banquets of gargantuan dimensions. Unfortunately, some of the journalists fared too well and this lowered our prestige somewhat. But then the Lord Mayor of London arrived, with his mace-bearer and aldermen, and their presence helped. One evening we attended a dinner at the British Embassy, an old palace, to meet President Masaryk. Wells, Mrs. Vandervelde, the wife of the Belgian Minister, my wife, and myself went by car. The rest of our party were coming by char-à-banc, but their driver was drunk and drove the British Mission furiously round and round the town before they discovered what he was doing. They eventually arrived somewhat late, and we had to hurry over our dinner, as the President was by that time expected at any minute. Things were progressing nicely when the Lord Mayor of London was seized with the gift of tongues, and to everybody's embarrassment made a speech. When he came to his final word and was sitting down, Sir George Clark rose, so that they passed each other in mid-air. He replied with extreme

146

brevity while we all got ready to run.   In sixty seconds we were all dashing upstairs, and we were just in time.

After this affair we seemed invariably to be children of misfortune.   One poor Czech hostess awaited the Mission for hours, mortally offended.   The fault was not ours but that of our programme master, an American publicity man, who had confused his dates.   That made us feel uncomfortable; but I wonder what were the Lord Mayor's feelings when, at a gala performance of a Dunsany play at the Opera, he mistook H. G. Wells for the Mayor of Rome and congratulated him on his English.   On another occasion one of the journalists became involved in a drunken brawl.   He was of the American party, but the authorities discovered that he was a German by birth, and we all felt a little unhappy about *that*.

Then a maid in the hotel went down with smallpox, and we were all vaccinated and put in quarantine.   This meant that with the exception of an occasional trip in a special bus which took us for rides in the country, we had to stay in the hotel.   Soon Ward Price went down with chicken-pox, and of course everybody thought at first it was smallpox.   Then a South American journalist collapsed across my wife's knee and was instantly suspected of smallpox, too.   We spent a miserable twelve hours wondering whether we should catch it, as we had been next to him all day.   Nobody but the maid caught the disease, and at last our quarantine was up.

We hastened from Prague: a very ignominious departure. There were no gay Hosannahs for us when we reached the railway station, but on the platform we saw stretcher cases of typhus.   We boarded the train with a thankfulness that we had escaped.   My only regret was that I had not broken my quarantine, as Konody and Sharp had done, and gone to Vienna with them.   When we arrived at Strasbourg the German-American journalist was forbidden to travel through France, American though he was, and he was left to smell his way home through Germany.   We broke our journey at Paris, and the rest went on, feeling horribly ill through vaccination.   The return was certainly an anti-climax after the welcome at Prague; but this was one of the first, if not actually the first, of the propaganda missions for showing other nationalities the achievements of a new government. The mere fact that Russia has copied the policy is a proof that we were not as ineffectual as we felt.

14

Back in London, I settled down to paint for my second New York exhibition, and I scarcely went out until my paintings of the city were completed and ready for shipping, a thing that had to be done well ahead of our sailing date. This time Kathleen was coming with me, though she was very much against it.

Shortly before sailing I was the victim of a hoaxer who did me a lot of harm in America. One morning I was rung up by an American journalist representing a vast Press syndicate. He told me he had heard I was crossing the Atlantic again and he would be much obliged if I would let him come up for an interview so that he could send something across in time for my arrival. He wanted to know what sort of pictures I was going to exhibit, what I thought about America. I knew the value of keeping the Press on one's side. But I was very busy, and I suggested it would be better if he came along to the Café Royal that night and had a drink with me. He was glad to do so.

Unfortunately I was late, and a man we will call Mr. A. was early. He was a frequenter of the Café Royal who hung about for some one to stand him a drink, and therefore the friend of many artists and a greater number of scallywags; and when this American journalist, who was new to London, came in and looked about, Mr. A., from long practice, saw to it that he caught his eye.

'D'you know which is Mr. Nevinson?' asked the journalist.

Mr. A. pricked up his ears.

'I'm Nevinson,' he said. 'What do you want?'

'Well, I want some dope about that trip of yours to the States.'

Mr. A. invited him to sit down and the American invited him to have a drink. He got his story all right. It was, indeed, such a story that Mr. A. got a free dinner for it, and he left nothing to the journalist's imagination.

When I came in late they were eating. I looked round, hoping I had not missed my man, but he seemed to have gone. The American spotted me and asked: 'Who's that guy standing over there?'

'Have nothing to do with that man,' replied Mr. A., pointing at me. 'He's nothing but a Scandinavian scrounger who calls himself a poet.'

Long afterwards I heard all about it.

But in the meantime I sailed for America, to discover on arrival that Mr. A.'s story had preceded me, black-guarding American artists and saying a lot of most uncompli-mentary things about America. Montgomery Flagg, the Irish-American illustrator, wrote to the *New York Times* attacking foreigners, and especially condescending English artists who came to exhibit pictures in the country they openly despised. Of course, I knew nothing of the inter-view and was not quite clear what it was all about. But it put everything wrong and caused a Chauvinist movement among American artists, who also complained that Americans did nothing for American art.

While this row was going on, all my paintings were held up in bond, and my brokers insisted that I should have to pay a great many dollars' taxation. I knew this to be wrong, as Quin had altered the law, and original works of art were allowed into the country free of tax. Income tax alone was charged on sales. However, they would not budge. It was a serious state of affairs for me, as I was missing the season and my wife and I were living in New York with the pound worth thirteen shillings and the cost of living phenomenally high. Then I remembered Lamont, who was chairman of Morgan's, was a friend. We called, Mrs. Lamont, and explained our quandary. She immediately rang up Morgan's, who got on to my brokers and the Customs people, and at once the assessor saw us. He said *of course* there was no taxation on my paintings, as though I was to blame. All I need do was to sign an affidavit swearing that they were original works of art painted by me, and they would be released at once. I duly signed, took over the pictures, and then discovered that the clerk responsible for trying to hold us up for 'imaginary' taxation had been 'given the air', as he had taken me for an English sucker and was going to put the money in his own pocket.

We then hung the show at the Bourgeois Galleries in Fifth Avenue, and the private view cards were duly addressed. But instead of posting them ourselves we gave them to the coloured elevator boy to stamp. He stole the money and posted the letters down a drain. My dealer, who was handling the Press, stamped and posted his own letters, which got through. The journalists came, but they came to an absolutely empty Private View. This, after the interview and the delay, was the third disaster, but there was a fourth one. I had painted New York. This was the worst crime of all. That a foreigner should do this first and do it well, was something the Press decided they just could not stand. George Bellows had done a few sketches of the Bowery and Coney Island, mostly figure work; Pennell had done some etchings of the Hudson River; but no one had tackled the beauty of this modern city. All American painters had gone to 'Parus' for their inspiration, and even their landscape painters, such as Winslow Homer, had painted American scenery in the European tradition. My work caused an outcry.

I then had an example of American generosity. All manner of people who had been kind to me on my previous visit, when I was a success, now calmly cancelled their engagements, and I was treated as though I had some form of infectious disease. However, as is usual, some Americans stood by me, and one lawyer actually lent us his studio to live in. It was his love nest, but he had quarrelled with his girl, and that made it possible for us to continue our stay in New York. Even then we met the American hold-up. The lawyer explained that he was terribly busy and we would have to find our own bedding and cooking utensils, and, though a millionaire, he told us the cheapest place in Seventh Avenue to buy them. He also explained that the electric light might not be working, as he had probably forgotten to pay the bill, and would we mind arranging that ? We moved straight in; and in this penthouse on top of a twenty-story modern building, we lived with candles stuck in bottles waiting for the electric light to be turned on. Edison Light Company assured me that the account had been settled, but that made no difference. There was no light. At last, and how slow are American methods, I persuaded them to come and see to it, and it was then discovered that the janitor had deliberately pulled out the fuses in order to get a tip for putting them in again: such a common American method of raising the wind that by a recent law the janitor was liable to imprisonment. The janitor was polite to us afterwards, but we were always afraid of him, as he looked so vengeful.

In the end I was fortunate in selling a few pictures when buyers began to come to the show. Miss Bliss was very kind to us and lent us her box for the opera in the diamond horseshoe, next door to the Vanderbilts. I was younger then, but how shocked I was at the noisy, drunken behaviour of this exclusive New York society, even when Martinelli was singing.

Then came the first slump and that withered all hopes. It was by no means like the real depression that caught America in the heyday of hire-purchase some years later, but it was bad enough. It happened practically overnight. A millionaire who owned a portion of Fifth Avenue, and never speculated, took me out to lunch at the Union Club; and, as George Robey used to sing, ' What there was, was good.' We ate bread and cheese because this millionaire reckoned things were very bad on Wall Street and he thought it best we should all live frugally. We packed up and returned home second-class, with Italian emigrants, wounded, disappointed, and insulted.

It is significant that since then, though it has taken me ten years to do it, I have sold every one of my paintings of New York, and to such buyers as Sinclair Lewis, H. G. Wells, C. B. Cochran, Lady Latham, the Birmingham Art Gallery, Mr. Williamson Noble, a private collector in Pittsburg, and another in Philadelphia. Moreover, the German film director Stromberg, who made ' Metropolis ', has said that he owed something to my paintings. Since then dozens of painters have copied my technique in the rendering of modern buildings, American dancing, and negroid singers.

Brodzky had been right when he told me to clear out and never go back to America. I only wish I had taken his advice.

We returned to London, to discover that in our absence a studio above our flat, for which I had paid a large premium, had been turned into a night club. Sleep was impossible at any time, as the drums beat on every hour until the morning and dancing lessons were given during the day. The landlord said he would do what he could because of the quiet tenancy clause in my lease. It was impossible to find another place. With three other tenants of the block of flats, I complained to the borough council. They thanked us profusely, but did nothing; and, whether by a coincidence or not, they increased our assessment for rates.

One night Clifford Sharp, the editor of the *New Statesman*, had been dining with the Asquiths, and on his way home, as it was quite early, he thought he would drop in to see us. The police, vindictive at our complaints, saw him ringing our bell and immediately arrested him. Before the magistrate next morning he was charged with disorderly conduct and naturally he pleaded not guilty. The magistrate, of course, was deaf, and thought he pleaded guilty, so fined him five pounds. Fuming with indignation, Sharp went to see Asquith, who only told him he was very lucky in having an ordinary name, as the newspapers did not realize who he was and he had got out of a nasty form of publicity very cheaply. Further, he said perhaps it was a good thing the magistrate *was* deaf. I believe Sharp then went to see the Commissioner of Police about it, but what happened I do not know.

I went to see my own lawyer, who told me there was nothing to be done but cut my losses, find another studio, and clear out. I was fortunate in finding the lovely place where I now live, far away from the West-end and the ' gay life '. I got it cheaply, too, as the coal strikes and the railway strikes and the American slump were depressing everything, including property. My offer was accepted, although our relations thought we were mad to take what appeared to be a ruin. However, I saw it needed little but a general clean up, and we moved in. Imagine my despair when, after a week or two, a studio across the garden started a sort of drinking, dancing club. It seemed too awful to be true. But it went broke after a short time, as it was too far off from the centre of things. At present I am surrounded by professionals and R.A.s.

My health started playing me up again and my nerves were all awry. I was overwhelmed by a feeling of futility that dried up my creative urge. The black pessimism to which I am always liable engulfed me now. No longer did I associate with any artists, and I avoided every sort and kind of intellectual contact. The only oasis I had was in the friendliness and generosity of Oswald Greene, brother of the present Master of the Rolls, who used to drive us every week-end to his houseboat at Hampton Court, or take us down to the sea to swim. He was a queer character. Trained as a Jesuit, he had drifted into publicity, and was working for the firm of Benson's, of which he was a moving spirit. He was immensely wealthy, but an Oxford man with a genuine love for literature, sculpture, and painting, arts which he considered too fine for the public even to see. This attitude I never resented in him, although I detested it in Roger Fry. Greene was a private person, while Fry was an art critic and always writing and making money out of the public through art, and therefore not entitled to despise it.

Besides this, I felt that all the Bloomsburies, now dominant in the London Group, were too cliquey, too pretentious, for me to meet. Their love of affectation for its own sake was too vulgar and indiscriminate for a professional artist. The amateurishness and attitudinizing were more than I could stand, and it was for this reason eventually that I resigned from the London Group. Wyndham Lewis was, of course, still 'carrying on', but that counted for very little, as he was quarrelling with his best friends such as Ezra Pound and Wadsworth.

In my new studio I had difficulty in starting work again, quite apart from the despair and the intellectual battle that was going on within me, though I was to have an exhibition at the Leicester Galleries during the autumn, for which I wrote the following preface to the catalogue:

> *Again I wish thoroughly to dissassociate myself from all the modern movements, ' neo ', ' post ', ' ism ', or ' ist '.*
>
> *I have particular antipathy towards* DADAISM—*The gregarious striving for peculiarity and ' nouveauté ', which has ended in utter monotony and the loss of individuality.*
>
> GAGAISM—*The international curse of the senile who dominate all official Art Societies, especially in France (possibly because the French are the militarist nation they possess the largest battalions of ' Pompiers ').*
>
> PAPAISM—*The paternal patronage and fostering of the good boys of the Slade by the New English Art (Teachers') Club.*
>
> MAMAISM—*The tedious maternal boasting of Monsieur Clive Roger of the angular and deformed babe christened Post-Impressionism, which is slowly dying in the grimy atmosphere of the London Group.*
>
> BABAISM—*The propagandist sheep who bleat of pure art and significant form, and butt inanely for little periodicals.*
>
> TATAISM—*The tendency of most of the moderns to group themselves together only to break away with loud and abusive farewells.*
>
> *I hope my pictures make it clear that I paint what I love, how I like, for the joy of painting a motive so rarely suspected in living artists, either by the public, or by its echo, the journalist.*
>
> C. R. W. NEVINSON

I felt an ever-increasing dislike for the limitation which abstract art was imposing upon painting. The Impressionists had always been my gods, Renoir and his prettiness were appealing to me more and more. I was becoming wearied of my contemporary intellectuals and the ease with which they appreciated ugly-ugly pictures which lacked draughtsmanship, and displayed nothing but ignorance of craftsmanship, and the self-complacent rubbish which was being written about all forms of art, bored me, the sort of nonsense that was written by Clive Bell, Roger Fry, Middleton Murray, Marriot Raymond Mortimer, Popoffsky, and Wilenski. Taste and judgement seemed entirely distorted by fashion and cliché.

My great handicap has always been that I have known so much about the various schools of painting. I am absolutely incapable of airily dismissing all the work since the Renaissance and the realistic paintings of Velasquez; while many of the portraits of Titian and Van Dyke fill me with awe; and all this in spite of the fact that the Primitives arouse my emotion by their clarity of form and colour. Unlike most of the moderns, classical sculpture and the portraits of Gainsborough still maintain an achievement far greater than the distortions which have come about since Paul Gauguin tried to rediscover the fundamentals of artistic expression. My taste has always been too catholic, and this has been reflected overmuch in my painting, which at this time was inclined to box the compass. Secretly, I envied the limitations of such men as Wilenski and Herbert Read, who have only one rule for taste—a rule which has been broken by the great masters of Europe, India, and China. Now, out of this fog and confusion, I can discover for myself at least two links with all great art.

One link is immediacy of appeal, or what I call completion. This can be done by two entirely different and opposite methods. One is often achieved by the man who knows when to stop, and it accounts for the beauty of the sketch or of the spontaneous drawing or painting, the *premier coup,* as Matisse calls it; and the other is achieved by the highly finished artist who by use of accentuated detail is able to beautify a surface by elaboration. The second link, I am now inclined to believe, is an expressionism which, by virtue of its own inherent quality, is always and inevitably decorative, and a painting which has nothing at all but decorative intention seldom succeeds. For example, when a cave-man used drawing to express or describe the animal he was not able to catch, the result was far more decorative in effect than a drawing of an animal done merely for decorative purposes. Or again, by reason of its inherent quality of expression, a portrait by Holbein, which aimed at little more than exact likeness, is far more decorative than a portrait by Reynolds, which was intended to enrich the setting and create an atmosphere of grandeur for an English milord.

It is interesting to think that the Surrealists have now destroyed the art theories of yesterday, and are re-introducing what amounts to literary or symbolic content into their paintings, as opposed to the ' pure ' decorative art preached by the followers of the Post-Impressionists or abstract painters. They are almost coming back to Aristotle's definition of a work of art as being something which should create horror in order to purge the onlooker of pity, denying the existence of beauty, at any rate as an intention. I would hate to see an art as ugly as a Velasquez dwarf or a Rembrandt nude. To me, because modern art is now so permeated with the grotesque through the influence of Raoult, Picasso, Spencer, Epstein, and others, the chaste beauty of Botticelli, Leonardo, Clouet, and even Ingres, is more satisfying by reaction.

About this time I had an encounter with the late Lord Birkenhead. He had made a famous after-dinner speech which was widely reported in all the papers, about the ' glittering prizes ' of war, so I entitled my sketch of Passchendaele, ' Glittering Prizes ' and dedicated it to ' Our Noble After-Dinner Speakers '. The picture showed some wounded men wandering back to the dressing-station between a ' holy grail ' of champagne glasses and crossed cigars. Old Lewis, of Lewis & Lewis, the solicitors, who seemed to represent the whole of the aristocracy, went to the galleries and threatened them, not me ; and, not wishing to risk a lawsuit, they withdrew the picture. What any court of law could have done I do not know to this day, but there it was, a piece of bluff that came off. Indeed, Lewis went back to the galleries later, and thanked them for withdrawing the picture and admitted he had no case, a thing, of course, Birkenhead well knew.

The picture is now the property of the French Government. General Joffre wrote and personally thanked me for doing it. Of course, the champagne and cigars have been painted out, but I wonder how long it will be before they come through!

Incidentally, it was then I discovered that my flying pictures were in the Louvre, an honour kept only for the dead. This was due to the fact that in translation I had been described in some official catalogue as C. R. W. Nevinson, *late* R.A.M.C.

In the artistic muddle I now felt myself to be in, I decided that the only thing possible for me to do was to break from all studiotic theory and find my way as best as I could. I avoided all art chatter and settled down to study nature. I had a motor caravan built for me. In this I was a pioneer. The caravan was a development of my motor ambulance in France, when I was sleeping on the stretchers and more or less living in it as well. It was built on a Ford truck, and inside it was furnished with bunks and a little kitchen, papered in pale pink, with black beams, and little cretonne curtains with rosebuds on them, tied back with blue bows. It was a regular Marie Lloyd interior, the antithesis of all sophisticated decoration, and very pretty it was.

As I could not afford two cars, I also used it for driving about London, and unfortunately it was too conspicuous. The Press tried to work up a stunt. One or two journalists even suggested that I never slept in it, but only used it for purposes of advertisement, an idea that was difficult to follow, as the caravan did not look so vastly different from any other van. Nowadays, of course, we meet trailer caravans all over the country, but there was nothing like that in those days, and people undoubtedly were interested. The life has always attracted me and I have seldom been without a caravan since. But my first attempt marked a turning-point in my career, a break-away from the artistic *milieu* in which I had always lived, a snapping of all my social links, and the beginning of a search for a way out of the aesthetic cul-de-sac which modern art had led me into.

Inevitably my work changed. I settled down almost

158

entirely to do landscapes, abandoning my painting of cities. What figure work I did was almost entirely of young girls, or figures ' *en plein air* ', and differing from the Impressionists only inasmuch as it was impossible for me to forget my training in making a pattern or design. Thus did I achieve a structural quality which greatly strengthened my work, and for this I shall always owe a debt to my experiments in the abstract painting between 1914 and 1920. I gave an exhibition at the Leicester Galleries, and the critics were completely bewildered. They seemed to mistake art for some kind of political party system, and they accused me of leaving the so-called progressives and becoming a reactionary. In my own mind I felt I was progressing, and, thank heaven, so did many picture buyers; once again I sold every picture. Most artists, I find, have now followed my lead; even P. Wyndham Lewis mentions the tyranny of abstraction, and those painters of the Left, who grimly stick to modern art, now appear to be terribly old-fashioned. But what accusations of insincerity, of lack of conviction, and even of breach of faith, were levelled against me at the time.

It is always satisfactory when the truth comes out. Roger Fry and the professors had, I knew, often discussed my American trips, and in art circles they had dismissed me as ' merely commercial '. My last trip, of course, had been very nearly disastrous. After deducting my travelling expenses, frames, and freights, and even when I had lived rent-free in a millionaire's love nest, my profits amounted to five shillings a week. Through my highly excitable friend Blewsher, a crime reporter, this got into the papers and knocked the intellectuals, amateurs, and professors (who never think but in the form of money) groggy. Those of them who had disparaged me in public, while they had made secret plans to visit the United States, hastily rearranged their ideas. The chatter stopped, and even the hangers-on of the Café Royal, Chelsea, and Fitzroy Street, were struck dumb. For them only was the glory of never doing any work and never selling any pictures, borrowing half-crowns from all and sundry, and starving romantically in a garret because of their misunderstood genius and the integrity of their aesthetic ideals. It was also a blow to the amateurs of Bloomsbury, although they, too, painted only for the glory of art and the necessity of expressing themselves.

One of the most persistent and one of the most charming of those people who have tried to sell pictures for me was Mrs. Aria, the great friend of Henry Irving. Her wit had a world-wide reputation and I always looked forward to seeing her. One day she said to me, 'Hundreds of girls seem to have been very kind to you, and as you are not a cad or a bounder, I can only presume you're a genius.'

She was very naughty in one respect, and although I laughed I could not help feeling embarrassed at her persistent efforts to persuade Lady Wyndham to buy one of my pictures. Poor Lady Wyndham was known to be careful, and there was really no reason why she should buy a picture of mine if she didn't want to, yet she was never allowed to forget there were always some for sale. When I jokingly chided Mrs. Aria for bothering the lady, she gave me a wicked look and said, 'My dear young man, you mustn't mind. It's such fun for me.'

Here I met George Moore a great deal, and he agreed with me that he hated the way Parisians dramatized genius such as Modigliani, by making them dissipated, half-starved rats after their death. He startled me by saying that was why he left Paris years before I was born ! Paris never changes, though old de Lara loved meeting me at Aunt A.'s as I was always able to tell him something he did not know about his beloved Paris.

I was in Paris when I heard again that the Tonks movement to remove my picture 'La Mitrailleuse' from the Tate Gallery had been revived. The artist who told me is a man of reputation and known to every one in the art world, but I will not have him dragged into the controversy. It is enough that I believed what he told me. I was in a fury about it this time. For years I had been gossiped about and reviled. Every form of abuse had been heaped on my head by this man who was now objecting to the work which had been gladly accepted by the Contemporary Art Society.

White hot, I wrote to that old schoolmaster Aitken, Curator

of the Tate Gallery, demanding that the 'Mitrailleuse' should be taken down. I said I did not like the picture, but even if it were the worst one in the world, the Tête-à-Tête behaviour was still worse. I made every comment on the way artists and others were behaving in the Tate Gallery, and pointing out that their proposed action was most offensive to the purchaser of the picture, who I understood, was an American who had generously given it to the Contemporary Art Society.

A few weeks' afterwards Sir Robert Witt opened an exhibition in Manchester, and in the course of his speech he stated that an artist, whose name he would not mention, had asked for the removal of one of his own paintings from the Tate Gallery, as he considered it the world's worst picture. That night the newspapers rang me up and asked me if I knew who the artist could be. I was astounded and mortified to think the matter had been made semi-public and my letter misquoted, and I denied all knowledge of it. Further, I suggested Professor Tonks and Roger Fry as possible candidates for the honour. Then one newspaper sent a man down to the Tate. He simply tipped a custodian and asked if any of the pictures had been removed lately. In two minutes the cat was out of the bag. And what a ballyhoo the Press of the whole world made out of the news. Even *Punch* heard of it.

Sir Robert Witt fled into the country and refused to come to my rescue. I became an object of ridicule. My dealers rang me up and complained of damaging my reputation, and my enemies enjoyed themselves by keeping the joke going. Then the very people who were responsible for the picture's withdrawal turned on me, and with that self-righteousness I have come to know them by, 'accused me of raising the storm' to quote Professor MacColl. The whole thing was, of course, the most lamentable breach of confidence. My letter was marked 'Private and Confidential', and nobody had any right to disclose anything. In the long run I know that this plot against me and my reputation actually did me good. 'La Mitrailleuse' had many champions in spite of the fact that they believed I had condemned it, and I found

161

my work and my modesty appreciated in the most unlikely quarters. Shortly after this, a new personnel came into being at the Tête-à-Tête, and the ' Sladish Corridor ' with all its petty favouritism and vulgar personalities ceased in art politics for a while.

15

While the world was looking black for me, I formed a friendship with Boyd, who became a great patron of mine, and I was able to sell enough pictures to enable me to carry on. I continued to work, and when I gave another show at the Leicester Galleries he bought several more paintings and presented them to various museums. This interest and generosity did something towards restoring my self-respect and repairing the damage done.

We spent many week-ends with H. G. Wells at Dunmow, where we met a number of delightful people, Sir Richard Gregory, the scientist, and Arnold Bennett in particular. I had known Bennett for some years, but he always seemed to be at his best with Wells, and the gentle teasing of Jane—Mrs. Wells—made him beam with satisfaction and tell stories of his past, when it appeared he always bought something expensive and afforded it afterwards. I have also seen him quite peevish when he told us he had just finished a book and nobody took much notice of the fact. He repeated the news time after time until somebody showed an interest and allowed him to talk about it. Authors have warned me that as a race they are much better when they are known only in cold print, but I can recall occasions at my studio or elsewhere when Wells, Bennett, and Somerset Maugham, talking quietly together of many things, have made the hours minutes. Bennett was very interested in a new car of mine. I had sold my caravan to a Scots commercial traveller. By means of detachable seats I had the new saloon made into a sleeping-car, while for a kitchen we had a large trunk at the back with everything in it. We used this form of camping *de luxe* for some years. As a comment on the man who was always interested in the price and make of motor-cars, I noticed that in Bennett's memoirs he described my car as a Ford. It was not a Ford; it was a Chrysler, and a new one at that. Very hurtful.

The artist, Arthur Watts, who was later to be killed flying, used to come and help in the charades organized by Jane. Sometimes these were of the most realistic description, and I remember a surgical scene, invented by H. G., where the intestines were removed from a patient and yards and yards of garden hose were extracted from him. On another occasion Sir Richard Gregory got so carried away that, although in the audience, he became post-Rheinhardt and walked the joy-plank to join the actors; reversing the convention of the actors joining the audience.

I took enormous pains with the interior decoration of my studio, an experience which I found of value to me afterwards when I came to arrange the hanging of so many exhibitions and the arranging of houses and clubs. I also took up gardening, and my flower paintings date from this time. I also gave a lot of parties. It would be quite impossible for me to make a list of all the interesting people I know in London and in Paris, and although I was completely detached I found it amusing to gather in my studio all sorts and conditions of men and women. It is remarkable to think of the people who honoured me in coming. One would never have imagined I was intensely lonely.

Among those who used to come were such people as the Sitwells, H. G. Wells, Mark Hambourg, Sinclair Lewis, Goossens, Michael Arlen, Firbank, Arnold Bennett, the Countess of Drogheda, Josef Holbrooke, the Cochrans, Noel Coward, Lady Melchett, Gracie Fields, Mrs. Guinness, Lady Hulton, Diana Wynyard, Jeanne de Casalis, Nigel Playfair, Ena Burrell, Morris Harvey, Constance Collier, Aubrey Hammond, Sir Stanley Woodwark, Gilbert Frankau, Natalie Sieveking, Ann Trevor, Harry Greene, a host of lords and ladies, M.P.s, Indian Rajahs, Japanese poets, Chinese painters, Cingalese journalists, actors, writers, scientists, Cockneys and South Americans, Spaniards and New Yorkers, and of course, such artists as John, Barney Seale, Munnings, Epstein, Strang,

164

Dyson, and Low; critics and patrons, great men and small. My studio is a large one, but its capacity was often taxed, as the newspapers would say, by the crowd. In one corner I have built a bar, which is also a cunning tool chest, although that is not apparent. I have discovered that a bar has the mysterious power of breaking down nervousness and constraint. Men and women will cluster round it and talk without any introduction or common cause; which is my idea of the way people should behave. And to help things out I often used to find a band of unemployed ex-soldiers or buskers in some part or other of London, and get them to come along and play in the gallery of my studio.

My gatherings were so successful that I found myself being interviewed as the man who gives the most wonderful parties; a humbling experience, considering that I have tried all my life to do a good painting. But, like so many other good things, the parties were overdone, and in the end I nearly abandoned them. So many people began to take them for granted that they never bothered about an invitation. That was bad enough. But while I never objected to friends coming along even if it did congest the studio, I would not have the uninvited strangers. At that time, gate-crashing was thought to be funny by many of the Bright Young People, who found it hard to think of something new, and there were so many interesting people in my studio that all sorts would drift in to see them. Their presence and behaviour infuriated me. Once my wife was actually struck by one of these gentlemen. He had arrived drunk, and when I spotted him I ordered him out. He simply walked out into the garden and came in by another door, and when Kathleen saw him and indignantly told him to clear out, he hit her and lurched past. Needless to say, his immediate exit was an undignified one. Twice I caught people stealing bottles of drinks. On such occasions I felt a fool for having asked any one, although there is nothing I enjoy more than being a host. Max Beerbohm has said that people are either born hosts or born guests. Of later years I have tried to teach myself to become a guest, but I was born a host and I shall end a host. My giving of parties is an indulgence that amounts to a vice. I must have entertained thousands during the sixteen years I have had these studios, and I would hate to think what must have been consumed on the premises.

Those years should, I suppose, have been the happiest. My health was good, I was financially unworried, and I was going everywhere; in fact, I often described the *wagons-lit* as our spiritual home. If we wanted to go anywhere we went, and my wife would often at a moment's notice pack in the afternoon and we would catch the night boat or 'plane for the South of France or the Pyrenees. I had a beautiful home and I had broken away completely from the intellectuals and art politics. Yet painting, or rather exhibiting, was making me profoundly unhappy. Gilbert Frankau had just commissioned me to work for *Britannia*, the new weekly he was editing, and at the same time I was working for another one-man show. The two types of work were entirely antagonistic, and gradually the strain bore me down until I had my first attack of pleurisy, which left me with a melancholy I could not fight off.

Then there appeared in the new edition of the *Encyclopaedia Britannica* a most insulting attack on me by Manson, the new Curator of the Tête-à-Tête. I was first shown it by Reginald Berkeley, the dramatist who died soon after he had gone to Hollywood doing the film version of ' Cavalcade '. Since my row with the Tate Gallery a picture of mine had been presented to it by H. G. Wells. I thought the fuss was over and forgotten, and that in future I should be allowed to earn my living without further attack from the ' connoisseurs ' who ran the place.

So strong were my feelings that I took counsel's opinion with a view to taking what was called a libel in trade; for, after all, if an unwarranted attack on me appeared in a publication which advertised that all its writers were authorities on their subjects, was it not more than likely that I should lose at least one sale ? Against that there were all the arguments for artistic criticism, and the risk that a judge might hold that the article came within its bounds. The upshot was that although counsel himself felt sympathetic to my case and thought a judge might do likewise, there was a real risk that in law my action might fail. I was advised not to proceed, as artists are always guilty in English law.

The result was that I became a victim of an *idée fixe*. I consulted a famous nerve specialist because I was honestly frightened of developing a persecution mania. On the top of my many illnesses I was being treated as I remembered no artist having been treated before. To prove to this man of science that my ideas were not based on the ridiculous I showed him the paragraph. He read it and these were his words :

' The only decent thing you can do to a man who writes like this is to kill him.'

I veered round then, and told him that in my thoughts I was murdering Manson asleep and awake, and that it was awful. I was labouring under a sense of injustice for which there seemed to be no redress in law, and that was what I came to consult him about. What could he do to help me ? As my wife kept telling me the creature was not worth swinging for.

The doctor told me that as we were living in a civilized community the best thing I could do was to make it up and forget it. I left him, five guineas the poorer.

Soon afterwards, at some gathering or other, the question of the article came up. All artists were disturbed by it, for no man knew when he would be the next to be attacked. I told the people near me how I had tried unsuccessfully to bring an action and what the doctor had said ; and Fincham, the assistant curator of the Tate, heard what I said. He came to me and told me that Manson was most distressed at what had occurred. It appeared that he had written a great deal about me and that, while the criticism had been left in, the praise had been cut out owing to lack of space. What was left in the publication constituted a distortion of the article he had done. Fincham assured me that Manson's original criticism was completely inoffensive. Could he not help me to make it up ? The relief to my mind on hearing his words !

I wrote to Manson and asked him to be my guest at a Saturday night dinner at the Savage Club, and the funny thing was that we did make it up. Towards the end of the evening Manson was sitting with his arm round my neck. The specialist was absolutely right in every particular and as good a psychologist as he professed to be. The breach was healed in spite of the fact that after dinner Manson became bitter in the bar and was attacked and even insulted by some hard-baked artists who deeply resented the whole tone of the aesthetes on the committee of the Tate Gallery towards English artists. I thought the row would blow up again, but Manson ignored the artists completely and we parted friends.

For some twenty years I have not been near the Tate, as I do not wish to arouse, or even to remember, the misery that gallery has caused me. I have never seen my pictures in that gallery. I can never understand why those in charge of artists' work should hate art as much as they do. Critics I can understand. The monotony of visiting shows, and the nausea that too many pictures can cause, are a sufficient reason for their attitude. But in the case of curators, and non-practising artists, I find a bitterness which I can put down only to a form of Puritanism, a suspicion which amounts to hatred of any form of beauty. The average member of the public puts it down to envy, due either to the fact that the chatterers are disappointed artists, or that they lack creative urge; but I myself think there is some sort of moral factor underlying their criticisms. A work of art is neither better nor worse because it is painted by a man who eats too much, drinks too much, or womanizes; while a vegetarian, a teetotaller, or an aesthete is quite as capable of doing as good a painting as a debauchee. Even this endless talk about sincerity is of no aesthetic value whatsoever. I could name two of our best contemporary painters who are incapable of any sincere thought or action and who yet maintain an artistic integrity that is beyond all doubt. And I know many others who are profoundly conscious of their sincerity, and almost protest it too much, yet whose paintings are definitely tainted by a conscious or subconscious desire to attract attention by a sensationalism or a deformation which mars the aesthetic value of their work. To read a great deal of contemporary opinion on the arts, one might be led to believe that sincerity was enough. If only it were! This would be a golden age for the arts. Actually, it has as little to do with artistic creation as the fact that a man is red-headed or dark. Even commerce has little effect, one way or another, upon artists. There are exponents of the fine arts who never think of their work except in terms of cash, just as there are commercial artists with a genuine feeling for beauty and an enthusiasm for art unknown among the highbrows.

Ever since Whistler coined the phrase, ' Art for Art's sake ', a new, and in my opinion a wrong, standard of judgement has been introduced to bear on the function of an artist.

We have opponents to all modern art, such as de Laszlo and Sir David Murray, who describe painters as decadents, degenerates, and impostors, merely because some have preferred to do pictures that in no way resemble the visual world. Many of these painters were Jewish, and it is only during the last century or so that they have been allowed by their religion to make any image at all. In Persia, Turkey, and in Northern Africa it can clearly be seen how the second commandment influenced Mohammedan art and produced nothing but the abstract or geometric pattern. In England, where the seventh commandment is most reverenced, many of the greatest lovers of this de-humanized art were either Quakers or Methodists by birth, and they were always suspicious of the flesh or any sensual appeal. This suspicion is ever-present in the Englishman and is one of the many fruits of the Reformation and the later excesses of Oliver Cromwell. If only an ancestor of mine had saved the life of Henry the Eighth's son when he was court physician at Greenwich Palace, England might have been saved from Puritanism. As it was, the Stuarts came to the Throne and were followed in reaction by Cromwell, who saw the devil in everything that was beautiful. Art could be forgiven only if it had some moral or ethical purpose, or at least if it did not glorify a beauty that was seductive or sexual. Hence this common ground on which the Jews and the Bloomsburies judge a work of art. One kind is shocked because nature or the imagery of God is faithfully and humbly mimicked; the other kind is delighted when form is stripped of its sensuality and all allure is eliminated by distortion or mathematics.

This application of a standard which can never rightly be applied to any work of art is largely responsible for the present antagonism.

The Quaker and the Jew will always fight, although their points of view and love of being misunderstood have on the surface much in common; but of course the old Cockney song, 'The Jews were a match for Quakers' is still true as regards money-making.

A great change was made to my life when Philip Page, Aubrey Hammond, and Basil Cameron proposed me to the Savage Club. When my name came up an objection was made to me that I was aggressive. The talk of the art circles was known everywhere. I only wish I were aggressive. I am cursed with always seeing the other point of view, and the chief thing I like in life is easy company and good fellow-ship. I am indifferent to other people's beliefs, and the only fights I have ever had have been against a certain form of highbrow who has invented slanderous stories against my personal character, the integrity of my artistic intention, my parents, and my home life. Thanks to my supporters, I was given the benefit of the doubt by the Savage Selection Com-mittee and allowed the usual month's probation, so that members could judge for themselves. My supporters advised me to visit the club as much as possible, and I did.

My membership of the Savage was an entirely new experi-ence for me. No longer did I feel the outcast among the set I had been brought up with—demi-socialists who wrote for unimportant little reviews; painting people who exhibited in obscure places; men and women who for the most part had been too superior to take any active part in the affairs of the day, who were proud of saying they never had anything to do with the War because their objections to a German policeman were no stronger than their objections to an English one. These people had a vague love for Russia simply be-cause they knew nothing about it, and an avowed detestation of England simply because they were English. Yet they professed to be international. It was a class which could be summed up as Fabian Shavians, vaguely connected with political economy and the *New Statesman*. They hated the realism of the French, but praised any art, no matter how bad, as long as it came from Paris. They wrote about English bad taste in French magazines, often accusing the English of failings which were common to all nations and thus demonstrating their insularity. Most of them had allowances from their fathers. They seldom worked; they used the arts as a refuge for their laziness, taste as a hedge to screen their inferiority as craftsmen, and economics as an excuse for their incapacity to meet creditors. They were intensely envious of any one capable of earning his living. No wonder the trade unionists despise the intelligentsia of the Labour Party. Nearly all are without scruple, and rely on their superior education to grab power from an ignorant democracy, which they despise and misunderstand even more than 'the ruling classes'.

These people now faded into the distance as far as I was concerned. In the Savage Club I was able to mix with numbers of great doctors, eminent scientists, actors, writers, musicians, artists—sensible, hard-working men, all busy at their arts or professions, all men of the world, and generally speaking all possessed of X-ray eyes and capable of stripping a highbrow of all poses, affectations, and pretensions. There is no other collection of men in the world to compare with it. There are field-marshals and fiddlers, mummers and millionaires, and when they enter those dignified doors in Carlton House Terrace they leave all differences behind them and meet their fellow-members on common ground. I found myself in an atmosphere I loved. It reminded me somewhat of the early art days before the War, when tolerance and artistic camaraderie were accepted facts among practising artists.

For the first time for some years my health was all right, and I was able to go everywhere, see people, stay up at night, and eat and drink what I liked. On the advice of a great doctor I was able to join the Savage Lodge, and feel men could be with me rather than against, and I soon began to know many of the members and came in contact with two professions which I find the most likeable in London: the theatrical and the scientific. It has been said that actors are insincere. Perhaps they are, although it is always a mistake to label a profession. Perhaps they have forgotten one's existence within half a minute of leaving, but then perhaps it is this very insincerity that makes them delightful company. It is a matter of indifference to me that they happen to be playing a part, for the older I get the more I prefer good manners to good morals. I have long been wearied of those be-bearded, spectacled gentlemen who are so vain, so convinced that they resemble D. H. Lawrence, and so overwhelmed by their own sincerity that they are unable to hide their contempt for others, or restrain themselves from saying a wounding thing, however untrue.

The scientist has always appealed to me because in the artistic world, which to-day lacks all standards, it is a relief to come across a mind which accepts nothing but fact and is even doubtful of that; which realizes that nothing can be established without constant experiment. Unlike literary people, scientists know what people are really like, and they accept humanity as it is, without that censoriousness which seems the main urge of many writers.

Sometimes the Savage reminds me of my early life, when journalists used to come to my father's house and discuss the news which did not appear in the papers. Here men come from every sort of queer place and speak authoritatively on every subject.

16

During this period I came to know a number of film people. Maurice Elvey I had known for years, but through Reginald Berkeley and Donald Calthrop I met Wilcox and saw the real birth of the British film industry. Mervyn McPherson asked me to the most extraordinary functions. There were first nights at the new Tivoli or the Palace; there were parties to meet the stars, grand affairs where men and women from every walk of life were present, apart from the usual dead-heads; and there were receptions like the one given to the Talmadge sisters at the Savoy, where the guests solemnly filed past two very commonplace women, while thousands outside clamoured to see these goddesses.

Then there were dinners like the one I attended in a private room at the Carlton, where the Home Secretary listened gravely to David Waulk Griffiths making a speech of the profoundest banality in which he said he was just a simple, hairy-chested American loaded up with a freight of love. Once I found myself on a committee for a beauty contest, organized by the *Daily Mail,* with Arthur Bouchier, Laurillard, and Pomeroy; and when the winner of the Golden Apple looked at us, she just cried and cried and cried.

It was a funny world I found myself in. Once when I was down to speak at a lunch I was sitting next to Fay Compton, who was upset because when she was coming in with Leon Quartermaine the mobs recognized him but not her, and then she heard some all-knowing typist ask: ' Who is that little bit with him ? ' To which another girl replied: ' I don't know, but she's always about with him now.' And Quartermaine was her husband !

On another occasion I had to get to Leicester Square to

see a *Daily Sketch* girl who was being sent to Hollywood to be trained as a film star.

I had difficulty in getting through the crowds to the banquet at the Carlton. All over the place there were reminders of the *Daily Sketch*, and no one was permitted to forget that this feast was organized by that great paper in honour of their beauty prize-winner. I was just in time; and when W. L. George, *not* having read his *Daily Sketch* that morning, rose to make his speech he inquired who the new star was. The silence was dreadful. Not long afterwards I followed suit by making a remark on the lavatory theme of film at a banquet given to Emil Jannings at the Piccadilly. Those 'propagandinners' are no longer given, but for me they were marvellous opportunities for meeting all sorts of people. I felt I had to go everywhere to destroy the myth spread by the art circles.

One of my difficulties has always been that the art world is a village and that a certain set of 'arty' writing men have made personal attacks on me by attributing to me a character which bears no relation to mine and publishing their beliefs to three million people. I then meet some of the readers, and they are bewildered when they see at once that I do not fit in with the newspaper paragraphs. It often takes them some time to adjust their preconceived notions. People approach my work in the same way and are startled when they see nothing aggressive or repulsive about it. As many artists know, its chief quality is a love of nature and a hypersensibility. Only occasionally do I indulge in satire, although I admit to a regret that I have never been able to cultivate the fantastic and imaginative side of my painting, on the lines of 'The Inexperienced Witch', 'Castles in Spain', and 'Pan Triumphant'. Thanks to the Society for Adult Education, the oil-painting 'On Seeing a Swallow for the first time in Summer' is at last receiving appreciation.

I am not commercially minded, but to paint pictures that never sell and simply cause all other kinds of work to be misapprehended is a task which I find stultifying. Every artist always has too many pictures, and for some reason imaginative pictures are now entirely out of fashion with the critics, the buying public, and the general public. I do not think any artist can be expected to use what talents he has only to kick against the pricks. One day there will be a reaction, and artists will be able to paint fantasies, which are the inventions of the mind, using realistic form. By that I mean that trees will look like trees, and human beings like human beings, but they will be of such a nature that no photograph could produce the same result. The Surrealists are pointing the way towards this, but unfortunately their work is marred by a debauched Freudianism ' gone gay ', and by a revolting grotesque that makes Goya appear almost pretty-pretty. Not that I necessarily wish to condemn this offshoot of art, because it is obvious that the Chinese, the Japanese opium painters, the later Indian, and many of the German and Italian Primitives like Dürer, Raphael, Leonardo, and Holbein, have all been attracted by macabre.

It is often a marvel to me how I get enough time to do everything. At this period I was painting hard all day, gardening, cooking, attending to my affairs, travelling, and camping, and meeting hundreds of people each week. I was making speeches, and writing articles on all kinds of subjects for the morning papers, the evening papers, and for the magazines, American and English. I was becoming a famous character about town, dining, dancing, carousing, and theatre-going, recognized everywhere, never having to take a number for my coat and hat in any restaurant or hotel, and known by name to the waiters of the entire West-end, the City, and as far East as Limehouse. I knew a Harley Street doctor who had to abandon his practice for health reasons and take a cruise round the world, and when he came back he told me a curious thing. He had discovered that if he mentioned my name on board ship, or in any bar, be it in China, Australia, South America, San Francisco, or Panama, either he would become involved in an argument about me or my work, or somebody present would have met me personally and have recollections of me at a party in London, Paris, or New York. When I mentioned this to my Father his comment was : ' To be known in every bar all over the world is certainly fame indeed.'

My life was so different from that of the average artist. In the War my work had put me in touch with hundreds of French, Canadian, Australian, New Zealand, and British troops. My family life kept me in touch with the journalistic and political life of England; and as an official war artist I had met regular officers of all ranks, besides innumerable 'Society' people. The Café Royal, the Savoy, the Eiffel Tower, and Kleinfeldt's had enabled me to meet artists, demi-journalists, and paragraphists, business men, the theatre and film worlds, and the riff-raff. In Montmartre and Mont-parnasse, too, I mixed with all manner of men, from members of the Jockey Club to bookmakers, from American racketeers to writers such as Gertrude Stein, Sisley Huddleston, Ford Maddox Ford and their coteries, and James Joyce.

One night Kathleen and I were dining at the Petit Trianon, opposite the Gare Montparnasse, when we noticed James Joyce and his wife at their customary table. I had been an early admirer of his *Ulysses* and had been able to tell him that H. G. Wells was interested in his newer form of writing. When we had finished our meal we went over to join them, as I was aware that Joyce was always glad to see people. We were then thinking of living in Paris for good, and at once my wife and Mrs. Joyce started a discussion on French flats. On the contrary, I was tongue-tied in the presence of a great master; and as Joyce is a very shy man and I always catch the mood of the person I am talking to, the conversation was somewhat hesitating. Suddenly he turned to me. 'My wife has been complaining,' he said, 'because there is no light literature in our flat. She has never read my *Ulysses*, which, after all, is light, humorous stuff.'

As his book had shocked the world I was dumbfounded, and there was another pause. Then I remembered that he was fond of champagne and that we both had a natural palate for it. He liked to discover unknown marks, some of which are so much better than well-known ones. I looked at the empty bottle in front of him, and asked if it was a good one. To my amazement he informed me that because of his bad eyesight he had given up drinking champagne. His wife had not helped him, as she had half a bottle of hock.

He then inquired about my work, and I told him that sometimes I was overwhelmed by its futility. He heartily agreed with me. The next morning I painted harder than ever ! *Ulysses*, of course, was banned, and the author was regarded by the Puritans as a dreadful person ; yet when his wife had to spend some weeks in a nursing home, James Joyce could not bear to be parted from her and occupied a room next door to hers. Could anybody demand a more charming proof of domesticity than this ?

Sisley Huddleston and I were great friends. He was a man of enormous stature. We have dined and wined together in all parts of Paris, roared with laughter and teased ' the girls '. On one occasion Sisley, Clive Bell, and I had eaten *poulet au riz* and had drunk wine with it. Being a large man, Sisley had a large appetite. We took one of those tiny Parisian taxis to Boulevard St. Germain, and when we arrived outside Lipp's we discovered that the rice had swelled so much inside Sisley that it was impossible for him to get out of the door. We pushed and we pulled, but he seemed to be growing larger before our eyes ; and at length the driver opened the roof, and Sisley came out through that and over the back. By that time he and I and the driver were so hysterical with merriment that they refused us admission to the Brasserie Lipp's in the belief that we were drunk ; and Clive Bell, who had stood by, shocked and exquisite, was furious because he had a rendezvous there with Derain.

Once our relations were strained over a picture of mine. H. G. Wells had presented ' Montparnasse ' to the Tate Gallery, and Sisley wrote to the Press protesting at the exhibition of my picture as there was a nude in the studio and the studio was his. I think he did it largely as a *blague,* as he was able to connect the Tate Gallery, Wells, and a nude with his own name. On the other hand, he was European editor of the *Christian Science Monitor,* and he was possibly afraid that some good American might ' think things ' if his studio was recognized in the Tate Gallery. In a way he was right. Actually it was unrecognizable and there are hundreds of studios in ' Montparnasse '. But of course the connexion between my name and the Tate was more than suspicious, and once again the Tête-à-

Tête people accused me of trying to work a ' publicity stunt '
on them.

Some months later, I came across Sisley in Harry's bar, and
I carefully made no reference to the trouble over the picture.
Then up came Gilbert White, the diabolical American wit
of Paris, and when he saw us together he turned to me and
said : ' Wall, Nevinson, I know why you painted a " noode "
in Sisley's studio, though I am sure you never saw one there.
But just as Swaffer sees spirits all around him from never
drinking, you kind of felt nudes all around his place.' We
all looked extremely piqued, and Sisley was about to become
pompous when somebody laughed and we all joined in.
Our friendship was once more cemented. I now know that
if I had been editor of an American Christian paper in a
wicked city like Paris, I would have been livid if a nude
had been introduced into a painting of my home. When
I worked on the picture and put in a nude I was thinking
only of the design. But then I always forget the interpretation
the average member of the public puts on a nude. Nothing
startles me more than when the Mayor and his aldermen
representing various municipal galleries come to my studio
to choose a picture, and they arrive all agog and begin lifting
the curtains and peering into cubby-holes in the hope of seeing
a naked girl.

I was now doing a great many portraits ; and, among
others, I painted Edith Sitwell, a grand woman, completely
unlike the absurd legends told about her by the envious and
the petty. Her courage has always been a tonic to me ; and
her *débonnaire* wit, her feminine shrewdness, and the nobility
of her character make all her vilifiers appear the most revolting
of literary parasites. How she worked to earn her living by
her pen. Once she said to me : ' I always felt that success
would be the one thing that would do me good.' And it
has, though I never thought it possible that anything could
improve a lily. At dinner with Osbert one night we were
talking about Noel Coward, and another guest happened to
say he wished some one would exterminate the little *patiche*.
Osbert at once turned and said : ' I wish you would. Edith
would be so obliged.' Another time I was giving a dinner

178

at my studio to some of the most distinguished men in London, all leaders in their own spheres. My cook was then a man, an ex-batman, and I impressed on him the fact that he must spread himself for such company. He appeared in no way interested until he saw Osbert Sitwell, when he found an opportunity to ask me who he might be. I explained and all he said was, ' I can tell a master of men when I see one.' The others, famous leaders of thought and progress, seemed to make no impression on him, and, of course it was Osbert who led in the settlement of the general strike. After the dinner he asked anxiously if the captain was pleased.

I painted Mrs. Bonner, the famous beauty; and her Florentine perfection inspired me to do one of the best heads I have ever done. Afterwards I did Josef Holbrooke, who spent his time attacking the Jews and the Scots.

It was a privilege to paint Mark Hambourg, a dear friend. His Russian zest and wit never cease to enthrall me, and everything he says is worth hearing. Never have I met a man with such a gift for penetrating to the heart of things, and by the use of a few vivid phrases he will lift any conversation out of the ordinary. I remember sitting beside him at an after-dinner concert, when Moiseivitch was playing. The audience, all men and women of "culture," were anything but attentive, smoking, drinking, coughing, picking, wriggling, but the waiters and waitresses stood entranced, their eyes on the master. ' Look,' said Mark. ' Look at the effect of education. It kills all concentration. The " lower classes " are the only people left who can listen, and can respond to the highest emotions.'

Another sitter of mine was Sinclair Lewis, the strangest literary man I have known. He was restless, clownish, and intense as only Americans can be, and he prowled round my studio incapable of sitting still, while all the time he poured out the most remarkable monologue of love and hate, shrewdness and sentimentality, that it can have been the lot of any portrait painter to hear. He used to leave me with a sense of exhaustion and elation that I have never known any other human capable of producing.

He was obsessed by a dread of the future and of his own

in particular, fearing that his creative faculties would dry up; and all this before he wrote, *Babbitt*, *The Man Who knew Coolidge*, and *It Can't Happen Here*. His irony was devastating, and I wish I dared write some of the thrusts he made at contemporary writers, French, English and American, but I have been warned that it is possible in this country to write the truth only of the dead. All the time I am struggling with the awful fear that anything I have said will be held in evidence against me.

I have sometimes wondered if Sinclair Lewis looks back on that particular visit to England with dissatisfaction. Never have I met a man so sensitive and yet with such a gift of putting his foot in it. He would break all the snob rules laid down by the mumbo-jumbos of English literature, and infuriate everyone with a taint of preciosity. Sometimes it would seem that a devil possessed him, although I recall two occasions when he was worsted.

Once we were at dinner with Somerset Maugham, and among those present were Mrs. Maugham, Knoblock, McEvoy, Osbert Sitwell, and Eddie Marsh. There was nobody in the party to whom Sinclair Lewis could take exception; and as for our host, I have always noticed like many others that he is the one man admired by all authors. After dinner, Sinclair Lewis took Eddie Marsh's monocle, stuck it in his own eye, and began parading up and down with Eddie Marsh following like a dog on a string. Then, to amuse himself, he parodied high-brow conversation in the best Oxford manner, at times imitating McEvoy's cracked voice, which was sometimes bass and sometimes treble. All of us were embarrassed, as the parody was grotesquely realistic, and I saw McEvoy pull his hair over his forehead and begin to look like a village idiot, a danger signal in him.

I knew it would come, and sure enough McEvoy suddenly interrupted the parody and inquired if Sinclair Lewis was an American. Sinclair Lewis looked taken aback at the question, but fell right into trouble.

'Yes,' he said. 'That is what makes me so sick with you condescending Englishmen.'

'I don't care if you are sick,' replied McEvoy calmly. 'In

fact I should be rather pleased. But you are just the man to tell me why old Americans are so much nicer than young ones.'

Poor Lewis. The eye-glass fell from his eye and he was silent until we left.

I took him on to a night club and he began to regain courage. A little Chelsea girl joined us; and, still sore, he began boasting. I knew this Chelsea girl to be a terror and by no means as innocent as she looked, but in spite of all my efforts to silence him he would talk about himself. With murmurs of disbelief the girl urged him on until he was announcing to the world at large that he was the author of *Main Street*, which had the largest circulation, bar the Bible, throughout America. The wicked little girl looked at him with wide-open eyes and asked, 'Are you a writer?' By now he was in a mood to repeat himself. 'Sure I am,' he bellowed. 'I am telling you I wrote *Main Street*, that has the largest circulation, bar the Bible, throughout America.' With a look of complete innocence the girl went on, 'You an author? I thought you were an American! But surely you were a publicity agent once?'

Another time talking with Lord Beaverbrook, Sinclair Lewis kept on saying, 'What do you think, Max?' Beaverbrook grew tired of this form of address after the eighth time and suddenly snapped at him, 'What do you think, Sinc?' Little humiliations, maybe; but Americans are very touchy, and to be worsted by 'a limey' is no fun.

17

During this time England was being mismanaged by a Socialist Minority Government, a curious set of men, with their ideals in the sky and their hands in the till, utterly ignorant of European mentality, but bemused with the best of intentions, and, as the General Strike proved, sublimely indifferent to the laws of contract.

We were in Paris when the General Strike occurred. It was not at all pleasant to be abroad at that time, because we were kept utterly without news except for the sensational stuff which was joyfully printed by the French papers. The air was full of the wildest rumours of murder and sabotage. George Slocombe was then foreign correspondent for the *Daily Herald*, and he told me the pound would not be worth twopence by the end of four days. Then a man on *The Times* told me the British Navy had been mobilized.

However, I had been caught before in a panic like this, and I determined to go home to London. When I dropped into Cook's to inquire the best way, I was told that forty people had been killed at Victoria Station alone, that it was inadvisable to travel by train owing to the bands of determined wreckers, and that only air travel was possible at an increased rate. I went to my bank and demanded to see the manager, in the certain knowledge that he would have been in telephonic communication with his head office in the City. He assured me that everything was quiet in London and throughout the country, that all the stories of murders and riots were false, and that the pound was going up.

The pound was the answer to everything. If it was going up—and no bank manager would lie about such a sacred subject—then all was well. I thought of the excitement in

Zelli's in rue Fontaine, which was full of wildly rejoicing Russians, Jews, Germans, Austrians and Italians, who were all grinning because England had fallen at last. If any one had any doubts about the depths of the dislike and distrust in which this country was held all over Europe, here was an answer.

That evening I saw Sisley Huddleston and told him what the bank manager had said. He seemed surprised that I was prepared to take the manager's word and said that bankers always talked like that. Next morning Kathleen and I went to the Gare du Nord and asked for two tickets to London as though nothing had happened, and we had a most comfortable journey, especially Kathleen, who joined the entourage of the Duke of Connaught by accident and even used their special gangway. We were safely deposited in London by over-courteous undergraduates, who drove the train well, but the journey was a great disappointment to one milord who was marvellously dressed in a check ulster and a deer-stalker's cap with ear flaps, and who expected to be shot at every level crossing. All the way from the coast he complained bitterly about the miners, and demanded to know why, if they disliked their job so much, they always insisted on putting their sons into it, and too many of them at that.

In London the anti-climax was bewildering. There certainly had been much more excitement in Paris. Incidentally, I learned from Brown and Phillips, the art dealers, that the stories in Rome were even more fantastic than those in Paris. They had actually received telegrams from connoisseurs instructing them to have certain pictures delivered for safety to the Italian Embassy, as a protection from the mob that was looting and burning the West-end.

Few people realize the effect on my moribund generation of these upheavals. Artists, writers, sculptors, musicians, have all suffered. Old men simply cannot understand it. They have never known what it means to have their careers cut short, not once, but frequently, by forces over which they have no control, so that they have suddenly to turn their hands to work for which they are unfitted. The young are utterly unable to realize how sensitive the arts are to economic chaos. It has been said that no arts can flourish except behind well-armed frontiers, and it is perfectly true that art is the first to suffer and the last to recover when financial confidence has disappeared. This may sound as if artists are parasites living on a wealthy and stabilized community, but it is only partly true. All artists are dependent on their patrons. Good singers appear where there is a high standard of singing and a general appreciation of it. Tenors come from Italy not from the Sahara: English music-hall artists come from Lancashire or London; clowns from Milan or Whitechapel; literary men from the middle class; French painters from the rich *bourgeoisie*. When all forms of security leave the ordinary members of the public, interest in the arts dies. Even the theatre suffers, and it is used only as a distraction these days. It is not so much the lack of money, but the lack of interest, which is far more blighting; and I believe this is the reason why so few of the younger men have done any work that really counts.

Practically all the promising ones among our so-called young men, modernists and the others, are as old as myself, if not older. Even Ben Nicholson and Stanley Spencer were my contemporaries before the war at the Slade. T. S. Eliot I distinctly remember as a promising poet during the War. Even the Surrealists were Symbolists in Brussels in 1912. We hear much of modern art and new forms, but actually they have been able to remain modern only because of the stagnation of public opinion, which has allowed Christopher Columbuses like Herbert Read and Grigson to re-discover what the whole art world knew and argued about in the reign of King Edward the Seventh. The most striking example, of course, is Epstein, who in 1910 was doing much the same sort of work as he is doing now; and, after all, that is over a quarter of a century ago. And how well I remember P. Wyndham Lewis stalking up Boulevard Raspail about the same period and telling me how he was trying to make a work of art as hard, as repulsive, and as acid as possible.

After the General Strike the franc was still in our favour,

so I went down to Marseilles to paint, and later to Antibes. My legs were beginning to worry me again and I had the signs of another attack. But we stayed on hopefully. We spent a good deal of our time with Maurice Lane-Norcott, the humorous writer, and Rosemary, his wife. We were also mixed up with the crazy crowd at Juan les Pins. There were Russian princesses and film actresses from Ufa in Berlin : some with diamonds, some with marmosets, some with doves on their heads, some with husbands, some with keepers, and some with a roving eye ; but none with money. At times they professed to give cocktail parties, which in fact had nothing at all to do with them, but were given free by the management to attract more custom or to signalize the opening of yet another bar. There were monocled beachcombers who had a fixed scale for introducing young ladies to peers and millionaires, but who were extremely proud of being of Military rank. The whole place was un-believable, but never dull. There was a sensation when Guevara brought his wife along to the Casino to find us. We had missed them at their villa at Mougins and they had come on later. Guevara's wife was Meraud Guinness, but when they came on us Meraud was dressed like a little *fille de matelotte,* and Guevara was *au rapin.* Some silly English people looked very hot and haughty at the presence of those two tramps at our table, and when the Casino servants bowed low, they muttered among themselves and asked questions. Then Meraud, who had been sitting with her arms folded, stretched out one hand for a cigarette and the other for a glass. I have never seen such a transfiguration as that on the painted faces round me when they saw diamonds and emeralds on those two little hands. Their inquiring dignity changed to amazement and eagerness ; then unfortunately a waiter not only told them who Guevara was, but mentioned the word Guinness. At once it became impossible to sit at the table with all the people round, beaming on us and craning their necks to hear what we said. Meraud was wonderful. She remarked that the people were very dull, and would we go and sit with them else-where ? She took care to let them hear *that.* But English snobs will never learn, and they continued to beam. We left them at once; and, all in a better humour for the change, we ate *soupe de poisson* at Golf Juan in a beach restaurant frequented only by those who know the South.

Oswald Greene came down to join the Leslie Hensons and ourselves, but he was most distracted and prophesied evil for England all day long. The leg had eased somewhat, but I now suffered from a pain in my head. I presumed it to be caused by the glare of the sun, and we returned to London. Little did I realize it was to last for some four years.

To my amazement I discovered I had been elected as a member of the New English Art Club, having been nominated fifteen years before by Augustus John and Muirhead Bone. As a non-member I had been on the hanging committee, but I had almost ceased to think of myself as a candidate for the club. I think no honour gratified me more, and my spirits rose. It was the first time I had ever had any recognition from any established art society, and I no longer felt the outcast of art. The miserable years after the War were at last drawing to a close, and sneers and misrepresentations were dying down. Further, I had at last somewhere to exhibit outside my one-man shows, which are always terrible risks. Inevitably some works detract from others when one has to exhibit as many as thirty pictures. There was also the pleasing thought that the New English had also been lucky to me in selling my work.

I was seeing a good deal of Orpen. Either he would dine with me or we would go to the Berkeley to eat creamed haddock, seemingly his only idea of food. His strange impish humour, combined with his Irish shrewdness, made him the most delightful companion, but there were many sides to his nature. Up at my studio one evening he seemed in the best of spirits while he was quipping and ragging Theo Holland, whom he had known at G.H.Q. He was sitting among 'the lovelies', laughing and joking with everybody. when suddenly the Russian sculptress, Dora Gordine, leaned over to him and said softly: 'Sir Orps, why are you so un'appy?' Orpen was flabbergasted. Then he left us and sat with the Russian, with whom he discussed life with the intensity which one associates only with Russians. It was a queer scene. Instead of leaving at ten, which was his invariable rule, he drove away in his hired Daimler at four in the morning, obsessed by self-pity and behaving like a man who has never been his own master and has missed everything in life.

For some reason that evening seemed to seal our friendship, and often after that he would discuss with me all manner of technical difficulties, and sometimes help me in my painting. I have never known such a complex character. He was a victim of moods and self-conflicts, covered by a mask of flippancy which gave a wrong impression and in which he took a roguish delight. He was a member of the Arts Club, and as I was getting on very well with all kinds of men at the Savage, I thought I should like to join the Arts.

I discussed the matter with Orpen and he readily agreed to propose me, but my candidature had the most direful results. There appeared to be some artists who still bore me ill will, and first of all they suggested that I did porno-graphic work. Orpen wrote to me about this, and fortun-ately I was able to prove it to be a lie. I suppose no man has been more free from that sort of thing, possibly because my life has never been Puritanical. Then, to my amazement, came the old charge invariably made against all men who have attained a certain fame or notoriety. They said I was a pervert, I, of all people ! The charge was really too silly, and of course Orpen should have dealt with it at once and told the committee it was false. Instead, he wanted to go to law.

I stopped him from doing that. As I pointed out, no man of the world could afford to have that kind of nonsense printed in the Press. I don't mind speaking of it now, when every one whose opinion I value knows the charge to be only a shameful blot on the artists who made it, but then it was different. Even if we won the case, the public would say there was no smoke without fire. It was no use expecting the ordinary man to understand the depths of artistic jealousies. Fortunately, Orpen listened to me as I was the man concerned, but he was very bitter about it ever afterwards.

Some member of the Committee told somebody else and the story got round. It was a repulsive time for me, although, to be perfectly fair, I have never heard of anybody who believed it, possibly because it was so well known that I had always been attracted by women. The awful thing is that some modern art is associated with effeminate gentlemen, but why connect all living artists with *them*?

I am glad to say the story caused a great many very distinguished men to stand by me, and I have had the privilege of their friendship ever since. Maxwell Ayrton was one who wrote a most charming letter, and others have urged me to stand again. This I shall not do. I consider that this method of attacking an artist, no matter how much any one disagrees with his ideals or personality, is nothing short of infamous. Most of the men who tried to befoul my reputation are now dead and the story has died with them. I have often been to the Arts Club since as a guest, and one of the most charming things ever said to me was said there. Old Adrian Stokes came over to me. 'Are you Nevinson?' he asked. I said I was. 'Well,' he said, 'it is a lesson to me, even at my age. What a fool I was to believe what an artist said about another man's character. I shall always blame myself for having even listened. Why have I not met you before?'

When he interrupted an Academy banquet and asked that at least one of the speakers should mention English art, I sent him a telegram of congratulation, which he showed proudly to every one.

The Academy itself has altered during the last ten years, and we see a great increase of light and atmosphere and an improvement in draughtsmanship and the study of form. Any change like this is bound in the nature of things to come from the outside and reflects what has taken place throughout the entire world of art. In painting the pitch of colour has altered.

For many years now commerce has made use of the most advanced artists. Before the War Boccioni went to the Isotta

Fraschini motor people to design for them cars which are now known as streamlined. Americans lately told everybody that they had hit on something new, but as it happened they were just twenty years behind the times. It is the same with the films. Who would have thought of attributing all superimposition to Severini ? Yet this is what he was doing in 1912. Germany used his method for photographs, Russia adapted it years later for films, then America copied his technique from them and proclaimed the wonderful new process of super-imposition as another victory for Hollywood. Naturally they had never heard of Severini, but he was the man behind ' their ' idea. Fauvistes were employed by textile manufacturers to design the voiles, brocade and tweeds that modern women wear. Surrealists have designed carpets, while the modern architect and decorator owe much of their inspiration to the advanced school and particularly to Picasso.

Although I hardly dare to prophesy, it is now generally evident that painters of both the younger and the older generation have found neither photographic representation nor dehumanized simplification enough. A more lyrical note can be seen in the world of art ; a more perfect balance is being kept between ugliness and prettiness ; and a wiser and less hysterical outlook is now maintained between representation and unrealistic fantasy.

Throughout this epoch some artists have always been able to be of their epoch yet uninfluenced by art crazes. Augustus John is a genius who at once comes to mind. He is influenced by the tradition of draughtsmanship of the old masters, and, with the exception of Puvis de Chavannes, he has been little affected by the French Impressionists, Post-Impressionists or Cubist schools, except in so far as his colour is on a different scale or pitch from that of the Old Masters. The Impressionists studied light ; but they also studied the colours of the dark, and eliminated the heavy browns and blacks that have come to be associated with the paintings of the Old Masters. Though I am always called a Modern, I have always tried to base myself on John's example.

For the exhibition which I held at the Leicester Galleries at this time I had the honour of a preface by Thomas Earp, reprinted from the *Studio*:

RECENT PAINTINGS BY C. R. W. NEVINSON *

Mr. Nevinson's exhibitions always arouse an expectancy which they can be depended upon to satisfy. With him the increasing experience of life is accompanied by a development in expression; he is constantly widening the field from which vision makes its choice for the purposes of art, and at the same time enlarging the means by which those purposes are effected. Thus his work has the excitement of a successive novelty, where hand and eye work in unity to mark a steady progress in the artist's power. There is no sensation for its own sake, no chasing after a current mode or sporadic efforts at experiment; there is simply the logical growth of an invention and a craftsmanship which gradually gather up more and more material upon which to exercise themselves, and bring on each occasion a greater skill and variety to the process. But although Mr. Nevinson delights in projecting his point of view from fresh angles, and in surprising us by the fertility of his methods in transferring it to the canvas, he remains constant in his fidelity to certain subjects. We can trace in his work a predilection for the spectacle of modern cities, and a keen pre-occupation with their function as time-symbols. He sees them, not as receptacles of isolated examples of the picturesque, but as coherent units significant of the continuity of time. To this we may attribute the tendency of his recent work away from the detached incident or the exceptional appearance towards generalisation and synthesis. The later canvases are at once more compressed and more comprehensive. They have become emotional and epic, where previously their theme was all-sufficient to itself in its instantaneous realism. As a result, their strength of suggestion is immeasurably greater—that suggestion which is the vital property of classic art. In some cases the element of formal pattern is emphasised in them, perspective is summed up by the delimitation of

* Reprinted from the *Studio*, October 1930, by courtesy of the Editor.

planes instead of being graduated, and individual details of shape are reduced to a geometric unity. But such methods carry their conviction with them. They may vaguely be termed modern or cubist, as no doubt Giotto and Poussin were called by some such contemporary equivalents, and it may be remarked in passing that Mr. Nevinson is among the extremely few European artists who have made of this manner in painting something more than a technical exercise, and that with him it has the appropriateness of human expression. That he should have made use of a form which is particularly associated with his period should not deny him a place by the side of the great artists of tradition, for though the language be different, the statement is as clear and enduring as theirs. By the wide and independent survey of which this later work is evidence, he has co-ordinated the peculiar and varied features of his present-day environment into a coherent rendering of appearances which definitely captures a beat in the rhythm of time. He can face the years in safety by virtue of the breadth and intensity with which he has viewed his hour. It may be Fleet Street in the tumult of activity, with the roar of the traffic almost articulate upon the canvas, or the vast pattern of Paris viewed, symbolically enough, from an aeroplane, or one of those permanent moods and intervals of a city, as in the glimpses of Notre-Dame from the quays, which seem invincible against all change—in all these cases Mr. Nevinson portrays the forms created by massed human activity at an especial point in the evolution of the race. But along with this more epic aspect of his recent achievement, one should not lose sight of his happy gift in what might be called the intimate picture, the modern equivalent of the conversation-piece, in which he shows the still-life or the interior instinct with a personal humour, or so charming a psychological subtlety as ' Nothing to lose'. In its recondite emotions, as in its more universal appearances, he has triumphantly proved himself an interpreter of his epoch and a leader of its art.

T. W. EARP

The worry over the Arts Club did nothing to improve

the pain in my head, and although I consulted doctor after doctor I had become the despair of the medical profession. One of my eyes was now becoming useless and I went to see a brain specialist, who calmly assured me I had no tumour on the brain. I was rather startled, as I had never suspected it, but I suppose it was pleasant to know there was nothing wrong there. I was put on a diet of lettuce and Vichy, and this curtailed all my social activities and I was able to paint only with the greatest difficulty. So I took to writing, or rather to dictating articles for the Press, fortunately with ever-increasing demands. This infuriated the writers, who now began to praise me as a painter, and of course artists were no longer able to call me a journalist because I was one. And how polite everybody became! The power of the Press was a revelation to me, and I was invited to be a dead-head at all sorts of functions—political, theatrical, and financial. It was most unfortunate that my lettuce, my Vichy, and my general state of health did not permit me to make the most of my opportunities.

This journalism took me to Paris, and once I happened to be dining at the Tour d'Argent with my dear friend Francis Berry, the wine merchant and picture buyer, when who should come in but Germaine, a French girl I had known for years. She was a very intelligent girl and the mistress of a Senator, and when she told me that England was bound to go off gold in the autumn I was more than interested. I have always listened to the mistresses of French politicians.

Nobody had any idea, as early as June, that England was in real difficulties. 'If Germaine gives England until the autumn,' I said, 'it may be years before we can afford to travel again on the pound. Let's go to Venice. It was the first place to inspire me to be an artist and it may be the last.' Ill as I was, we went, and I did some of the best paintings I have ever done and sold them at Pittsburg. Sure enough, *The Times* began telling us in Venice that Germaine was right and that England was going wrong. We got back to London just in time, four days before the pound crashed.

My friendship with Wells became strained because of this journalistic phase. Once I was walking down Fleet Street and I met an international banker named Singer. Naturally we spoke of the political situation and I told him what I had heard months before in Paris. He said gold was pouring out of the country and that the Government was hard pressed to find the money for the unemployed. We could look for trouble if there was no dole. Half an hour later I met Wells in Bond Street and I mentioned to him what the banker had just said to me. Wells dismissed it as rubbish and said that even with that vain man Ramsay nothing was going to happen, although in a year or two he thought we should be defending our potatoes. At lunch I met Reggie Pound, who was then Literary Editor of the *Express*. When I repeated my morning conversations he offered me an article on it, and, I gather, invited Wells to write, too. I quoted Wells in mine and had a telegram from him saying he had no idea he was being interviewed. This is an example of the way an amateur journalist gets himself into trouble. Wells might not have spoken to a newspaperman as he did to me, and my last intention was to offend him. However, it was a lesson to me.

Then came pleurisy, culminating in pneumonia that nearly ended my life. The telephone was at my bedside, and in order that I should not be disturbed we were supposed to be cut off from all incoming calls. One night, however, when the night nurse had gone out of the room the bell rang. Instinctively I reached out my hand.

' Yes,' I quavered.

' Daily Blank speakin',' announced a very Cockney voice. ' Is 'e gone yet ? '

It hurt me to laugh and I maintained my gravity by thinking they should not have left it to the office boy.

' No,' I said. ' He's still with us.'

I then said that the patient had expressed a desire that certain matters should be remembered in his obituary notice, and I dictated a paragraph which the voice assured me it had taken down. I wished him ' Good-bye '.

'Good-bye,' said the voice. 'An' if 'e goes within the next hour give's a scoop, will yer?'

I promised to do my best in difficult circumstances, and rang off. I recovered, thereby proving I was no heavy drinker. I was by no means out of the wood, however; and when I tried to get back to work was in a state of despair because my hand seemed to have lost its cunning and I was doing work that would have shamed an amateur, I suddenly felt like a corpse and coughed up blood and more blood. I was then suspected of T.B., but the X-ray and the blood tests proved it was only a hole in my lung caused by an abscess. This was risky, as it might become infected, so I was sent out of London to live in the fresh air, and ordered to do no work whatever.

I felt my days were numbered, so I promptly bought a new car which I christened the hearse, and spent money like a fool. I became so bored doing nothing that I took on the whole *menage* of our bungalow at Shepperton; we entertained a lot. I cooked all the meals, did everything in fact. This not only put in my time but gave my wife a much-needed rest, as she was exhausted after the months of sick nursing and anxiety. I was deeply touched by a queer thing that happened then. One day a chauffeur arrived and pushed an envelope through the letter-box. It was an anonymous letter wishing me a speedy recovery, and inside were fifty pounds in bank-notes. I was honoured by letters from the King, the Queen, the Prime Minister, and all kinds and conditions of people from every class, from peers to pot-men, from princesses to prostitutes, congratulating me on my recovery. I had no idea that bulletins had been published in the Press.

Just as my convalescence was becoming assured, I was greatly shocked by the complete breakdown of my Mother, who tried in a moment of mental disorder to take her life. She recovered, but only to be the victim of hallucination, with periods of complete clarity. Her most distressing delusion was that people in the Tate Gallery and Wyndham Lewis were trying to murder me, a state of mind which showed how deeply she had felt my treatment, and in my weak condition I was so overwrought that I had difficulty in retaining my own reason. To see this strong mind groping in the darkness was dreadful. Fortunately, she died.

The weeks following were hateful to me. My Mother had been much in my life. It was some consolation to know that she had been beloved by some of the noblest thinkers in the land, and that her erudition, her wit, her integrity, and the life which she had devoted to great causes, had not been as wasted as she thought.

18

As I still had to live out of town, we continued our life on the river at Shepperton, but we could not complain that we were dull. At times things became even dramatic, and particularly so when my nurse was very nearly drowned before our eyes at a crowded regatta. She was rescued by the Russians who lived next door, and this led to hilarious nights and general absurdities. Farther upstream were Mr. and Mrs. Wolfe. He was chairman of the O.P. Club and kept open house for people connected with the theatre. His duties kept the neighbourhood lively.

Constant Lambert would come down to stay with us, and he would swim violently up-river, doing imitations of Rhine Maidens with Wagnerian gurgles complete, and he seemed to spend the rest of his time copying out orchestra scores in a confusion of noise. Often Wolfe's parties would join ours, or ours would join theirs, and there was a continuous companionship that made me lose my sense of forlornness. Cedric Hardwicke was a great swimmer, and through him and Wolfe's contact with the Malvern Festival I again met Eileen Beldon, now an actress, whom I had known when she was a child in the Isle of Man. Edna Davies, the film actress, was often there, too. She had been stricken down by T.B. It was ideal for me, as we were all of us determined to be light-hearted, although some of us felt pretty desperate.

In August I was invited to stay with Dr. Harris in Wales, but I had not been there more than a few days when I began to feel ill again, and one morning I woke up knowing I was in for serious trouble. As Harris's daughter was already ill, I telephoned to London to say I would be home in the evening. I left in agony, and drove like a madman, hoping to reach Cheltenham and get to hospital before I collapsed. At Cheltenham I determined to get as far as Oxford. At Oxford I decided to make a dash for London. My medical knowledge was enough to tell me that something awful was happening in my stomach, and I drove at a desperate speed, unable to use my left leg for the last hundred miles, so that I had to use my right leg for declutching and to brake by hand. One of my ancestors, Swift Nick Nevinson, the highwayman, did the famous ride on a horse from London to York, but my drive from Carmarthen to London with an abdominal abscess I consider to be a greater family achievement. When I reached my studio in Hampstead I was in a state of collapse.

Doctors and surgeons were sent for, and I was removed to a nursing home at once for an operation. I had driven all that way with an abcess on the peritoneum. Once again I did my dying act, and for ten days they could not tell whether or not the operation had been successful. I was threatened with peritonitis and suffered the agonies of the damned. As usual, I recovered, but this time very slowly; and when I was X-rayed once again to discover the cause of the abcess it was found that I had diverticulitis.

While I was ill I had the honour of being made a member of the Royal Society of British Artists, and a little later I became a member of the Royal Institute of Oil Painters. I was also elected President of the National Society. I was proud and most pleased about the National Society, as I had been one of the founders. It was a sort of ' united front ' that was trying to amalgamate all forms of artistic thought into one group, as many of us believed it was time to bridge the gulf, largely artificial, which existed between various contemporary artists.

I still think this exhibition one of the liveliest in London, though for some reason the critics detest it. This may be because it is the first society that has been formed since before the War. It makes no attempt to distinguish between the academic and the unacademic, and unfortunately so much of art is considered to-day in the terms of political parties, Right or Left, and so many artists are regarded as agitators on the one hand, or as reactionaries on the other.

My health would not permit me to make the most of the honours that had been bestowed on me, but in spite of my physical incapacity I attended all the hanging committees to which I had been elected, and suddenly I found myself famous among artists as a hanger of pictures. I do believe I have exerted an influence on the general appearance of contemporary exhibitions. My chief innovation has been to raise the height of the line. Artists are so terrified of being skied that year after year the line became lower, with the result that many pictures were nearly touching the floor, a position in which no picture is ever seen in a private house. I usually put pictures well above the line. I never look at the names of the artists, but try to make some arrangement through colour and size, and make as many centres as possible. It has also been my experience that artists are far too touchy about being hung in a corner. Pictures often sell in a corner, while centring pleases the painter but seems to repel the purchaser. An exhibition should look pleasant to come in to, and this is of far greater importance to the artists than the position of individual painters, for both the critics and the public are unconsciously charmed.

The great difficulty in modern art is to fight the antagonism people feel towards pictures. The curse of many modern paintings has been that they have aroused so much hatred and fury. People hardly expect nowadays to enjoy a picture, and it is treated as a problem. Far too much has been written about painting, so the average man has become frightened of it. People say, 'I understand nothing about painting.' Why should they? One does not go to the ballet to understand it. Nor is it the business of a theatre audience to understand the intricacies of elocution, movement, or Delsart. It is unnecessary to understand the workings of Gigli's larynx or breath control or his method of using his nasal passages as a sound box, in order to appreciate him.

Taste can never come from understanding about technique. Every one knows that too much knowledge of 'backstage' destroys all pleasure in the drama. In the case of art writing, most critics have little knowledge of technique, and I should hate to say how often in my own case they have failed to distinguish between an etching and a lithograph, although no one is more of a purist than myself in the matter of medium. Many a time, too, a tempera has been described as an oil because the critic has failed to take Whistler's advice to smell the difference. Again, the confusing of pastel and water-colour is pathetic; and this is only the A B C of technique.

Not long ago I was speaking to an experienced salesman of pictures at a famous exhibition, and when I remarked on the large attendance and the increase of sales he told me that since the death of Fry artists have sold better. He said so many customers came to him in the past and said, ' If Fry is right, then I am wrong. I have lost interest in pictures and am buying no more.' He went on to say that although Konody was a fine fellow he had the same effect. No wonder the art clubs of Chelsea, St. John's Wood and London were so relieved when they died. I was a little shocked, not merely because I had always liked Konody and disliked Fry, but because it was such an awful end to two lives which artists apparently regarded as parasitic. I still think both Fry and Konody loved art and really had no intention of ruining the livelihoods of artists by the setting up of theories as standards by which pictures must be judged.

George Bernard Shaw annoyed me by writing a stupid attack on artists, in which he accused us of being drunkards and drug-takers, driven to suicide through our own futility. He asserted that no artist should ask more than five pounds for any picture. I have been up to Shaw since childhood, when my Mother told me of a strange, pale-faced man who haunted the reading-room of the British Museum dressed in a jaeger suit and a red beard. When it comes to his own business, he knows it, but his hatred of beauty and artists always has made him talk nonsense.

It was suggested that I should reply to him in the *Daily Mail*. They asked me not to go for him too much as he was a very old man. The gist of my article was that it was no wonder Shaw was a Socialist because he was suggesting that we should sell pictures below the cost of production. It occurs to few people that quite a small picture is an expensive undertaking, even if no models are used. I mentioned that Shaw was getting on in years and was probably out of touch with modern conditions, and I instanced the rise in the prices of materials necessary for painting a canvas. Baroness Orczy wrote to the paper to say Shaw was really a very young man, so Charles Graves went round to interview him. Shaw simply told him that if we two walked down Bond Street together he would be taken for my son. I replied that he was now so childish that his remark was tragically true.

Every one seemed to enjoy the battle, and I found myself the recipient of hundreds of letters, not only from every kind of artist including R.A.s but from literary men, politicians, and people who were wearied of the babbling which Shaw was inflicting on us. It seemed to infuriate people to think that while Shaw had made a fortune out of books and the theatre, he would stoop to say things of artists, and make accusations that could apply equally to actors or writers. It was high time somebody attacked him.

When I went down to Nice I found Frank Harris in ecstasy, the naughty old man, because somebody had stood up to Shaw.

' He must be getting old to have shown his chin like that,' he said. ' He was asking for a knock-out. Of course he always hated artists and was suspicious of beauty. It's the bourgeois in him—the Irish Protestant bourgeois. George Barnum Shaw, that's what he is.'

Yet, for all that, Harris seemed to love Shaw and was writing his life. Shaw wrote to him almost daily, telling him exactly what to say. I am sure Frank Harris was as bad as he was painted, but I enjoyed the downy old bird, and I know I brightened his life, which was then drawing to a close. He was quite frank about himself, and he told me one story which I believe is new.

After coming out of gaol he decided that he would rather commit suicide than go in again; and as he always had a contempt for Court orders and ignored everything, he felt liable to arrest at any moment. So that he might not again suffer indignity, he carried with him a small packet of cyanide of potassium, which he proposed to swallow before the hand of the Law could touch him.

On his last trip to New York he was packing up at quarantine when a steward came along and told him he was wanted by the captain. Harris's heart fell. Here it was. He concealed the packet of poison in his right hand and followed the steward, and when he saw the captain talking to a tall, smooth, well-fed man he knew it could only be the worst.

'You wanted me,' gulped Frank.

The captain inclined his head towards the third man, who was eyeing Frank keenly.

'Mr. Frank Harris?' asked the American.

Frank wished he wasn't, but admitted the stigma.

'Pleased to meet you, Mr. Harris,' said the large man, extending his hand. 'I'm the mayor, and I've come right off in a tug-boat to tell you that because of the great work you have done we are honoured to offer you the freedom of our great city.'

Hastily Frank changed the poison packet into his left hand and greeted the mayor.

The last I saw of Frank Harris was at a lunch he was giving to a rich woman gambler who lived in the Hotel de Paris at Monte Carlo. He had written an introduction to her book, which seemed to consist largely of her troubles with gigolos; the fact that she disliked boating on the smelly canals of Venice, but thought the Lido simply gorgeous, especially when the orchestra from Antibes arrived; and how on her return to her beloved home, the Hotel de Paris, she had found the garden replanted, and her Pekinese had been terribly upset by the loss of some shrubs. Harris said it was a grand book. I am sure he was going to borrow money from her; but when I left she was using his car and chauffeur, eating his exquisite lunches, and drinking his champagne. She was Scotch.

The trouble about my breeze with Bernard Shaw was that I was always being asked to attack various institutions even more British than Shaw, and when sometimes I did consent to speak the audience went away disappointed because I had not been sufficiently bellicose. My last public appearance at that time was at a luncheon given by the Happy Thought

Society. Every one wished happy thoughts to every one else. How touched some of my detractors must have been when they heard of it.

The next day I went down with a return of my abdominal trouble and I lay in agony for weeks. It could not be decided at once whether or not I should undergo a very serious major operation. One great doctor took my X-ray photographs to no less than seventeen other doctors before he told me that if I wished to have it done I must settle up my affairs. He was a brother Savage and hardly charged me anything at all for the enormous amount of trouble he took. I should like to record here the extraordinary generosity I have received from the medical profession. Once a surgeon who operated on me paid for my anaesthetist. I detest that silly public that talks as though the medical profession regarded disease as an opportunity for grabbing money. I am a triumph of science. I could hardly tell how many doctors of all kinds I have been under, how modest their charges have been, and of the trouble they have taken day and night, even cancelling their holidays. The Medical Association permits the mention of no names. As a patient I know more about Doctors than Dr. Cronin.

At last it was decided that I might live without an operation, provided I observed the strictest rules, ate no vegetables, no health foods, and freed myself from all anxiety. Travel was forbidden, and I was to hang around, ready to be rushed off to hospital for an operation, if necessary, at a moment's notice. As I was confined to barracks, I began painting again. I was suffering from abdominal shock and I had swallowed lots of belladonna and other pain-killing drugs, and as a result my pictures of this period have a weird quality. I became obsessed by suicidal tendencies. For some months I would keep looking at the beam in my studio and arrange the drop for hanging myself, and I would go off absent-mindedly and sniff the gas, morbidly wondering what it would feel like. Then the telephone would go and some-body would ring up to say he was very down in the mouth and would I go and buck him up, as my laugh always did him good. Since that hateful time when I was humiliated at the Burlington House Exhibition of British War Paintings,

I have worn a grinning mask. Originally I adopted it as a form of defence, well knowing that laughter is always hated by the English intellectual and detested by the nonconformist critics who hide their trivialities behind much bemoaning and groaning. This probably accounts for the fact that while my work was becoming increasingly serious in philosophical content, most of my friends and acquaintances were clowns, professional and otherwise.

I was overwhelmed by the stupidity of Europe, which allows itself to be governed by braggarts and grabbers who are not merely preparing for another slaughter, but are using all the arts to distort truth, and all methods of reproduction to misinform. Liberty of thought has been killed and youth has been regimented. All Europe and Russia is whispering behind its hand. What hope lies in the immediate future? My chief objection to modern art is its horrible uniformity, of which the younger generation seems unaware. My creed has always been that the only value in art is individuality, not merely of technique, but of personal outlook and choice of subject, with its emotional reactions. There are cases where the personality of the artist is so strong that it is almost impossible to look at Nature except through his eyes. If we look at a ballet girl by Degas, a circus scene by Picasso, or twilight on the Thames by Whistler, we see how they exemplify Oscar Wilde's belief that Nature imitates Art.

I am always glad I fell under the influence of the Cubists and the Futurists when I was a very young man, and I am still more glad I did not lose my head. Undoubtedly the Cubists strengthened my work, and without them I now know it would have become increasingly flaccid, formless, and undisciplined through lack of design. I have a tendency, too, to over-elaborate, particularly form, and Cubism taught me to simplify. The greatest classical ideal to strive after is that of Pericles—beauty with simplicity, and culture without effeminacy. Though I am aware that I am called a modern artist, I consider myself an academic one; and by that I do not necessarily mean a Pompier or French Salon artist, who are not, in my opinion, traditional painters but merely carry on something which was established just before the French revolution. They were official painters, and they concerned themselves with the outlook of the Court or the milord, who introduced a Neo-Classicism as a result of the culture acquired during the Grand Tour.

I am modern only in the sense that Barbizon or Impressionist painters were, insomuch as they concerned themselves with contemporary life as lived by the vast majority, and not with an artificial coterie of aristocratic patronage. Although art critics never mention this, it was the Barbizon painters who were the cause of the first revolution in art; by painting Workers' in plain air then came the Impressionist painting the Bourgeoise in atmospheres; and the second one resulted from the attempt to express the possible liaison between the arts and our present-day mechanical ambience. Ruskin and Morris were merely attempting to put back the clock. We must accept our own age as it is. Our business is to beautify mechanical invention in every possible way, so that it will cease despoiling our lives, as it has done ever since we discovered a use for steam. The Greek ideals which have influenced the world are not dead and man will always demand something better than quick transit and hygienic comfort. Even America no longer idealizes the plumber as the symbol of civilization.

Not long ago a supercilious art critic informed me that I was more of a sociologist than a painter. I replied that I could not paint unless I believed that art supplied something more than pictures to decorate drawing-rooms. The tendency of late has been to regard all art as a drawing-room affair, out of touch with the ghastly aftermath of the last War. There is a general adoration for purely destructive things such as State and Sport. One kills man, the other kills time. Grossly encouraged by the State, Sport is encouraged because it produces soldiers, destroys integrity, and encourages that reckless optimism which is the fundamental cause of gambling. In passing, although I have met all manner of men, I have never trusted a man who proclaimed himself a sportsman.

I was still unable to go about and see people and I became a wireless fiend. On this invention I call down blessings, yet I fear it for two reasons. The first is that I am horrified when day after day I hear news blandly radiated of persecution and tyrannies that would have shamed the inquisition. I have seen death and torture, as other men of the War generation have, and I am appalled by the attitude of those people who hear the news grow worse and worse and yet don't care where we are drifting. The announcer is permitted to put no feeling into his voice, and as he tells us like a speaking machine of some animal behaviour of a great European figure, contemporary man fills another pipe and waits for the football or cricket results. We hear a great deal about the terrors of modern invention, with its power of indiscriminate slaughter, but what terrifies me far more is the modern mind.

The second reason why I fear the wireless is because broadcasting has made dictatorship possible. During the course of an election in the old days, a man was able to cover only a certain amount of ground, and it was impossible for him to make himself known to all the people. Consequently, there were always some people who opposed him, and we were certain of our minorities. But nowadays the Duce, the Führer, and the President of the United States can speak in every home every day if he wants to. If he has what they call a wireless personality he can wipe out all opposition and permit no one else to speak. Mussolini did it, Hitler did it, and Roosevelt could do it. To me minorities should be given a hearing in the State.

A discussion of these things led me to co-operate on a novel with Princess Troubetzkoy which dealt with third dimensional warfare on London. The book, entitled " Exodus ", was published too soon. If it had appeared now it might have been more in tune with public opinion, which at last is beginning to realize that space has shrunk and that industrial areas are vulnerable and the exodus of cities are more dangerous than gas and it prevents movement of troops.

Soon after the book was published I was asked to attend a lunch at which I was to help judge Strube's cartoons for some competition in the *Daily Express*. I sat between the editor, Beverley Baxter, and George Robey, and the other guests were Lady Snowden and Gordon Selfridge. Strube, of course, did not appear—dear, modest ' George ', and the luncheon party was made up by other members of the staff. George Robey told me a story which was certainly Robey-esque, then he turned straight to Lady Snowden and said, ' You can't take your daughter to the theatre nowadays. They're too immoral.' Lady Snowden acquiesed, but with-out much conviction, and Robey went on with his high moral talk. Impressed by his desire to protect his daughter, I men-tioned the fact that it had given me pleasure to hang one of her paintings well at the New English, but he turned to me sharply and replied : ' My daughter ? I haven't seen her for ages.'

I have often noticed this extraordinary lack of humour in comedians. Not long after this I met Charlie Chaplin again at one of Selfridges election parties. He was surrounded, as usual, by high-brows and sycophants, and I did not care to barge in, as I knew he was bothered by all sorts of people who all claimed to have known him in the ' Mumming Birds ' days.

However, Charlie remembered me, and just as I was shaking hands with him the news came through that Ellen Wilkinson had been defeated. I stopped and cheered delightedly. He did not hesitate to take me to task.

' I should have thought you were above that sort of thing,' he said in the most didactic manner. ' I understand you are now a successful artist, and I should have thought your sense of humour would not allow you to cheer at an election result.'

I am afraid I laughed, and I explained that I was cheering only for a personal reason.

' Besides,' I went on to say, ' you above all men should realize that no successful man has a sense of humour.'

After that it was like one of Charlie's films. He followed me about all over the place trying to explain himself, but I only laughed the more. It was fun being able to say that to the greatest clown the world has ever seen, but nevertheless there is a certain truth behind it. The man with a sense of humour often achieves little because of it. To succeed one must take oneself seriously, and I can imagine nothing more grotesque than that. This explains why heads of State make up in solemnity what they lack in brain power.

It was at one of those Selfridge election parties that Max Beerbohm was heard to make one of his delightful remarks. He and his wife had been asked to come to the party, which was attended by nearly all London. There were beautiful girls from the stage, striking ladies from the film studios, and others both beautiful and striking from addresses Mayfair.

He looked gravely round at the faces near him. All were painted, not with the art that conceals art, but with the determination to gain attention. This elderly exquisite looked again and shuddered, then he turned to his wife.

' My dear,' he said. ' You are looking so charming to-night that I simply must talk to you.'

19

In my fight against ill health, I came to regard myself as being as strong as other people and suddenly decided to defy the restrictions put on me and to risk travelling. I got to Paris, only to be taken very ill, and all I could do was to lie in the hotel bedroom and long for my surgeon again. I had counted on flying, but a gale blew with such violence that all services were stopped. That taught me a lesson, and when I got back alive I did not venture from my studio for some time, but worked for my new show at the Leicester Galleries.

This show was not a success. It was confused in outlook, and I, the famous hanger, made the great mistake of hanging too many pictures. But apart from that, everything seemed to go wrong. No doubt my illness made it difficult for the dealers to work with me, and I have found that co-operation between the artist and the dealer is the first essential for an exhibition. Moreover, I was no longer on terms with the picture buyers, the general public, or the Press.

People seldom realize the things an artist has to do besides paint pictures, especially to-day when there are hundreds of exhibitions. Unless an artist is in the swim he does not sell his pictures, and people do not even go to see them. The result of this exhibition was heart-breaking to me, as up to this time the Leicester Galleries had always sold my work very well, and on occasions had sold every picture on show.

On the top of this disappointment I went down again with pleurisy. I decided to reorganize my life. I could not go on as I was doing; I was a physical wreck incapable of work. It is impossible for an artist to leave a great city and bury himself in the country if he wants to live by selling pictures. So, trembling, I bought myself a second-hand caravan trailer, intending to camp within easy reach of London and spend as much time as I could living and sleeping in the fresh air. I could then feed on food it would be impossible to obtain in any English hotel, and use my studio when I wanted it.

This has been the turning-point of my life, as far as health goes, and I live in this way both summer and winter. I had been uncertain of the winter until I heard from Peggy Wyatt that a caravan was one of the few places in which one could keep really warm. This mode of life has entirely revived me, and there is no time for introspection or brooding. Every year we go farther and farther afield. I always return to London with dread, but in time I shall cure myself of that. I avoid all artists, and also all those people who in public places are to be found eternally discussing art and never spending any money on it and whose love of art seems to consist of living in rooms of unqualified hideousness with bare walls. I never so much as glance at my Press cuttings; and except for a few intimate friends and the men at the Savage, I associate only with strangers who do not know what I am. I remember my Father telling me that one of the reasons he was opposed to my becoming an artist was because it was a wretchedly lonely life. How right he was. Actors, musicians, architects, doctors, all have work to do with others, but a painter is essentially isolated. Half the bitterness for which sculptors and painters are notorious is due to the fact that the very nature of their work makes them isolated for long periods.

My life in the caravan has put me in closer touch with Nature than ever before, and, curiously enough, I have experienced far less loneliness. People will come to a caravan who would never come near a little country house or an hotel. The change for the better in my health has shown in my work; and when I had my exhibition at Coolings, Earp told me my pictures were by far the best I had ever done. He and Greig have often disliked my work, but those two are the only critics of knowledge and taste now writing for the Press or the wireless, and I regard criticism as a great art. I wrote this preface for the catalogue of the exhibition:

I suppose I should, but I will not, apologize for the fact that I

*am English, and that my name is Nevinson and not Nevinso ;
nevertheless, I hope this collection of paintings will prove at least
that I wish thoroughly to dissociate myself from all geometric
mumbo-jumbo, mathematical metaphysics, the pretentious Bloomsbury Belles, and affreux Intelligentsia, the New Shy, the Biblical
Commentators, and all the Illustrators of Art Theorists and Literary
Critics, who write endlessly on painting and aesthetics, and the pure,
pure art of the coca pinks and the chocolate browns ; abstract art
and geometric art, whether Jewish, Puritan, Mohammedan or
Persian, comes from the observance of the Second Commandment.
I am catholic, and therefore I have no fear of imagery in art.*

*The History of English Art is glorious, as it is and was, always
breaking away from the ' studiotic ', and from dead formulae, finding
refreshment in nature and its study. I am trying to follow in this
tradition, and I defy the myopic, city, one-room minds of the mid-
European or the flâneur of Paris.*

*I detest the cult of the ugly-ugly, the nonconformist, the esoteric,
the vulgar Parisian racket, and commercial exploitation of the
' misunderstood '.*

*The dreary, bare walls of to-day are due to intellectual prigs
writing and writing that painting is too difficult to be understood by
any but the writer and his tiny clique of ' superior persons '. For the
complete enjoyment of any art, knowledge of its works or backstage
is dangerous. Pictures are painted to be looked at, not explained ;
and nearly all rooms are better for a picture or two.*

CHRISTOPHER RICHARD WYNNE NEVINSON

This exhibition included a portrait of the Hon. Mrs. Baillie-
Hamilton. As a consequence, a new road seemed to open
up for me and I have since then had many requests for portraits. It is not a life I care to adopt, because sitters so often
have such strange preconceived notions of themselves, and
their relations have more curious ones still. I can well understand Sargent's bitter saying: ' Every time I paint a portait
I lose a friend.' One realizes the gulf that photography has
made between portraiture and the sitter. Modern photography is so unrealistic, and those strange girls who sit at the
back of a photographic studio and fillet a face they have never
seen have altered the entire conception of likeness. Orpen

has discussed this with me, and he agreed that the fact that the camera always lies, and so would make Holbein or Valasquez impossible as Court painters to-day. The moderns seem unable to see themselves as they really are. The medievals were under no delusions.

Major Holden, the stepfather of Wanda Baillie-Hamilton, was chiefly responsible for making this last exhibition of mine a success. Its first week had been ruined by the General Election, which had descended on us after all the arrangements had been made, so he gave the portrait a party. It was one of the most remarkable parties ever held in Bond Street. There were the new M.P.s, lords and ladies gay, great scientists, doctors, actors, actresses, writers, critics, connoisseurs, and millionaires. I would like to pay a tribute to Coolings for the way they stood up to it. The Embassy Club, which did the catering, was not quite accustomed to dealing with the great ones of journalism and the arts and to dispensing free drinks. Yet things went well, and I sold three-quarters of my work.

This friendship I formed with Major Holden began when I asked permission to pitch my caravan on his aerodrome at Norton Priory. I think he has helped me to grow up more than any man I have ever met. It was a delight to talk to him. After all the intellectuals I have known, with their tendency to mistake wishes for facts, muddles for achievement, and with all their queer views on economics, political situations, and international affairs, it was such a pleasure to meet a man with a real knowledge of what was going on, a gift for being able to explain the most intricate problems, which are the fundamental cause of the chaos of the world to-day, and an uncanny intuition in the affairs of men.

I was asked to be the guest of Lord Hyndley at a dinner which was to be given to Ramsay MacDonald. I did not quite know why I was asked, but I went. After the Archbishop of Canterbury had spoken, he was followed by the President of the Royal Academy, and then Ramsay made an eloquent and a noble speech, which he said would probably be his swan-song. The theme was, roughly, that now was the time to bury polemics because of the very real dangers that were ahead: it was most impressively done. After the banquet I went round to thank the President for his speech, and I said I thought it was time for me to take heed of Ramsay's warning and for my part to bury all polemics. Some Academicians then chaffed me about my attitude to the Royal Academy, and accused me of growing old and not moving with the times. They said that whatever objection I had to the Academy twenty-five years ago no longer held, that it was now representative of contemporary painting, except for merely freakish work—which I dislike as much as any one— and that the young men were taking advantage of the change while I behaved with middle-aged prejudice.

When I got home I wondered if I should try my luck. Up to the very last moment for sending in I could not decide, and then, nearly too late, I sent three pictures. I had one rejected and two hung on the line. I was delighted.

Personally, I feel that rows between artists do no good to art. They are incomprehensible to the public and they weaken both sides. The present condition of civilization makes it imperative that culture should be strengthened, even by the humblest. Until the modern mind learns to respect those who are trying to construct or create, rather than those who grab and destroy, there is no hope for Western civilization. It is terrible to contemplate how the prestige built up by the giants of the Victorian intellectuals has been thrown away by their successors, and it is the cultured people who are the most to blame. No doubt there was some pomposity in the behaviour of our immediate predecessors; but the reduction of all our writers and thinkers to pigmy size, started by Lytton Strachey, has been the feature of this epoch. I am sure their inability to face facts, or their dislike for doing so, is largely responsible for the very second-rate quality of those men who now lead the thought and action of the various nations.

I shall never live to see it, but on all sides I can sense the reaction coming in the hearts of men and the rebellion growing in the minds of all educated people against this destructionalism which permeates painting and all the other expressions of man. We have pulled down enough. We are beginning to distinguish between threadbare convention and the solid truths which are the foundation of tradition. Let us leave it at that. The Surrealists prove this to be the exhaustion of sensationalism, culminating in a vulgarity, regimentation of affectation, and mutilation that can please only the little minds who have obviously never known pure aesthetic emotion, but mere jaded theory. It was a phase that had to be lived through, and it has thwarted me a thousand times. I was meant to achieve something and not to rebel, and yet I seem to have been always forced into the position of a rebel, and I am quite unable to agree with those who want revolution for revolution's sake.

Flower painting has fascinated me, and when I held an exhibition my wife wrote this preface:

Women are said by those who know, to be by nature promiscuous. I solved the problem by marrying six men at one ceremony, but nothing surprised me more than when I discovered that one of them studied the habits of wild birds, and knew a great deal about flowers and botany. I knew my husband to be a painter, writer, mechanic, carpenter, and cook, well up in English and French politics, absorbed in backstage, with a restless mind incessantly devouring and memorizing intellectual theory, scientific fact, or general information, and hands capable of almost any kind of finesse : but I know that he is much more fond of Nature than he ever allows it to be known, and I am particularly grateful that Mr. Lockett Thomson has made him concentrate and produce an exhibition of a subject he so much loves.

Purely as a professional gardener, I do so appreciate the living quality of his flowers and the knowledge of their growth and species ; such a change from the glutinous blobs of rose madder applied to palette scrapings, without either form or design, and described not only as roses but as exquisite quality of paint. I hope I am not too much of a botanist, but it is irritating to see flowers of four petals painted casually with five or six, and then definitely named : it makes me suspect some artists must have as defective eyesight as some critics.

To those dear people who may think it pretentious of me to write a preface to this catalogue, I can but plead that many of the arrangements in nature were designed with my co-operation.

KATHLEEN NEVINSON, F.R.H.S.

The show was a failure, as King George V died on the day after the private view. National calamities always hit the arts first, and painting most of all. Nobody came to see my flowers. Nobody was expected. And so the hopes of two years withered and died.

After a quarter of a century as a professional painter, it is now obvious that some of my work has survived far longer than I ever expected it to. I have sold hundreds, if not thousands, of pictures, and I presume I have given pleasure to the purchasers, because, thank God, very few of them have ever come to that knacker's yard, the auction room. I wish I could meet my audiences, but I am prevented from knowing who buys my work. Dealers naturally keep patrons to themselves so as to retain the 25 per cent to 33⅓ per cent charged to artists on sales.

My prices have always been humble, but it has been possible up to the present to lead the life of a millionaire. Far from being a starving artist, a great deal of my time has been taken up in refusing food and drink, affaires with exquisite women, and wonderful offers of travel or hospitality. But I have always been driven mad by the itch to paint. Painting has caused me unspeakable sorrows and humiliations, and I frankly loathe the professional side of my life. I am indifferent to fame, as it only causes envy or downright insult. I know the necessity of publicity in order to sell pictures, because the public would never hear of you or know what you were doing unless you told them of it. But publicity is a dangerous weapon, double-edged, often causing unnecessary hostility and capable of putting you into the most undignified positions. Until of late I have had to fight an entirely lone hand. When I exhibited at the Royal Academy it was a revelation to me how well the publicity was done through the dignity of an institution rather than through the wits of an individual. But I suppose that now I shall always remain the lone wolf. I have been misrepresented so much by those who write on art that the pack will never accept me. Incidentally, because I painted I have earned something like thirty thousand pounds for the critics, curators, or parasites of art. Ninety per cent of their writings has consisted of telling the public not to buy my pictures and of charging me with every form of charlatanism, incompetency, ignorance, madness, degeneracy, and decadence. It is useless to deny that this has had its effect.

However, at last I begin to see signs that this fog is lifting. I have been re-elected a member of the Chelsea Arts Club, through the kindness of Rushbury, Barney Seale, and Dyson; I was even so far honoured as to be asked to do the decoration for one of their Balls at the Albert Hall.

Francis Dodd wrote me the following letter:

MY DEAR NEVINSON,

I boldly put down your name on the candidature list for the R.A. yesterday, but I now realize that I ought to have asked you first and obtained your consent. . . . I need not say what an advantage I think your presence would be to the Academy, nor how much I admire the way you have made a style for yourself. This you know already, but I should like you to agree to let your name go forward, and I will then get the other necessary names to support your candidature as soon as I can.

Believe me

Yours faithfully,

FRANCIS DODD

Sir Muirhead Bone has since written to the *Sunday Dispatch* -

SIR,

Mr. C. R. W. Nevinson in his interesting reminiscences in the *Sunday Dispatch*, makes a reference to myself which pains me acutely, even after some twenty years, for I am still ashamed of myself having referred in an unkind and quite unjust way to his large war picture now in the Imperial War Museum.

I am sorry he did not mention that I called on him the

next day (after an unhappy night), and apologized to the best of my ability.

One sees more clearly now in retrospect that Mr. Nevinson's war pictures were a bold and thoroughly interesting grappling with a most difficult subject matter, and are important contributions to the history of that time. Soldiers have told me indeed that his pictures conveyed to them the particular feeling of trench life better than any. He may rest assured that he had, and has, many admirers.

MUIRHEAD BONE

On all sides I see prejudice disappearing, and my paint being more appreciated, and I hope that this book will do a little to reveal me as I am—as Harry Tate described me: ' A pretty talker, because you think glum no wonder you laugh.'

And how I laugh at pale intellectualism, bellicose pacifists, internationalists who hate the English, and the aesthetic ugly-uglies !

After all my agonizing experience I can now reach a definition of beauty. Prettiness is caused by the under-accentuation of form, the under-statement of scene or character, and the modification of colour. Ugliness is caused by over-accentuation, distortion, or lack of proportion. And Beauty is the exact tight-rope act between the two. Experimentation is the cause of all regeneracy in art; an endless repetition of tradition the cause of its decadence. Nevertheless, many an old-fashioned picture is infinitely finer than those painted for mere experimental purposes. I consider there are only two kinds of art. To quote Goethe when he was asked about classic and romantic poetry: ' There is only good and bad poetry.' I feel the same timelessness with modern and Old Masters. There is neither old nor new—Left nor Right: only good and bad.

Printed in Great Britain by Butler & Tanner Ltd., Frome and London

SELF PORTRAIT
Tate Gallery (reproduced by permission)
Presented by the late Margaret Wynne Nevinson

LONDON BRIDGES

Presented by Eugene Gallatin, Esq., to Metropolitan Museum, New York

3 A.M.   CLOSSERIES DES LILAS, BOULEVARDE MONTPARNASSE
Purchased for a Private Collection, London

TITI

In the possession of the Artist

SINISTER PARIS NIGHT

Purchased for a Private Collection, London

SUR LE TERASSE, PARNASSE

In the possession of the Artist

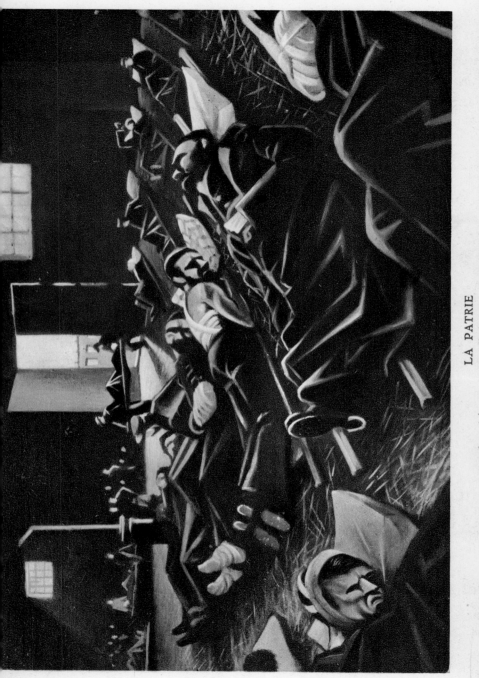

LA PATRIE

Purchased by L. J. Cadbury, Esq., Birmingham

COLUMN OF MARCH

First purchased by Prof. Sir Michael Sadler, Oxford

A TAUBE

Presented by the late Lord Melchett to the Imperial War Museum

THE ROAD FROM ARRAS TO BAPAUME

Imperial War Museum

IN THE AIR

By permission of H.M. Stationery Office (Crown copyright)

PORTRAIT OF THE ARTIST'S WIFE, KATHLEEN

Purchased by the late R. J. Boyd, Esq., London

GLITTERING PRIZES

Presented by General Joffre to the French Government

ANY LONDON STREET

Purchased by Sir Alexander Park Lyle

AMONGST THE NERVES OF THE WORLD
London Museum

THE SOUL OF A SOULLESS CITY
In the possession of Williamson Noble, Esq., London

THE TEMPLES OF NEW YORK

Purchased by J. Rosenberg, New York

WALL STREET, NEW YORK
Birmingham Art Gallery

THROUGH BROOKLYN BRIDGE, NEW YORK

Purchased by Sinclair Lewis, New York

NIGHT DRIVE

Purchased by Mrs. Fox Pitt, London

HENRY IV, L'ILE DE PARIS
Dublin Art Gallery

CHRISTINE

Purchased by G. Besky, Esq., London

FILLES EN FLEURS

Purchased by Alec Waugh, Esq., London

NOTRE DAME DE PARIS

Purchased by the Northern Arts Collection Fund for the Laing Gallery, Newcastle-on-Tyne.

A STUDIO IN MONTPARNASSE
Tate Gallery (reproduced by permission)
Presented by H. G. Wells, Esq.

ENGLISH LANDSCAPE IN WINTER

Walker Art Gallery, Liverpool

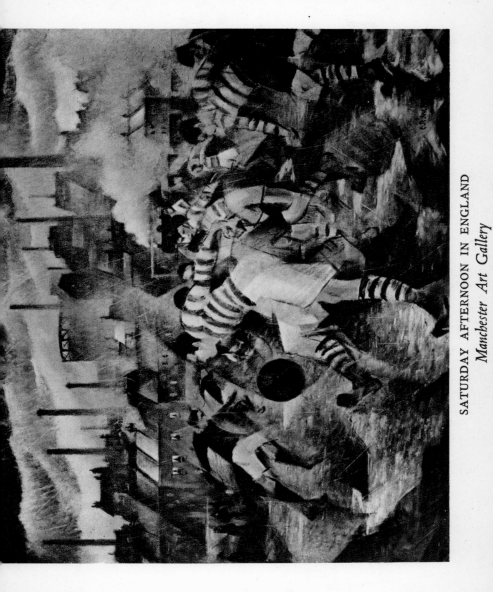

SATURDAY AFTERNOON IN ENGLAND
Manchester Art Gallery

THE CHARLADY'S DAUGHTER
Purchased by Miss Evelyn Sharp

CLOUD SHADOWS OF SPRING

In the possession of Hamilton Fyfe, Esq., London

STARLIGHTER
In the possession of the Artist

BATTERSEA TWILIGHT

Purchased by R. Temple, Esq., London

THE TWENTIETH CENTURY

In the possession of the Artist